MW01200215

3

LIGHTING THE
Eighth Fire

LIGHTING THE
Eighth Fire

The Liberation, Resurgence, and
Protection of Indigenous Nations

edited by
LEANNE SIMPSON

ARBEITER RING PUBLISHING · WINNIPEG

Copyright © 2008

Arbeiter Ring Publishing
201E-121 Osborne Street
Winnipeg, Manitoba
Canada R3L 1Y4
www.arbeiterring.com

Printed in Canada by Marquis Book Printing
Cover image by Rebecca Belmore, "Architecture for a Colonial Landscape."
Photo by Scott Stephens, courtesy of Aceart Inc.
Typeset by Relish Design Studio, Ltd.

Copyright notice

This book is fully protected under the copyright laws of Canada and all other countries
of the Copyright Union and is subject to royalty. Any properly footnoted quotation of up
to five hundred sequential words may be quoted without permission, so long as the total
number of words does not exceed two thousand. For longer continuous quotations or for
a greater number of words, contact Arbeiter Ring Publishing for permission.

With assistance of the Manitoba Arts Council/Conseil des Arts du Manitoba.

We acknowledge the support of the Canada Council for our publishing program.

ARP acknowledges the financial support to our publishing activities of the Manitoba
Arts Council/Conseil des Arts du Manitoba, Manitoba Culture, Heritage and Tourism,
and the Government of Canada through the Book Publishing Industry Development
Program (BPIDP).

Printed on 100% post-consumer-waste recycled paper.

Library and Archives Canada Cataloguing in Publication

    Lighting the eighth fire: the liberation, resurgence and protection of indigenous
nations / edited by Leanne Simpson.

Includes bibliographical references and index.
ISBN 978-1-894037-33-4

    1. Native peoples—Canada. 2. Land use—Canada. 3. Native peoples—Canada—
Politics and government. 4. Self-determination, National—Canada. 5. Traditional
ecological knowledge—Canada. 6. Native peoples—Canada—Ethnic identity.
7. Native peoples—Canada—Government relations. I. Simpson, Leanne, 1971-

E78.C2L545 2008   323.1197'071   C2008-904673-0

For Nishna and Minowewebeneshiinh.

Contents

Gchi Miigwech

LEANNE SIMPSON

GZHE-MNIDOO! Miigwech noongwa waabdaamaa miinwaa ngoding giizhigak. Miigwech kina gego gaa-miizhiyaang, kina kiig gaa-tooyin aw sa Nishnaabe wii-miigkadaawsod. Miigwech newiing nekyaa mebimiseg, miigwech newiing nekyaa mebiniseg, miigwech wesiinyag gii-miizhiyang wii-wiisiniyang, miigwech bineshiinyag noodoonogwaa nagamwaad, miigwech nbi biinaakizigoyang, miigwech gii-miizhiyang nokiiwin! Miinshinaag mina-de'ewin, wii-mina nokiitaadiyang, naadimooshinaag wii-ni-mosaadimaang Nishnaabe-naadiziwin, naadimooshinaag wii-ni-mna-maadizyaang! Miigwech Gzhe-mnidoo! Miigwech! Miigwech! Miigwech![1]

Gchi Miigwech to Nishnaabe-kwe Elder and Nokomis Edna Manitowabi, Nishnaabeg Elders Mark Thompson and Robin Greene, and Nishnaabe-kwe Elder and Nokomis Shirley Williams for her assistance with the Nishnaabemwin. Gchi Miigwech to the Indigenous academics and writers whose work has both influenced and inspired me, particularly Winona LaDuke, Vine Deloria Jr., Patricia Monture, Sákéj Youngblood Henderson, Leroy Little Bear, Linda Tuhiwai Smith, Kiera Ladner, Taiaiake Alfred, Andrea Smith, and Andrea Bear Nicholas. I will never forget sitting in the Hamilton Convention Centre at nineteen years of age, listening to John Mohawk, the first Native academic I had ever encountered, speak eloquently and passionately about Indigenous history. It was life-changing. And, of course, I have been profoundly influenced by the work of Trish Monture, which got me and most Indigenous women in the academy of my generation through our degrees, both intellectually and emotionally. I would also like to acknowledge Paul Driben, who taught me how to do research and write, and then believed in my intellect enough to send me back to school to do a PhD, and to Rick Riewe and Jill Oakes, who supported me once I got there.

Chi'Miigwech to the contributors to this book, who gave their time and their thoughts to make this project happen: Taiaiake Alfred, Glen Coulthard, Nick Claxton, Charlie Greg Sark, Laura Hall, Susan Hill, Paula Sherman, Renée Bédard, Fred Metallic, Eden Robinson, Jocelyn Cheechoo, Jackie Price, Isabel Altamirano-Jiménez, and Brock Pitawanakwat. Miigwech to all of you for being patient, committed, engaged, and honourable throughout the editorial and revision process. Thanks also to the two anonymous reviewers for engaging with the work and providing highly skilled and extremely important feedback that clearly made the essays in this book better, and to the folks at Arbeiter Ring for getting this manuscript out there. The mistakes, of course, are mine.

Thanks to the Indigenous students whom I have had the honour to teach and to learn with at Athabasca University, Trent University, the University of Manitoba, Inter-Universities North (in Sagkeeng First Nation and Pimicikamak Cree Nation), the Centre for Indigenous Environmental Resources (in Hollow Water First Nation) and at the University of Victoria. Many of you are contributors to this book, and many more have inspired my intellectual dreams. Thanks also to Norbert Hardisty, Judy DaSilva and Betty Riffel, who continually invite me to work with their communities—work that keeps me grounded in the reality of reserve life.

And finally, Chi'Miigwech to Kiera for countless discussions regarding Indigenous politics, governance, and Indigenist theory, and for generously allowing me to google her mind for a variety of sources, page numbers, and other helpful bits of information. To Steve for his constant support of my politics and my professional life, and for his patience and love, to Nishna and Minowewe for tolerating me "tip typing on the puter for 50 hundred hours," to Aaron for numerous headshots, and to my parents for providing our little ones with hours of entertainment while I completed this project.

[1] This prayer was original written by Shirley Williams and quoted in Paula Sherman's PhD dissertation, *Indawendiwin: Spiritual Ecology as the Foundation of Omàmìwinini Relations* (Department of Indigenous Studies, Trent University, Peterborough, ON, 2007). It is used here with permission.

Kulu, Cops, and You

CHARLIE GREG SARK

Kulu danced in the sky,
with stars and moon.
He carried your ancestor
maiden to land above the sky.
They glided beyond the reach of time
and memory, as the maiden sang her song.
She shed tears as they circled the moon,
her tears fell,
melted into the earth's atmosphere.
Tears escaping petrified space and
gracing the turtle with an ocean to drink.
Caressing his back
as we wept
with the knowledge
that the maiden no longer
belonged to ocean's song.
The instant she sang to the moon,
the ocean heaved as her essence
flew in infinite directions, through the stars

and found the universe asleep, shivering and
alone.
Kulu's maiden-voyage was his last.
Earthly desire melted his wings.
He fell in the vacuum of space,
with loneliness and change.
The sun sliced his vision
into finite knowledge.

These voices
carve flesh from
bones fed
by innocence and harmony.
These voices
slice and rip
with claws fed
by blood and misery.
As if the giant children of watchers
gained their freedom to slaughter,
torture, and rape,
with the murder of Jenu.
Who knows not evil,
or innocence, he is
your pet cannibal.
Emerging from your hell,
our world beneath the world.
Hatred so pungent that
a simple glance from
passing authority
bruises flesh. Leaves it
clinging to ancient bones,
trapped in arid lungs.
The generations that come and go
from our world
can stitch these wounds,

but 500 odd years
trapped in one memory
will leave scars
for ancestors to ponder.
Weakness and fear
hammer the surface of these scars,
bruising flesh.
Transforming desire
into a need to retreat,
run, hide on Kulu's back.
Escape
toward your heaven,
our world above the sky.
We are
lost in-between two worlds,
lost in two words,
echoing our voice.
They belong to time,
and ulnoo.
The time that
breaks metal,
pride, and fear.
The time that
named thunder and rain.
Ulnoo know
that hate will not pass,
but retreat into shadows
beyond fear.

On the edge of your lip,
your supple respect,
rests the intimate memory and knowledge.
Balanced between
the wealth of mortal memory and
Indian knowledge of poverty.

Your grandmother was thunder, and
your children the storms that rage
in your heart.
And, your grandchildren spoke through you
while we flew close, quiet, and content.
Allowing the world its measure
to pass, through change and birth.
Their voices embody the darkness
that lifted you from my wing.
I heard your song,
your breath echoed, as it moved between the
stars and moon.
Your tears froze in the coldness
of newcomers.
The shallowness of time
opens my memory
to distance
between touch and taste,
and closes with intimate truth.
The tradition that broke their reality
it pounced on your soul
on your self,
and broke the sky into
tiny pieces of my heart.
And their lips
the steel
that bends our
will, as warriors,
to belong.

AUTHOR'S NOTE: A previous version of this poem was originally commissioned by the Canadian Broadcasting Corporation for the Poetry Face-off Competition in 2004. It later appeared in Charlie Greg Sark's *kitpu apteket* (Cardigan, PEI: Saturday Morning Chapbooks, 2005).

Opening Words

Taiaiake Alfred

As a scholar who has strived to understand and convey the depth and power of Indigenous Knowledge in my own engagement with colonial mentalities, and as a person who is committed to the liberation and resurgence of Indigenous Nations on Turtle Island, it is immensely gratifying to witness the regeneration of ancestral wisdom and the rebirth of the warrior spirit that the words in this book represent. My generation stands as a link between the groundbreakers of Indigenous scholarship and the emerging scholars in this volume. I am fortunate to have known, been mentored by, and worked with Vine Deloria, Jr., Leroy Little Bear, Beatrice Medicine, and John Mohawk. And now I am a mentor and colleague to this new generation. From where I stand, I say with pride that the intellectual strength of our scholarly warriors is on the rise!

The essays in this book point directly at the main problem of history; they describe its effects and lay bare the truth about the present reality of Indigenous Peoples. The problem that we have inherited in this generation is our disconnection from what it is to be Indigenous. This problem has been framed in many complicated ways, but really, what is colonization if not the separation of our people from the land, the severance of the bonds of trust and love that held our people together so

9

tightly in the not-so-distant past, and the abandonment of our spiritual connection to the natural world?

In thinking through this problem and in offering us strong words about ways to reconnect to our lands, cultures, and communities, these good minds are teaching us more than how to recover; they are teaching how to survive and *be* Indigenous. These emerging scholars are serving a crucial role for Indigenous people and for society as a whole because they are doing something no one else can. As Indigenous scholars who are culturally rooted and connected to their communities, they are doing what Euroamerican scholars simply cannot do for us: they are showing us forms of thought and pathways of action that are beyond the boundaries of a colonial mentality. Settlers have serious difficulties thinking thoughts that are outside foundational premises of their imperial cultural background. Very few of them can overcome the ingrained patterns of authority and dominance that are the heritage of empire and colonialism. So, we have to do it for them. And for us. These essays contain some of the best of the new generation's anti, non, de, and un colonial thinking.

Now, then, and forever, the fight is for the land. The land, and all it has to teach, to give, and all it demands, is what it means to be Indigenous. Living our responsibilities as humans, struggling for balance, demanding respect is the Indigenous way. In a sense, it's so simple, yet so few people seem to be able to disentangle themselves from the teachings of the church and state to see clearly again a human being's place in creation. Alienation and disconnection from the land create confusion and discord in our minds and souls. These manifest in the social and psychic discord that defines our contemporary existences. The threats to our people come in all forms and they are all real. But fighting for our survival in the twenty-first century is less about defeating the aggression of an external enemy than it is about finding new ways to love the land, and new ways to love ourselves and our people.

Many of my own generation of scholars and activists hold on to ways of thinking and acting that are wrapped up in old theories of revolution. Those theories centre on convincing the settler society to change their ways and restructure their society, through the use of persuasion or of force. But in the twenty years of my involvement in politics and academia, grounded in such revolutionary notions, I have often asked myself, "What if the settlers choose not to change their ways?" It is becoming more and more apparent each day, as capitalism and materialism grow into ever more powerful and arrogant forces and continue to roll over landscapes and cultures with impunity, that restoring a regime of peaceful co-existence with settler society and believing in the settlers' potential for friendship and enlightenment is impossible. The strength of these essays is that, facing this situation, they do not surrender to despair and advocate collaboration with colonialism or stoke mindless rage. They have a stronger vision of liberation. They are guided by ancient teachings—they are patient and wise and they recognize the futility of "revolution" and turn inward to focus on the resurgence of an authentic Indigenous existence and the recapturing of physical, political, and psychic spaces of freedom for our people. In this, they are a powerful truth that our people need to hear.

When I think of liberation, I think of how our grandparents and great-grandparents lived. It seems so clear, when we reflect on the words of our ancestors, that liberation is all just a matter of getting back in touch with a way of life that has respect, sacrifice, love, honesty, and the quest for balance at its core. The words of an Elder from my own nation drove this point home for me, when he spoke of his own belief about how people are returning to balance, and when I listened.

> I see little glimpses of the old ways coming back, so I always have hope. I think part of the answer about things getting back to their original value is when we start with our individual selves. When we start to respect ourselves again and demand respect from our children and everything else, I believe this will trickle down so that we will respect what the Creator put on earth for our use.

These are stories of the coming liberation of our people, a time when we will respect ourselves once more. They are all about our indigeneity coming back to life again.

Oshkimaadiziig, the New People

Leanne Simpson

Indigenous Peoples whose lands are occupied by the Canadian state are currently engaged in the longest running resistance movement in Canadian history; indeed, one that predates the formation of Canada itself. In the times prior to colonization, Indigenous peoples lived in independent, sovereign nations governed by complex political and social systems. Rooted in the land, with a strong spiritual and religious foundation, these systems ensured our citizens were taken care of and that contentious issues were resolved in a peaceful and just manner. Our Ancestors worked toward maintaining peaceful international diplomacy with other Indigenous Nations, with mass mobilizations leading to many of the Confederacies and political alliances we still see today.[1] When colonization and colonial policy threatened our Indigenous ways of being, our peoples resisted, organized, and mobilized at every point in history—we were not passive victims of colonialism. Indigenous politics of contestation, dissent, and a mobilization spanning nearly five centuries in some nations are the very reason we have survived as *Indigenous* Peoples as we enter the twenty-first century.

During the process of reading the first draft chapters for this book, I was reminded of a well-known Nishnaabeg prophecy,[2] a series of

13

sacred predictions that have foretold our history since the beginning of Creation. The later part of that prophecy relays that we are currently living in the Seventh Fire, a time when, after a long period of colonialism and cultural loss, a new people, the Oshkimaadiziig, emerge. It is the Oshkimaadiziig whose responsibilities involve reviving our language, philosophies, political and economic traditions, our ways of knowing, and our culture. The foremost responsibility of the "new people" is to pick up those things previous generations have left behind by nurturing relationships with Elders that have not "fallen asleep." Oshkimaadiziig are responsible for decolonizing, for rebuilding our nation, and for forging new relationships with other nations by returning to original Nishnaabeg visions of peace and justice. According to the prophecy, the work of the Oshkimaadiziig determines the outcome of the Eighth Fire, an eternal fire to be lit by all humans. It is an everlasting fire of peace, but its existence depends upon our actions and our choices today. In order for the Eighth Fire to be lit, settler society must also choose to change their ways, to decolonize their relationships with the land and Indigenous Nations, and to join with us in building a sustainable future based upon mutual recognition, justice, and respect.

For Nishnaabeg people, our prophecy is the foundation of our resistance and of our resurgence. For me, it is both hope and a crucial mandate for action. If we are to take seriously our current responsibilities, our generation has a profound ability to contribute to the recovery and rebirth of Indigenous Nations, and to peaceful and just relations with our neighbouring nation states. Political decolonization, cultural reclamation and resurgence, liberation, and peaceful co-existence with the other nations of the world—this is the work of the Oshkimaadiziig.

Oshkimaadiziig and the Academy

Within the Western academy, or, more accurately, from the margins of the Western academy, the Oshkimaadiziig operate within a web of liberation strategies grounded in the intellectual traditions of their perspective nations. Indigenist thinkers have advocated for the recovery and promotion of Indigenous Knowledge systems as an important process in decolonizing Indigenous Nations and their relationships with occupying states, whether those strategies are applied to political and legal systems, governance, health and wellness, education, or the environment. Recovering and maintaining Indigenous world views and applying those teachings in a contemporary context represent a network of emancipatory strategies Indigenous Peoples can employ to disentangle themselves from the oppressive control of occupying state governments. Combined with the political drive toward self-determination in our communities, these strategies mark resistance to cultural genocide, vitalize an agenda to rebuild strong and sustainable Indigenous national territories, and promote a just relationship with neighbouring states based on the notions of peaceful and just co-existence embodied in Indigenous Knowledge and languages and encoded in the original treaties. These strategies are the foundation of this book.

This collection builds upon the work of the Indigenous scholars and activists who nurtured us, inspired us, informed us, and supported us in our early interactions with the academy, including John Mohawk, Sákéj Youngblood Henderson, Vine Deloria Jr., Leroy Little Bear, Winona LaDuke, Linda Tuhiwai Smith, Taiaiake Alfred, Haunani-Kay Trask, Trish Monture, and many, many others. Most of us are the first generation of Indigenous scholars who have access to established Indigenous scholars to nurture, inspire, inform, and support us. This community has encouraged us to take their work further down the path of decolonization, grounding our work in the languages, philosophies, and ethical principles of our respective nations. In some ways, the collective intervention of this book is theoretical—our work does not rely on Western theories, or even post-colonial theory, to frame our research, analysis. and writing. We rely heavily on the growing, yet still marginalized, body of fourth-world theory—theories, strategies, and analysis strongly rooted in the values, knowledge, and philosophies of Indigenous Nations. But the contributors are also committed to a particular politic: putting the freedom of Indigenous Peoples as their highest political priority. This Indigenist theoretical framework promotes liberation, the retraditionalization of Indigenous institutions, and the decolonization of Indigenous Nations and the Canadian state. It privileges Indigenous intellectual traditions, Indigenous Knowledge Holders, and the "research" agendas of communities, nations, and traditional governments. But it is not just about theory, it is also about following our own intellectual traditions, working with traditional governments and Knowledge Holders, protecting the land and our knowledge—thereby contesting the foundations of colonialism and the academy itself.

Another significant intervention shown in many of the essays in this book involves a direct challenge to the hegemony of the politics of recognition. Several of the contributors contest our collective search for recognition within colonial institutions, both as a strategy (or lack of strategy) and as a pastime of continually responding to the demands and agenda of the colonizer. While recognizing that community- and nation-based activists may be forced to negotiate with settler governments and the legal system to immediately protect their citizens and territories, the contributors also claim that this cannot be the *emphasis* of our work. To do so is, as one of our reviewers wrote, to engage in a "death dance with the colonizer."

Our Indigenist Principles

The works of the Indigenist academics, writers, and revolutionaries who have come before us have most certainly influenced the writers brought together in this collection. But even more importantly, the contributors to this project have been profoundly influenced by their relationships with the land and the Knowledge Holders of their respective nations. The contributors to this work are protectors of our lands and protectors of our ancient knowledge systems.

This commitment leads us to reject pan-Aboriginalism, because we believe that the uniqueness and diversity of our cultural teachings and ways of knowing, rather than some manufactured hegemonic "Aboriginal" culture, hold the answers to the questions facing Indigenous Nations in contemporary times. We cherish the diversity of Indigenous cultures and believe that it is necessary to protect and promote that diversity. We honour the Indigenous Knowledge Holders of our respective nations and consider them to be the experts regarding Indigenous intellectual traditions. We are skeptical of the power our role as academics affords us in colonial society and we often have tenuous relationships with the university, because we reject its very foundations, its role in colonialism, and its contemporary relationships with Indigenous Nations.

We do not believe that it is helpful to freeze our traditions in the past, or lock them into an appropriated fundamentalism designed to control and exclude. We believe it is our *responsibility* to interpret those teachings from an Indigenous lens or, rather, Indigenous *lenses*. Some of our people have relearned our ways, but have not necessarily reclaimed the pre-colonial Indigenous context within which those traditions operated. I will give you one example from my own nation. Nishnaabeg society had a strong ethic of respect for individuals, as evidenced in our parenting philosophies and in the ways we conceptualized gender. This created a fluidity regarding gender similar to that observed in other Indigenous Nations.[3] This was combined with an equally strong ethic of non-interference, creating a culture where individuals were encouraged and supported in developing and fulfilling their destinies, as long as their actions did not have a negative impact on others or on the community in general. If, for example, a woman had a strong desire to hunt, she hunted, despite the fact that this was often considered to be a male's responsibility. In contemporary times, these values have not always been practised, particularly in the southern and eastern portions of our territory. Too often, spiritual "leaders" revitalizing traditional culture have appropriated the fundamentalism of our Christian colonizers to exclude women from ceremonies and practices—ceremonies and practices from which, in many parts of our territory, women were never traditionally excluded from.[4] This is not decolonization. This is not resurgence.

The contributors to this book conduct their research according to the intellectual traditions of the respective nations, in spite of the fact that many of the institutions we work for rarely support or even acknowledge this approach. This approach means we spend time connecting to the land, nurturing lifelong relationships with Indigenous Knowledge Holders, and have strong commitments to learning our languages, cultures, and intellectual traditions. We hold responsibilities to our clans, communities, and our nations, and we hold these responsibilities close to our hearts. Our work is *embedded* in community.

The Contributors

Haudenosaunee scholar Susan Hill begins. In "'Travelling Down the River of Life Together in Peace and Friendship, Forever': Haudenosaunee Land Ethics and Treaty Agreements as the Basis for Restructuring the Relationship with the British Crown," she uses Haudenosaunee epics to examine the basis of Haudenosaunee land ethics, how these ethics guide relationships with all other beings, and the centrality of those ethics to the treaty relationships of the Kaswentha (Two Row Wampum) and the Covenant Chain. This approached is echoed in Chapter 6 by Paula Sherman from the Omàmìwinini Nation, who explores the ways in which Omàmìwinini people within the Ardoch community have begun to revive traditional governance, relationships, and processes for interacting with the land and nation-states. Sherman describes the challenges in putting our theories of decolonization into practice given her community's resistance to uranium prospecting on their territory, and she encourages us to have the confidence to live out our teachings in the face of contemporary colonial adversity.

In chapter 2, Nick Claxton, a fisher from the WSÁNEĆ Nation, knows that the core of WSÁNEĆ governance and WSÁNEĆ lifeways was the complex reef-net fishery. Speaking through his own language and through WSÁNEĆ fishing culture, he deconstructs mainstream interpretations of the Douglas Treaty and deepens our understanding of the meaning of this treaty for the WSÁNEĆ Nation. Fred Metallic is a Mi'gmaq speaker and comes from a Mi'gmaq family of fishers. His family lives in the traditional territory of Gespe'gewa'gi, the seventh district of Mi'gma'gi, and, in Chapter 3, he broadens Nick's analysis by discussing traditional Mi'gmaq concepts of governance and relating to the land, again speaking through his own language. Fred discusses the necessity of understanding and living governance that is based on the teachings of our Elders so that we may reconnect with the land and continue to build relationships that have maintained balance and harmony for thousands of years.

In Chapter 4, Leanne Simpson, a Mississauga Nishnaabe-kwe, turns her attention to the academy and discusses the revitalization of

Indigenous Knowledge systems in contemporary times as necessary pre-requisites to Indigenous resurgence. She presents a strategy for reviving Indigenous Knowledge systems based on Indigenous ways of knowing. This theme is echoed later in Chapter 12, in which Dene political scientist Glen Coulthard challenges the idea that the colonial relationship between Indigenous Peoples and the Canadian state can be transformed via the hegemony of the politics of recognition. Both contributors argue that Indigenous Nations should put their own agendas first rather than continually responding to the demands of colonial institutions that refuse to fully recognize Indigenous Peoples and our knowledge.

Four chapters are written by young Indigenous women who are successfully finding ways of honouring their cultural and political values in contemporary times. In Chapter 5, another Nishnaabe-kwe, Renée Bédard, turns our focus to the responsibilities of Nishnaabeg women in protecting water and waterscapes, and she discusses what contemporary Nishinaabe-kwewag Water Walkers are doing about it. Jackie Price is an Inuk from Nunavut and, in Chapter 7, she challenges the very creation of Nunavut—an agreement in which the Canadian state secured the legal right to 83% of Nunavut's land mass and also secured a governing framework based on settler values. She explores Inuit traditional governance as a way of indigenizing governance in Nunavut and responding to the immediate threat of climate change. Jocelyn Cheechoo has been speaking out about environmental issues in her home community of Moose Cree First Nation since she was ten years old. Now the Old Growth Organizer for a large San Francisco-based NGO, the Rainforest Action Network, Jocelyn shares a personal narrative about her love of the land and protecting what is means to be Ehlileweuk, people of the land. In Chapter 9, Laura Hall, a Kanienkehaha PhD candidate at York University advocates for a revitalization of sustainable, culturally based, economic systems by honouring the Three Sisters and recentering Haudenosaunee lifeways.

In Chapter 10, Brock Pitawanakwat, an Nishnaabeg scholar living in Winnipeg, turns our attention to considering how we might live genuine Indigenous lives in urban environments by honouring the diversity of our ancestral ways and rejecting the seduction of settler society. He proposes that by speaking our languages, practising our ceremonies, and following Indigenous teachings wherever we reside, we will be able to maintain our Indigeneity. In "The Colonization and Decolonization of Indigenous Diversity," Zapoteca academic Isabel Altamirano-Jiménez diagnoses the colonization of both geographic space and how Indigenous Peoples interact with each other. She discusses colonial and post-colonial strategies aimed at domesticating diversity by redefining borders, reconstructing, and homogenizing/dividing "the Indigenous." The internationalization and reproduction of these strategies have produced uneven and dominant relationships among Indigenous Peoples, to the extent that we have even reproduced North/South relations. For Chapter 13, Leanne Simpson brings us back to our personal responsibilities in planting the seeds of resurgence, reflecting on the sanctity the land provides for this resurgence, through her experiences in her own territory as both a women and as a mother. And, to conclude, Eden Robinson, a Hailsa/Heiltsuk writer previously nominated for both the Giller and the Governor General's awards, writes in "Go Fish" about what it means on a personal level to recover our traditions so that we might pass them down to the next generation.

The essays in this book are in conversation with other Indigenous scholars, theorists, community-based and nation-based activists, and our allies. They are also conversations with the Oshkimaadiziig, both inside and outside "the academy." The issues presented within this collection will resonate with scholars and students in Indigenous Studies, in addition to the disciplines of environmental studies, political science, Canadian studies, women's studies, and cultural studies, and nation-based and community-based organizers. But the voices within the volume will also resonate with Canadians who have an interest in justice and in making things right with their Indigenous neighbours—Canadians interested in learning *Indigenous* solutions to the problems continued colonialism creates.

These essays build on five centuries of Indigenous resistance, contestation, dissent, and mobilization that have gone before us. The philosophies and ideological underpinnings presented in these essays are not new. They are what have sustained our families, communities, and nations for countless generations. Each time they come around, they bring with them the teachings and responsibilities of protecting the land, protecting our knowledge, and realizing justice. They are necessary prerequisites to building relationships of solidarity with other Indigenous Nations and to begin the journey toward peace with other nation states. They are the seeds of resistance that we will pass on to the next generation. Some of these stories have allowed themselves to be caught on paper. These are the stories that are meant to be shared with the ones that read, or rather, the ones that *only* read.

Miigwech
Leanne Simpson

AUTHOR's NOTE: Oshkimaadiziig (eastern Ojibwe dialects) is the same as Oshkibimaadizeeg (western Ojibwe dialects).

[1] Kiera Ladner, 2008, "Aysaka'paykinit: Contesting the Rope Around the Nations' Neck," in *Group Politics and Social Movements in Canada*, ed. Miriam Smith (Peterborough, ON: Broadview Press, 2008), 227–28.

[2] This is only a small portion of the prophecy. For a more complete discussion of the prophecy, see Sally Gaikesheyongai's *The Seven Fires: An Ojibway Prophecy*, (Toronto: Sister Vision Press, 1994); Benton-Banai's *The Mishomis Book* (Hayward, WI: Indian Country Communications, 1988); and Thomas Peacock and Marlene Wisuri's *The Good Path* (Afton, MN: Afton Historical Society, 2002). I have been instructed by Nishnaabeg Elder Edna Manitowabi that it is appropriate to share this prophecy in the context of my own life, and what is presented here is my own interpretation of that prophecy and its meaning.

[3] Kiera Ladner's "Women in Blackfoot Nationalism," *Journal of Canadian Studies* 35, 2 (2000): 35–60.

[4] See also Taiaiake Alfred's *Wasáse: Indigenous Pathways of Action and Freedom*, (Peterborough, ON: Broadview Press, 2005).

Chapter 1

"Travelling Down the River of Life Together in Peace and Friendship, Forever": Haudenosaunee Land Ethics and Treaty Agreements as the Basis For Restructuring the Relationship with the British Crown

Susan M. Hill

Haudenosaunee[1] land and environmental ethics shape our relationships with other humans and the natural world. The epics[2] of our cultural history embody the basis for these ethics. Since the beginning of time, these ethics have informed the way we interact with each other and with the rest of Creation. In this, they became central to the new relationships we created with Europeans who settled amongst us in the last four centuries. The ensuing treaty relationships were informed and defined by the lessons of Haudenosaunee cultural history. They created a framework for respectful relations that both sides agreed would exist for perpetuity. The colonial period[3] witnessed major offenses to the treaties, but the treaty relations still exist. As with marriage vows, transgressions do not nullify the original agreement. Today, as Canada and the United States seek to improve relations with the Haudenosaunee with reference to issues of land rights, the treaty relations need to be "polished" and once again serve as the lenses through which we view and understand the principles of the relationship between our nations. Revitalizing Haudenosaunee land ethics is critical for decolonizing our relationships with our territory and the Canadian state, and for us to collectively assume our responsibility to protect our lands to the best of our abilities.

This chapter will examine Haudenosaunee land and environmental ethics, how those ethics guide relationships with all other beings, and the centrality of those ethics to the treaty relationships of the Kaswentha (Two Row Wampum) and the Covenant Chain. Through these lessons of our shared past, Canada (and the United States) can find a respectful way to interact with the Haudenosaunee as we continue "down the river of life" together as neighbours and, once again, as friends.

Creation

Calvin Martin wrote that Indigenous people are "people of nature," and not people of history.[4] What this ethnohistorian has missed in his assessment of Indigenous Peoples is the fact that, while the natural world is central to Indigenous identities, our understanding of the relationship between humans and the rest of nature is held within our historical consciousnesses. He was attempting to make a point about the centrality of nature to Indigenous realities, but, in so doing, he negated Indigenous historical conceptualizations. The lessons of Haudenosaunee cultural history embody the basis for our relationship to nature. Without our history, we cannot understand how to interact with the natural world. Our historical consciousness, our land, and our environmental ethics are inextricably connected. For the Haudenosaunee, history on this earth begins with Creation. The Haudenosaunee Creation Story is a detailed epic, taking days to tell in its entirety. Additional side stories relate to the time of Creation and help explain how other entities of this world came into being. A very short summary is included here to provide a background for understanding Haudenosaunee land and environmental ethics.

The story begins in the Sky World at a time when this world was covered in water and inhabited only by water beings. A portal opened between the Sky World and the Water World, and a pregnant woman from the sky fell to the water below. Waterfowl became aware of her descent and flew up to catch her while animals in the water chose a giant sea turtle's back as the location upon which to set her. The muskrat brought dirt to the surface from the bottom of the sea, which, with the transformative powers of the turtle and the Skywoman, grew into Turtle Island (North America). She soon gave birth to a daughter (Zephyr), who, upon reaching maturity, gave birth to twin sons. The first-born twin, known as Sapling, was born through the birth canal, but his brother, Flint, was impatient and chose to come out of their mother's side, killing her in the process. The two were raised by their grandmother (Skywoman) and both possessed the ability to create new life. Sapling's creations embodied positive traits, while Flint's creations were typically aggressive and negative. In short, Sapling and the beings he created advocated for life on the earth, while Flint advocated for an absence of life. The two eventually held a contest to determine who would be in charge on earth. Through a game of chance—and with the support of all the beings he created—Sapling won the gamble. Shortly thereafter, Sapling completed his work on the earth and gave the humans their instructions for life before he returned to the land of his grandmother, the Sky World. He directed humans to plant, to be kind to one another, and to give thanks for all of Creation. The rest of Creation would provide for their needs as long as humans remembered to be thankful and respectful for the continued gifts of sustenance. Because of his central role in finishing the work set out by his grandmother, and especially because of his role in creating humans, Sapling is commonly referred to as Shonkwaya'tihson—"he completed our bodies."

The lessons of the Creation Story—also referred to as the Original Instructions—are numerous. They include many related to land and environmental ethics. First, after Zephyr died in childbirth, her mother and sons buried her body under the ground, and Skywoman planted corn, beans, and squash seeds from the Sky World over her grave. In honour of Zephyr and the food plants that grew from her grave, the earth became known as Yethi'nihstenha Onhwentsya—our mother, the earth. Second, Shonkwaya'tihson instructed that humans should plant food crops. This provides for their sustenance and keeps them connected to the land. A people dependent on their land understand the need to treat the land with great respect and conservation. Third, Shonkwaya'tihson reminded humans they had been given everything they need to live a good life on earth and the only thing requested in exchange was that the other life on earth—and all the elements of earth, herself—always be treated with thanks and respect by humans.

Kayaneren'kowa

Several times over the course of history, the Onkwehonwe (original humans) lapsed in their fulfillment of Shonkwaya'tihson's directives. Each time, Shonkwaya'tihson sent a messenger to remind the people of their primary duties to each other and the rest of Creation. One of the most critical times saw the Onkwehonwe of five distinct but neighboring nations—Mohawk, Oneida, Onondaga, Cayuga, and Seneca—embroiled in blood feuds and wars of revenge. This is the story of the establishment of the Kayaneren'kowa, the Great Law of Peace. The entire story takes between eight and eleven days to tell, so, again, the retelling here is a very short summary of key points relevant to the discussion of land and environmental ethics.

At the time of the great blood feuds,[5] a messenger was born to the people living on the north shore of Lake Ontario. He grew up with his mother and grandmother and upon maturity, travelled across the lake to the lands of the warring Five Nations. There he set out on a journey to convince the people to use their minds to resolve disputes rather than physical force. Through his Good Message of Power and Peace,[6] the Peacemaker advocated that the people of the Five Nations bury their weapons of war, agreeing to never take up arms against one another again. He was aided by a Mohawk leader, Ayenwahtha, who developed words of condolence to help the people move beyond the grief experienced in the ongoing blood feuds. This process of condolence allowed people to work through their grief, in order to see, hear, and speak clearly once again. The final result was a united people—the Haudenosaunee[7]—who were committed to use reason over might as their self-governing principles.

The governing process established by the Peacemaker, Ayenwahtha, Tsikonhsaseh,[8] and other leaders was built on principles of balance and consensus. They created the Grand Council with representation of the Five Nations via forty-nine matrilineal clan families. A powerful Onondaga leader, Tadodaho—who had ruled through sorcery and violence—was transformed by the Good Message of Power and Peace and was named the fiftieth Hoyaneh (male leader/Chief), completing the Grand Council membership. Under the Kayaneren'kowa, the Haudenosaunee agreed to deliberate issues affecting all the Five Nations in order to reach the best decision for all. Within this system of consensus, any leader may dissent with popular opinion and is given three chances to convince others of his position. If he fails to gain support for his position after three attempts, he must concede to the will of the others. Within this system, there is a mechanism for minority voices to be heard that does not allow for a "tyranny of the majority." Further, at the time of the founding of the Great Law, the Peacemaker instructed the Council that their decisions must be made in the context of the "coming faces"; in other words, the Hotiyanehson (plural form of Hoyaneh; Chiefs) must consider the impact of their decisions on all future generations.[9]

Specific aspects of the Kayaneren'kowa were recorded in wampum belts and strings. The principles these wampums recorded can be seen as internal treaties made between the Five Nations of the Haudenosaunee. Among these internal treaties are three directly relevant to the discussion of Haudenosaunee land and environmental ethics. First, the Ayenwahtha Belt documents the connection of the lands of the Five Nations. While nation-based territorial distinctions continued to exist, the lands were now governed by the Council as a whole and decisions affecting the land of one or more nations were deemed to affect all. Second, the Dish with One Spoon Wampum commemorated the agreement to share in the bounty of the hunting grounds. In this, the Haudenosaunee agreed to never again fight over hunting (economic) resources; instead, they would view the harvesting of resources from the forest in common. All had a right to share in that harvest and none had the right to take more than nature could sustain. Third, the Circle Wampum documented the internal kinship relations created under the Kayaneren'kowa. One string hangs in the middle of this wampum for each of the fifty Hoyaneh titles. They are encircled and held together by two intertwined strings, one representing the Law, the other representing the Peace. The strings are grouped together based on several different types of relationships, including national groupings and "brother"/"cousin" relationships within the national structures. These relationships organize the Grand Council and create the structure for deliberation. Of extreme relevance to this discussion is the interdependence created in this treaty through the extension of family relations outside direct bloodlines. Family became more than direct relatives, and mechanisms were created to add to those families where and when necessary. The lessons of the Kayaneren'kowa have guided the Haudenosaunee for centuries and served as the basis for interactions with the European settlers who came to our lands over 400 years ago. Among the traditional Haudenosaunee,[10] these continue to guide our internal governance and our external relations.

Gaiwiyo

A third Haudenosaunee epic relevant to the topic of land and environmental ethics is the Gaiwiyo,[11] commonly referred to as the Good Message (or Code) of Handsome Lake. This aspect of Haudenosaunee cultural history is more recent and is based on visions experienced by the Seneca Hoyaneh Ganiodaiio (Handsome Lake) between 1799 and 1815. In his visions, Ganiodaiio was shown both how the world had changed as a result of European infiltration into Haudenosaunee country and how the world would continue to change in the future. He was instructed to tell his people how they should reform their lives—primarily through a return to original values and ceremonies—and how to protect themselves against a destructive future. Included in these visions were prophecies about environmental destruction. The visions vibrantly described what has since proven true about the physical state of much of the Haudenosaunee territories (including lands presently occupied by non-Haudenosaunee). For example, he was shown water that was not drinkable and a river on fire. Two hundred years ago, the Haudenosaunee could not imagine such things being possible. The actions of human beings today against the rest of Creation have demonstrated a lack of thankfulness, and as accorded in the Creation Story, when the people become ungrateful and disrespectful, the Creator's control over this world will slip away. However, Ganiodaiio was also told that each generation of Haudenosaunee had it within their hands to put

28

off the earth's destruction by adhering to the Original Instructions, the Kayaneren'kowa and the Gaiwiyo. The principles of these teachings informed the treaty decisions our ancestors made, and, as a result, the treaties also hold the key to repairing those damaged relationships in a way that will benefit all, including the rest of Creation.

The instructions of the Creation Story, Kayaneren'kowa, and the Gaiwiyo explain proper ways of relating to, and harvesting for, the purposes of human sustenance. In general, the relationship described in the instructions is based on standards of respect and sustainability. It is taught that these life forms will continue to provide for the humans as long as the humans treat them with respect. These lessons of respect comprise the Haudenosaunee land and environmental ethics.[12] In essence, these ethics are based on the belief that as long as the Haudenosaunee people treat the rest of Creation with respect and gratitude, all the elements of Creation will ensure that the Haudenosaunee will continue to survive.

While these balanced relationships are essential for the survival of the current generation of people, the Original Instructions outline that our primary responsibility is not for the survival of the people currently alive but for the continuation of all life so that the future generations will be adequately provided with all they need to survive. As noted previously, the Haudenosaunee are directed to make decisions based on the impact for all future generations. The responsibility to the future is the source of the land and environmental ethics discussed herein. The duty to conserve those life forms that provide the sustenance necessary for human life is primarily focused on the ability of future generations to enjoy the bounties of Creation—and they are expected to practise conservation for the benefit of the generations that will follow after them. This duty to ensure sustenance for one's descendants is a primary element of Haudenosaunee ethics that has informed Haudenosaunee decision making since the days of Creation. The contemporary historical record demonstrates how the Haudenosaunee utilized these lessons from the Original Instructions in making their decisions regarding the lands of their territories,[13] and the ability of that land to sustain the future generations. Unfortunately, their ability to protect those lands for the future sustenance of their people was greatly impeded by actions of many Euro-American people and governments.

Environmental Ethics Expressed in the Treaty Record

Europeans travelled near Haudenosaunee territory as early as 1535, but the first significant settlement directly affecting the Haudenosaunee was the Dutch trading post at Fort Orange (present-day Albany). The presence of this post and the Dutch fur-trading enterprise led the traders at Fort Orange to suggest a treaty relationship with the Haudenosaunee for trading purposes. While the Dutch were interested in brokering a business deal, the Haudenosaunee insisted on a relationship similar to those they had created within their own people as well as in treaty agreements with other Indigenous Nations. The ensuing treaty is known as the Kaswentha,[14] or Two Row Wampum. It was created in 1613, was transferred to the British in 1664, and continues to guide Haudenosaunee foreign policy to the present day. As noted, the Dutch were seeking a formalized alliance for trading furs but the Haudenosaunee decided that the only way a healthy relationship would exist was to become family with the Dutch traders, as the Peacemaker had taught them.

Within the oral record of the Haudenosaunee, it is noted that the relationship was to be as two vessels travelling down a river—the river of life—side by side, never crossing paths, never interfering in the other's internal matters. However, the path between them, symbolized by three rows of white wampum beads in the treaty belt, was to be a constant of respect, trust, and friendship. Some might say this is what kept the two vessels apart, but in fact, it is what kept them connected to each other. Without those three principles, the two vessels could drift apart and potentially be washed onto the bank (or crash into rocks). This agreement was meant to provide security for both sides. In essence, they agreed to live as peaceful neighbours in a relationship of friendship, predicated on an agreement to not interfere in each other's internal business. The contemporary oral record of the treaty also notes that individuals could choose which boat to travel in with the understanding that one must be clear in one's choice and avoid "having a foot in both."[15] The premise of non-interference, within the concept of brotherhood, demonstrates the desire to be allies rather than to have one side be subjects of the other.

The Dutch were replaced by the British in North America in 1664. They quickly sought to treat with the Haudenosaunee, seeking to step into the place formerly occupied by the Dutch within the Kaswentha. The 1664 Fort Albany Treaty stipulated that the British would provide the same goods to the Haudenosaunee as the Dutch had before them. The British also promised to provide refuge to the Five Nations if they were defeated in their war with the "River Indians" (the Mahicans).[16] Additionally, the treaty included stipulations for separate criminal jurisdictions, with both sides accepting responsibility for their own citizens should they commit a crime against either Natives or colonists.[17] Of great importance in the text of this treaty is the recognition of the distinct status of each party, similar to the principles of the Kaswentha. The 1664 treaty recognized both the British and the Haudenosaunee as sovereigns with their own "subjects" and laid out the principles upon which these two governments would work together but remain as allies, neither becoming subject to the other. Like its predecessor, the Kaswentha, the 1664 treaty foreshadowed the later Covenant Chain of Friendship that was developed in the 1670s and nurtured over the decades that followed its inception.

As with the 1664 treaty, the council held at Fort Albany in 1677 articulated a British desire to assume the Dutch responsibilities agreed to over sixty years previously. The negotiations involved trade provisions, but in accordance with Haudenosaunee diplomatic principles, the heart of the treaty involved the relationship that would flow from the formal agreement. While the colonies appeared to be focused on the economic relationship the treaty guaranteed, the Haudenosaunee were intent upon expanding the foundation (started in 1664) for the family-like relationship that would govern the interactions between themselves and the British for the rest of time. In order to do this, they used deeply metaphorical concepts in their discussion to describe the relationship they were building together with the British. For example, the treaty record documented the following statement from Garakondie, speaking on behalf of the Haudenosaunee:

> (we) do thank the gentleman there that they do exhort us to
> peace, for we are so minded ... we desire now that all that is
> past may be buried in oblivion, and do make now an abso-
> lut covenant of peace, which we shall bind with a chain. For
> ye sealing of ye same do give a belt of 13 deepe.[18]

In his reference to "burying the past," Garakondie was utilizing symbols from the Great Law. In the years between this treaty and its 1664 predecessor, there had been disagreements between colonists and individual Haudenosaunee, resulting in losses of life and property on both sides. In this peace treaty, the two sides offered condolences for those losses they had inflicted upon each other. This treaty did not negate the previous relationship; it used the original treaty as a basis for reconciliation and further development while acknowledging how both sides had been responsible for damaging their agreement and relationship. The treaty relationship did not end because of violations by either party; instead, the subsequent treaty addressed the wrongdoings and created a means to rectify the wrongs.

While the ideas contained in it were not new to the Haudenosaunee, the metaphor of the Covenant Chain as representing the treaty relationship was. From that point forward, the concept of the Covenant Chain continued to develop and was eventually described as a silver chain holding both the British sailing ship and the Haudenosaunee canoe to the "Great Mountain" (Onondaga). It was described as a three-link silver chain representing "peace and friendship forever." These metaphors became central to the ensuing relationship of the Haudenosaunee and the Crown. Furthermore, the Crown borrowed this ideology and terminology in their treaty making with other Indigenous nations in North America. British and Indigenous treaty records documented the Crown's application of the Covenant Chain relationship to many other nations throughout the Northeast, including the Ojibwa, the Mississaugas, and the Delaware, to name but a few.[19]

The treaty record also holds evidence of Haudenosaunee values regarding land and the rationale behind their land-sharing decisions. In a famous speech made at the Treaty of Lancaster in 1744, Canasatego, an Onondaga Hoyaneh, declared the following: "We know our lands have now become more valuable. The white people think we do not know their value; but we know that the land is everlasting, and the few goods we receive for it are soon worn out and gone."[20] Canasatego put the British on notice that they were not dealing with a people ignorant of Western economics. At the Albany Conference ten years later, Hendrick (Mohawk Royaner Tekarihoken) echoed similar sentiments:

> What we are now going to say is a matter of great moment, which we desire you to remember as long as the Sun and Moon lasts. We are willing to sell you this large tract of land for your people to live upon, but we desire that this may be considered as part of our Agreement that when we are all dead and gone your Grandchildren may not say to our Grandchildren, that your Forefathers sold the land to our Forefathers, and therefore be gone off them. This is wrong. Let us all be as Brethren as well after as before giving you Deeds for Land. After we have sold our land we in a little time have nothing to show for it; but it is not so with you, your Grandchildren will get something from it as long as the world stands; our Grandchildren will have no advantage from it; they will say we were fools for selling so much land for so small a matter and curse us; therefore let it be a part of the present agreement that we shall treat each other as Brethren to the latest Generation, even after we shall not have left a foot of land.[21]

This "sale" was prefaced by a promise by the British that their future generations would respect their Haudenosaunee peers. In other words, the treaty bound the British and the Haudenosaunee to treat each other as brethren for all time. Hendrick's words about Haudenosaunee land loss were prophetic, but his reminder to the British about their vows of brotherhood was soon forgotten by the Crown.

Also at the Lancaster Treaty Council, Canasatego explained key aspects of Haudenosaunee land philosophies:

> When you mentioned the Affair of the Land Yesterday, you went back to Old Times, and told us that you had been in Possession of the Province of Maryland for above one hundred Years; but what is one hundred Years in comparison to the length of Time since our Claim began? Since we

came out of this ground? For we must tell you that long before one hundred years our Ancestors came out of this very ground, and their children have remained here ever since. … You came out of the ground in a country that lies beyond the Seas; there you may have a just Claim, but here you must allow us to be your elder Brethren, and the lands to belong to us before you knew anything of them.

It is true, that above one hundred years ago the Dutch came here in a ship … During all this time the newcomers, the Dutch, acknowledged our right to the lands…

After this the English came into the country, and, as we were told, became one people with the Dutch. About two years after the arrival of the English, an English governor came to Albany, and finding what great friendship subsisted between us and the Dutch, he approved it mightily, and desired to make as strong a league, and to be upon as good terms with us as the Dutch were …

Indeed we have had some small differences with the English, and, during these misunderstandings, some of their young men would, by way of reproach, be every now and then telling us that we should have perished if they had not come into the country and furnished us with strouds [blankets] and hatchets and guns, and other things necessary for the support of life. But we always gave them to understand that they were mistaken, that we lived before they came amongst us, and as well, or better, if we may believe what our forefathers have told us. We then had room enough, and plenty of deer, which was easily caught; and though we had not knives, hatchets, or guns, such as we have now, yet we had knives of stone, and hatchets of stone, and bows and arrows, and those served our uses as well as the English ones do now.

We are now straitened, and sometimes in want of deer, and liable to many other inconveniences since the English came among us, and particularly from that pen-and-ink work that is going on at that table.[22]

In reference to "coming out of the ground" it seems that Canesatego was speaking to the Haudenosaunee Creation Story, wherein the Creator formed human beings from clay and brought them to life with his breath.

This statement also attests to a strong belief that one's rights to a territory stem from one's origins and extensive interactions with a particular place. In addition, the speaker's words demonstrate the continuity in recollection of the history of his people with the British—an important example of historical consciousness and continuity. Finally, Canasatego's message summarizes many of the ecological changes resulting from European colonization. In this, he asserts that treaties and other agreements have had a direct impact in causing the "poor" times the Haudenosaunee were then faced with, and he urges the British to return to the original path of peace and friendship their ancestors helped to create with his ancestors.

A third Haudenosaunee-British treaty directly relevant to this discussion was made in Albany in July 1701, known as the Nanfan Treaty or Beaver Hunting Grounds Treaty. In this agreement, the Five Nations were seeking the protection of their northern and western hunting grounds, which had come under major attack in recent years. They called upon the provisions of the Covenant Chain, wherein the British promised to protect Haudenosaunee interests. The terms of the treaty are highly debated because, on the surface, the agreement appears to be a surrender from the Haudenosaunee to the British. However, British interpretation at the time (and throughout the next six decades, at least) was that the Haudenosaunee understood the treaty to place these territories under the protection of the King—following under the provisions of the Covenant Chain, wherein the Crown promised to protect Haudenosaunee interests. In the 1701 treaty, the Five Nations were specifically referring to their hunting territories and saw the agreement as a commitment by the Crown to protect Haudenosaunee use of those lands in perpetuity—an agreement of economic security.[23] Later British colonial documents explain that the Haudenosaunee saw this as a promise of protection by the British against the French, their allies, and any other people who might encroach upon those lands against the wishes of the Haudenosaunee.[24] In this promise of protection, the British were echoing the words of their predecessors, who had offered similar protection to the Haudenosaunee in the 1664 Fort Albany Treaty.

When considering the 1701 treaty, one must also recognize the dependence of the British upon the Haudenosaunee at that time. The

British had just declared war on the French again, and they knew they were dependent upon the Haudenosaunee to assist them should that war spill over from Europe to North America. The Covenant Chain alliance had also accorded the British prominence in the northeastern fur trade, an economic reality that provided invaluable assets to the Crown in order to help finance their worldwide imperial endeavours. The leadership of the New York colony was well aware of the British dependence on the Five Nations, as evidenced by the May 13, 1701, letter of Robert Livingston, New York Secretary of Indian Affairs (1675–1721):

> of the Five Nations, I need not enumerate the advantages arising from their firmness to this Government [New York], they having fought our battles for us and been a constant barrier of the defence [sic] between Virginia and Maryland and the French, and by their constant vigilance have prevented the French from making any descent that way.[25]

It would be simple to view the 1701 treaty as a surrender of territory by a "weak Indian Nation" to a "strong European power," but that was not at all the case. The Haudenosaunee and the British had truly become intertwined through the Covenant Chain, and while they remained separate peoples, they depended on each other like family.

The Tarnished Chain

In many ways, the 1701 Albany Treaty is symbolic of the change in the Haudenosaunee-British relationship following the American Revolution. In 1784, Sir Frederick Haldimand—on behalf of the British—offered the Six Nations a tract of land along the Grand River as reparations for land loss in their original homelands—which the Crown had surrendered to the Americans without Haudenosaunee consent in the 1783 Treaty of Paris.[26] The territory of the 1784 proclamation, known as the Haldimand Tract, falls within the lands of the 1701 Albany Treaty.[27] In other words, Haldimand was simply reaffirming a promise made to the Haudenosaunee eighty-three years previously: to protect Haudenosaunee interests in our own land. In 1755, the British recalled this treaty to convince the Haudenosaunee to join their cause against the French.[28] Without Haudenosaunee support—which probably would not have been given if not for the 1701 treaty—the war would likely have gone the other way. In less than three decades, the Haudenosaunee had gone from being invaluable allies to an afterthought in their North American empire. Unfortunately, it was the start of a negative turn in Haudenosaunee-Crown relations. Except for momentary shifts back to the language of allies (most notably in the War of 1812, but as recently as World War I), the Crown took a steady course away from recognizing the Haudenosaunee as allies to treating them like subjects or, even worse, wards of the state.

Haudenosaunee communities fell on both sides of the US-Canada border created at the end of the American Revolution. The Crown initially invited all Haudenosaunee to move to its side of the border (noting that several Haudenosaunee communities already existed on that side), mainly suggesting the Grand River and Bay of Quinte lands as new homelands. Eventually, the Crown broke off relations with Haudenosaunee communities on the US side of the border. On the Canadian side, the Crown continued relations with the Haudenosaunee communities located within those boundaries, but in a continually diminished fashion. While each community has a distinct history of decline in Crown relations, Ohswe:ken[29] (the Grand River Territory) is looked at here for examples of the tarnished relationship.

While the Haldimand Proclamation was merely a promise to uphold a limited portion of the 1701 Albany Treaty, it was in the same spirit of the treaty. It recognized Haudenosaunee autonomy over their territory and promised British protection of Haudenosaunee land rights. However, in less than seven years, Crown authorities were questioning the legitimacy of Haldimand's Proclamation because they determined that he had not used the proper seal[30] on the 1784 document. In 1793, Lord Simcoe issued a new "deed" to the Grand River lands, cutting off the upper third—over 300,000 acres—of the territory. The Six Nations Council quickly and defiantly objected to Simcoe's reassessment of their lands. This assertion, known as the Headwaters Claim, persists to the present day. Over the next fifty years, the Grand River lands were reduced to 55,000 acres, with most of the land losses coming under blatantly illegal transfers or leases conferred to sales without Haudenosaunee consent.[31]

The reduction of the Grand River lands was adamantly opposed by Confederacy leadership at every possible turn. Undoubtedly, it was one of the reasons that the Canadian federal government sought to replace the Confederacy Council with an elected band council system in 1924. The Six Nations Band Council, as defined by the *Indian Act*, would have to respond to Indian Affairs directives and would be limited in their ability to protest against actions of the governments of Canada since they, too, were a branch of the Canadian system. While they found minimal support within the Six Nations community for this system in 1924 (27 men—out of an estimated 1,000 eligible voters—voted in the first election), the majority of the community adamantly opposed the change in governance. The Confederacy Council continued to meet and govern the territory, despite the transference of funds and Canadian recognition to the Band Council (by the Department of Indian Affairs). This Indian Affairs action continues to be a major problem for the Grand River Haudenosaunee, but opportunities have recently arisen to rectify some of the past wrongs inflicted by Canadian governments.[32]

An Opportunity to Polish the Chain

While Indigenous Peoples have typically expressed their continued rights and responsibilities to their territories and corresponding environments throughout colonial times, the Oka Crisis of 1990 inspired an increase in Indigenous activism in Canada. The Oka situation was one in a series of actions within Haudenosaunee territories that also raised the concerns of Canadian and United States authorities regarding Haudenosaunee land rights. Many of these actions remain unresolved, leaving all parties involved unsettled. For example, the questions of land title for the Kanehsatake Mohawk territory remain unanswered[33]—which was the root of the problem leading to the standoff. There is hope, however, that other sites of conflict or potential conflict may be resolved utilizing Haudenosaunee principles and aspects of treaty relationships.

Since the early 1980s, the City of Hamilton, Ontario, planned to build a new highway on the eastern border of the city to alleviate traffic pressures associated with urban sprawl. Environmental activists from in and around Hamilton had joined efforts with a Six Nations environmentalist, Norman Jacobs, hoping that Haudenosaunee land rights might provide the key to saving a creek and surrounding forest from development, the last "undeveloped" land within the city. Years of lobbying the city council and educating the public proved unsuccessful in stopping the expressway. Even the federal government had sought to stop the project, but lost their case in federal court. Shortly before his untimely death in 2003, Jacobs urged the Haudenosaunee to negotiate with the City to see if a compromise could be reached. At the same time, Native and non-Native environmentalists moved into the Red Hill Valley, hoping their occupation would stop development. Most of the protestors eventually left the site, with two hold-outs being removed by police in September of that year. The road is still under construction, slated to open in 2008.

Critics would argue that the City was going to do "what it wanted" in the Red Hill Valley, but the final result has been something quite different. Instead of a standard highway project, the agreements negotiated between the Haudenosaunee and the City of Hamilton have resulted in a unique partnership (and series of partnerships) based on Haudenosaunee ethics and treaty principles. The General Agreement, signed November 17, 2003, articulates key aspects of Haudenosaunee land and environmental ethics such as the following:

> 1.4 Haudenosaunee law acknowledges the land and living things, not as resources or assets intended for the use and enjoyment of humans, but as vital parts of a larger circle of life, each entitled to respect protection. In Haudenosaunee thought, it is not possible to separate "land" from the rest of life—the waters, grasses, medicine plants, food plants, berries and trees; the insects, animals, birds and people; the winds and other unseen forces that benefit the world. Our relationship with all these is one of gratitude and humility. We acknowledge that each part of the natural world seeks to fulfill its responsibility, as we humans do.[34]

Related to this, also, is the Haudenosaunee acknowledgement that "while [they] cannot agree with the environmental loss that may be caused by the Roadway...they are entering into this Agreement to help mitigate that loss and to help protect the Valley for the future."[35] In this the Haudenosaunee were asserting their responsibility to protect the natural world to the best of their ability.

The agreement addresses the treaty relationship and how the City of Hamilton fits into it:

> 2.1 The Haudenosaunee and the Crown have a treaty rela-
> tionship that has lasted several centuries. Hamilton, as a
> municipality created by the Crown's laws, respects and shares
> in that relationship. The central symbol of that relationship,
> the Silver Covenant Chain, signifies mutual respect, sharing
> and help. The Covenant Chain relationship forms the basis
> and informs the principles of this Agreement.[36]

This statement clearly delineates the position of Hamilton as a government of Canada bound by the ancient covenants of the Crown. Of extreme historical significance, this agreement marked the first time a government of Canada had recognized the governing authority of the Haudenosaunee Confederacy Council since 1924.[37]

The General Agreement also articulates a unique approach to describing the relationship created by the agreement and the ensuing projects:

> 3.4 Rather than approach their work in the Valley from the
> perspective of legal rights and title, the Parties have agreed
> that the concept of joint stewardship ... shall be their guide.
> The Parties acknowledge that they each carry unique and
> different knowledge and resources, and that bringing these
> together is in their mutual best interests, as well as in the
> interests of the Valley.[38]

Of final note is a section that summarizes the complexity of the highway project and its implications for both parties:

> 3.7 The Valley has presented the Haudenosaunee and
> Hamilton with both a challenge and an opportunity. For
> Hamilton, the challenge has been to find sustainable solu-
> tions to its transportation and development needs while
> respecting the rights of both the natural world and its own

> future generations. For the Haudenosaunee, the challenge has been to find ways to accommodate Hamilton's transportation and development needs consistent with Haudenosaunee obligations to the ancestors, to future generations, and to the natural world, and consistent with Haudenosaunee rights. For both the Haudenosaunee and Hamilton, the opportunity lies within the relationship of mutual respect and assistance that has historically assisted the Haudenosaunee and their settler neighbours to find solutions that enable them to work together and to learn from each other.[39]

In outlining the possibilities for the project, they also recognize the stresses, especially those faced by the environment.

This agreement (and the ensuing sub-agreements) marks the first time the Haudenosaunee were allowed by a Canadian government in recent times to negotiate under the Great Law. It was precipitated by a shift from confrontation to negotiation, and the products to date have been a significant shift away from development norms by municipalities neighbouring the Grand River Haudenosaunee. While not perfect—it even recognizes that mistakes will be made[40]—it is a pragmatic solution to a situation that easily could have devolved into a standoff that would have probably "'nded" in highway development and extreme environmental loss. It may have also come to the loss of human life in the process. Instead, there is a highway, but there are also a series of environmental restoration projects, led by Haudenosaunee individuals, that serve as a model for what can be achieved when Euro-American governments work with Indigenous Nations, respecting their mutual obligations to each other. The Joint Stewardship Board membership is 50% Haudenosaunee appointees and 50% Hamilton appointees. Paul Williams, one of the Haudenosaunee negotiators for the Red Hill Valley Agreement, has described the partnership as an example of "careful reciprocity," a pragmatic solution to a seemingly unsolvable conflict.

Closing Thoughts

Clearly, I see a lot of promise in the model of the Red Hill Valley Expressway Project. Its grounding in Haudenosaunee land and environmental ethics in conjunction with the principles of Haudenosaunee-Crown treaty relations provides a road map to resolving areas of conflict, especially where land rights are at issue. However, it seems other governments of Canada have not learned from the experiences of the City of Hamilton.

As I write, my community is involved in talks with the Ontario and Canadian federal governments in an attempt to correct past wrongs on the part of the Crown against the people and land of Ohswe:ken. This negotiation process, instigated by the events of the Six Nations-Caledonia Reclamation, has the potential to be unlike any other land-related discussions held between governments of Canada and a First Nations community. For the first time since 1924, both the Province of Ontario and the Canadian federal government have recognized the Haudenosaunee Grand Council as a legitimate entity with the authority to represent the Ohswekenhronon.[41] On the other hand, both the Province and the federal government have attempted to undermine the authority of the Grand Council in this process. In some cases, they have insisted on the presence and participation of the Chief Councillor of the elected band council on behalf of Six Nations, despite the statement of the Band Council itself declaring the Confederacy as the body to take the lead in the negotiations process.[42] In this and other sleights of hand, the governments of Canada have shown a persistence of patriarchal ideas regarding the Haudenosaunee.[43] If they continue on that course, they will undo the work and efforts of everyone involved in the process since April 2006. So, as the governments of Canada and the Haudenosaunee Grand Council continue down this river, what exists in their shared history to use as a base for reconstructing healthy relationships between the Haudenosaunee and the Crown? Where might this river lead us if we travel it together in peace and friendship? What will our shared forever look like?

Author's Note: Community legal experts were consulted for accuracy and legal implications of the text; however, the author accepts sole responsibility for all words and does not speak on behalf of the Ohswekenhronon.

[1] The Haudenosaunee are a confederacy comprising five original member nations—Mohawk, Oneida, Onondaga, Cayuga, and Seneca—and several "dependent" nations, including the Tuscarora (officially the "Sixth Nation"), Delaware, Nanticoke, and Tutelo. The Haudenosaunee are also known as the Iroquois Confederacy, the Five Nations, and the Six Nations.

[2] The term "epic" is not intended to infer mythology. Rather, it refers to the size and scope of these stories that comprise the cultural history of the Haudenosaunee.

[3] "Colonial period" discussed herein roughly references events occurring between the years 1600 to 1800. I would argue, however, that the colonial period continues to the present day in many cases as a direct result of Western imperialism against the Haudenosaunee.

[4] Calvin Martin, *Keepers of the Game: Indian-Animal Relationships and the Fur Trade*, (Berkley: University of California Press, 1978).

[5] An actual date for the founding of the Kayaneren'kowa is unknown as Haudenosaunee methods of dating do not easily transfer into Western calendar systems. Many Haudenosaunee people date the founding of the Confederacy between 1000 to 2000 years ago.

[6] Karihwiyo (Good Message), Kasehstenhsera (Power), and Skennen (Peace) in the Mohawk language.

[7] At the founding of the Kayaneren'kowa, the Five Nations became one collective people known as the "Haudenosaunee," meaning "people who make a house," referencing the Peacemaker's metaphor of all the Five Nations living together in one longhouse, as one extended family. This house is also a metaphor for the peace built between the Five Nations through the Kayaneren'kowa.

[8] Tsikonhsaseh was the first person to accept the Law and, as a result, the Peacemaker directed that women were to play a critical role in the new government created under the Kayaneren'kowa. He directed that women, as leaders of their families, would select the male speakers to represent their clans in the Grand Council. As Clan Mothers, these women choose their male speakers and monitor their activities to ensure they conduct themselves with honour and respect. Since leaders serve for life, the power to name new leaders and the power to depose an errant leader rests with these women.

[9] Some people report that decision making must be made in the context of the impact for seven generations to come. Other experts in the Great Law assert that the decisions of the Council must be made in the context of all future generations.

[10] In most Haudenosaunee communities today, both Confederacy government and imposed elected systems exist. People choose which government they will honour, but it is often difficult to live in these communities without at least some connection to the elected systems, as they control the majority of resources and community services. Traditionally minded individuals, however, work toward strengthening the traditional governments in their communities in an effort to return the communities to a state of true self-governance under the Kayaneren'kowa. For a detailed discussion of these issues, see Oren Lyons and John Mohawk, eds., *Exiled in the Land of the Free*, (Santa Fe: Clearlight Publishers, 1992).

[11] This is the Cayuga and Seneca spelling of the word. In Mohawk it is "Karihwiyo," the same name for the message of the Great Peace discussed earlier.

[12] For a detailed discussion of these environmental ethics, see Haudenosaunee Environmental Task Force (HETF), *The Words That Come Before All Else* (Akwesasne Haudenosaunee Territory: Native North American Traveling College, 2000).

[13] For further discussion of this, see Susan M. Hill, "The Clay We Are Made Of: An Examination of Haudenosaunee Land Tenure on the Grand River Territory," Unpublished PhD dissertation, Department of Indigenous Studies, Trent University, 2005.

[14] This is the Mohawk spelling for the treaty; in Cayuga it is spelled 'Guswentha'. A second Mohawk name for the treaty is "Teyohate," meaning "two roads."

[15] For example, see Oren Lyons, "The American Indian in the Past," in Lyons and Mohawk, eds., *Exiled in the Land of the Free*, 40–42.

[16] E.B. O'Callahan, *Documents Relative to the Colonial History of the State of New York* (NYCD) (Albany: Weed, Parsons and Co., 1853–1887) I: 67–68.

[17] For a detailed discussion of this, see Paul Williams, "The Chain," LLM thesis, Toronto, Osgoode Hall, 1982.

[18] [British] Public Records Office [PRO], Kew, England, Colonial Office Papers [CO] 1/40; see also NYCD XIII: 510.

[19] For a discussion of this, see Francis Jennings, "Iroquois Alliances in American History," in F. Jennings, ed., *The History and Culture of Iroquois Diplomacy: An Interdisciplinary Guide to the Treaties of the Six Nations and Their League* (New York: Syracuse University Press, 1985), 37–65.

[20] Julian Boyd, ed., *Indian Treaties Printed by Benjamin Franklin, 1736–1762*, (Philadelphia: Historical Society of Pennsylvania, 1938), 78, as cited in Ronald Wright, Stolen Continents (Toronto: Penguin Books, 1992), 128.

[21] Pennsylvania Archives, Ser. 4, 2: 698–707, as cited in Timothy Shannon, *Indians and Colonists at the Crossroads of Empire: the Albany Congress of 1754* (Ithaca: Cornell University Press, 2000), 166.

[22] Treaty Minutes, Pennsylvania Council Minutes, 16 June 1744, 4:706–709, as cited by Wright, *Stolen Continents*, 129–130.

[23] For a detailed discussion, see Hill, "The Clay We Are Made Of," 194–202; Paul Williams and Curtis Nelson, "Kaswentah," research report prepared for the Royal Commission on Aboriginal Peoples, January 1995, from *For Seven Generations: An Information Legacy of the RCAP* (Libraxus, 1997), n.p.

[24] For example, see William Johnson, The Papers of Sir William Johnson (SWJP), I, (Albany: University of the State of New York, 1965), 530.

[25] *Calendar of State Papers, Colonial Series, America and West Indies, Preserved in the Public Record Office*, vol. 1701.1896; as cited in Richard W. Hill, Sr., "Cultural History of Haudenosaunee Sovereignty," unpublished manuscript, 1999.

²⁶ The British originally suggested land along the Bay of Quinte, a spot that many Mohawk families accepted as a new homeland. The majority of Six Nations people who decided to move to the Canada side of the border, however, selected the Grand River lands.

²⁷ The Bay of Quinte lands also fall within the 1701 treaty area.

²⁸ NAC, RG 10, volume 1822, 22; as cited by Williams and Nelson, "Kaswentah."

²⁹ Ohswe:ken is the Mohawk name for the Grand River Territory, also known as Six Nations. It refers to "the place of the willow trees," a defining characteristic of the riverbanks and neighbouring areas.

³⁰ Haldimand had used his personal seal-at-arms rather than the Great Seal of the Province. For a detailed discussion of this see *Doe dem. Jackson v. Wilkes* (1835) 4 UCKB (05): 142; and *Doe dem Sheldon v. Ramsay* (1852) 9 UCQB: 105.

³¹ For further discussion, see Hill, "The Clay We Are Made Of."

³² Similar treaty infractions have been committed by the United States government in violation of treaties they negotiated with the Haudenosaunee after their formation.

³³ Technically, these questions were "answered" in the Canadian legal system, in the 1920s, in the Privy Council (*Corinthe v. Seminaire de St. Sulpice*). The problem is deeper: the decision itself was clearly unfair. Any real solution to land claims has to approach fairness from an extra-legal (outside Canadian law) perspective in order to adequately address the purposely narrow interpretations of law in favour of Crown governments.

³⁴ City of Hamilton and Six Nations Haudenosaunee Confederacy, *The Red Hill Valley Project: General Agreement*, November 17, 2003, <www.myhamilton.ca>, 4.

³⁵ Ibid., 7.

³⁶ Ibid., 5.

³⁷ In October 1924, the Visiting Superintendent of Indian Affairs (Brantford Office) was accompanied by RCMP officers to the Village of Ohswe:ken where they decreed the Confederacy Council to be illegal under the *Indian Act* and implemented an "elected" band council system. This has been a point of great contention and upheaval for the Grand River Haudenosaunee since that time.

³⁸ City of Hamilton, *The Red Hill Valley Project: General Agreement*, 6.

³⁹ Ibid., 7.

⁴⁰ Ibid., 6.

⁴¹ Meaning "People of Ohswe:ken."

⁴² In other words, Canada and Ontario are again trying to tell Six Nations who should be their leaders, in the same spirit as did their predecessors in the 1920s.

Chapter 2

ISTÁ SĆIÁNEW, ISTÁ SXOLE
"To Fish as Formerly": The Douglas Treaties and the WSÁNEĆ Reef-Net Fisheries

Nicholas Xumthoult Claxton

The WSÁNEĆ (Saanich) people occupy a territory that encompasses what is now known as southern Vancouver Island, the Gulf Islands, the San Juan Islands, and across to the Fraser River.[1] The WSÁNEĆ traditionally lived in a highly developed culture with an intricate social system and model of governance. A major component of this system was the SXOLE, or reef-net fishery. This system allowed the WSÁNEĆ to live and prosper within the bounds of the WSÁNEĆ territory for many thousands of years. In British Columbia, it is only within the past 150 to 200 years that contact and colonization have had a detrimental impact on the WSÁNEĆ way of life. Despite the supposed protection of the Douglas Treaty of 1852, nearly everything that defines what it means to be WSÁNEĆ—the SENĆOŦEN language, culture, governance, and even fisheries—has been eroded to near extinction. In this chapter, I will analyze and interpret the implications of the Douglas Treaty for the WSÁNEĆ in such a way that I have not found in the literature, past or recent. My findings come from interpreting this agreement from a WSÁNEĆ perspective rather than from merely a Western legal or scholarly perspective. Of particular interest for me is the significance of the explicit statement in the treaty that promises the WSÁNEĆ the "liberty to carry on their fisheries as formerly."

The Douglas Treaties are well documented in both legal and historical literature. Firstly, British Columbia only joined Canada in 1871, and it appears that since and even prior to this time, extinguishment of Aboriginal title to the land has been a paramount concern of the Crown's, and it is with this emphasis on land title that nearly all the literature on the Douglas Treaties is focused. As a result, an analysis is required that goes beyond the land title implications toward a clearer understanding of what the treaty means for the WSÁNEĆ and the Crown. In my analysis of the treaty, it has become evident that the treaty protection of WSÁNEĆ fisheries "as formerly" protects much more than just fisheries. It protects a system of governance and jurisdiction within the WSÁNEĆ traditional territory.

The Douglas Treaties

Beginning in 1850, the Hudson's Bay Company (HBC) was authorized by the colonial office in London to establish a colony on Vancouver Island. The significance of Indigenous Peoples' relationship to their lands and resources was completely disregarded, and all the colonizers could see was an empty land that harboured boundless wealth for the taking. In the following four years, James Douglas, chief factor of the HBC, completed fourteen purchase agreements with Vancouver Island Indigenous Nations. These documents are often referred to as the "Fort Victoria Treaties" or the "Douglas Treaties." James Douglas did not explicitly use the word "treaty" in these agreements; however, the Supreme Court has ruled that these agreements were then, and remain to be, valid treaties, since Douglas, who was acting as an agent of the Crown at the time, arranged them with the Indigenous Peoples.[2] The Crown's intent was to abolish the Aboriginal title of those signatory nations, but, in exchange, allow those Indigenous Peoples to carry on their fisheries as they formerly had for millennia. It has been argued that for the WSÁNEĆ people and for all Indigenous Peoples on the Pacific slope, their fisheries were, and still are, necessary for their existence as independent nations.[3]

The northwest coast of what is now called North America was home to Indigenous Nations for many thousands of years before contact.

White people began to arrive on the coast of British Columbia in any significant numbers only in the 1850s. During the early contact period, the fur trade between Indigenous Peoples and Europeans developed without much colonial control. Trading companies established fortified trading posts, but Europeans at this time remained vastly outnumbered. Robin Fisher, in *Contact and Conflict: Indian-European Relations in British Columbia 1774–1890*, contends that during this time, control over Indian lands and societies remained in Indian hands, well into the recent history of British Columbia.[4] It was not long before the British Crown endeavoured to exercise its sovereignty over Indigenous Peoples and their lands, which was to become the driving force behind the Douglas Treaties.

Paul Tennant thoroughly recounts the time preceding, and including, the signing of the treaties in his book *Aboriginal Peoples and Politics*, albeit from a colonialist perspective.[5] He states that, after the establishment of the colony of Vancouver Island in 1849, the Hudson's Bay Company had been granted control of land and settlement of the colony. Regarding the land and colonization of the land, explicit instructions were sent to James Douglas from Archibald Barclay in London, who was the company's secretary at the time. It read:

> With respect to the rights of the natives, you will have to confer with the chiefs of the tribes on that subject, and in your negotiations with them you are to consider the natives as the rightful possessors of such lands only as they are occupied by cultivation, or had houses built on, at the time the island came under the undivided sovereignty of Great Britain in 1846. All other land is to be regarded as waste, applicable for the purposes of colonization. The right of fishing and hunting will be continued to the natives, and when their lands are registered, and they conform to the same conditions with which other settlers are required to comply, they will enjoy the same rights and privileges.[6]

The above passage reflects the colonial mentality and principles regarding land and land use that founded policy concerning Indigenous Peoples and their lands, and which pervades policy to the present day. The colonial assumption that the land was waste by simply appearing to be unoccupied was incorrect. Thus the Douglas Treaties, not unlike subsequent colonial policy, simply and devastatingly disconnected Indigenous Peoples from their land. The assimilative notion is also expressed in the reference to how Indigenous Peoples would be absorbed into the dominant society, to "enjoy" the same rights and privileges as the white people. The colonial vision of domesticating Indigenous Peoples and their rights was the main objective of that policy: the "Douglas System."

Paul Tennant states that James Douglas departed slightly from the instructions he was given for his negotiations with Indigenous Peoples.[7] He was instructed to regard the unoccupied land as wasteland suitable for colonization; instead, he regarded the Indians as rightful owners of the whole of their territories. Tennant bases this claim on the wording of the treaties themselves. Tennant states that Governor Douglas was purchasing these territories through treaty, on behalf of the Crown, excepting Indigenous village sites and enclosed fields. Therefore, Governor Douglas recognized Aboriginal title as the whole of an Indigenous community's traditional territory, and it was his intention to extinguish all this title except to that of the "village sites and enclosed fields." Tennant states that even though these treaties left only a few acres per family, it did leave it under title of the Aboriginal people who signed it. However, Tennant states that "the treaties plainly indicate that Douglas did not regard any land as un-owned" and that the "text of the treaty indicates that the Indian community owned the whole of the lands of their territory."[8] Tennant further states that a map of the treaty areas around Fort Victoria showed no gaps between the Indian communities.[9] However, what the author does not realize, in the case of the WSÁNEĆ, and likely in all cases of Indigenous villages and nations, is that it is only a small fraction of the WSÁNEĆ territory that is mentioned in the treaty and represented on that map. Therefore, from a WSÁNEĆ point of view, it is only the lands in the immediate vicinity of Victoria that have been sold, and the vast majority of the WSÁNEĆ territory, which includes the Gulf Islands, the San Juan Islands, and the waterways in between, still belong to the WSÁNEĆ. Tennant further justifies Douglas by saying he was more generous in fisheries, acknowledging the unqualified and unlimited right to "carry on our fisheries as formerly."[10] As mentioned earlier, Indigenous fisheries were central to Indigenous societies and to their identities as independent nations.

To further confound Douglas's apparent generosity to Indigenous communities, James Hendrickson presents an account of the unusual way the treaty itself was created.[11] Douglas initially had the Indigenous leaders of the community sign their "approval" at the bottom of a blank sheet. In search of the appropriate text to complete the document, Douglas used text that was virtually identical, except for the addition of appropriate names and dates, to the Treaty of Waitangi, signed a decade earlier in New Zealand.

This alludes to another discrepancy ignored by Tennant: whether the Indigenous representatives fully understood the implications of signing the treaty. Chris Arnett speaks to the WSÁNEĆ situation on that question. Unlike the other agreements, the WSÁNEĆ agreement was made with the actual text of the deed in place at the time they were signed. However, the oral history of the WSÁNEĆ states that the leaders "did not know what was said on the paper."[12] Even if there were interpreters available to the WSÁNEĆ, the promises that their winter villages, food-gathering sites, and, most importantly, their fisheries were to be protected would have led the WSÁNEĆ leaders to assume no threat in signing an agreement with the newcomers. Arnett also argues that the Indigenous Peoples perceived that the agreements were only a confirmation of ownership of village sites, food-gathering sites, and their fisheries. From an Indigenous perspective, entering into agreements with the colonists represented an arrangement whereby Indigenous Nations and the white people could live side-by-side, together sharing the land.

Conversely, I allege that the colonial settlers imposed their concepts of land ownership and use on the Indigenous Peoples who signed these agreements, and their intention in doing so was the domestication of Indigenous Peoples in Canada. Despite the apparent deception tactics and imposition of European principles of land ownership, the Douglas Treaties still guaranteed the Indigenous fisheries as formerly, and reaffirmed WSÁNEĆ title to the majority of WSÁNEĆ traditional territory. This right has largely been ignored and infringed upon, right up to the present day, despite protection of the treaty.[13]

Departing from the view that the Douglas Treaties are land-cession treaties, there is the view that the Douglas Treaties were treaties for peace. In her recent Master's thesis, Janice Knighton draws upon the oral testimony of a couple of WSÁNEĆ Elders, in which she concludes the WSÁNEĆ interpretation of the treaty was that of a peace treaty.[14] Knighton writes that one WSÁNEĆ Elder was taught at a young age through oral history that a WSÁNEĆ Hereditary Chief, whose father was present at the signing of the treaty, said that the signatories were of the understanding that "their way of life was never going to be disturbed, and they would be able to take their food and travel as they always had."[15] This WSÁNEĆ Elder also makes reference to ĆELÁNEN—traditional WSÁNEĆ laws and teachings that form the basis for the governance structure—could never be sold; in actuality, they were only reinforced and respected by this treaty for peace. This interpretation of the Douglas Treaties is closer to what I understand the treaty to mean for the WSÁNEĆ. The WSÁNEĆ reef-net fishery was not unlike the WSÁNEĆ ĆELÁNEN, in that it was part of an overall system of WSÁNEĆ law and governance.

Reef-Net Fishing

Very little is documented in literature about the reef net and the few sources that do exist are generally written from a Western historical perspective. Indigenous fishing for the most part was centred on salmon rivers such as the Fraser River. However, for the WSÁNEĆ, and all of the SENCOEN speaking peoples, reef net fishing was the primary and most significant fishery.

At the time of signing the Douglas Treaty—actually, well beyond this time up to the 1940s and 1950s before it was outlawed—the WSÁNEĆ people had in place a unique traditional fishery that had been annually carried out since time immemorial. This was the reef-net fishery, and it had implicit in its practice a well-established system of management and governance of the fisheries and land. Since salmon was a staple in the WSÁNEĆ diet, and a critical component in the WSÁNEĆ economy, the reef-net fishery formed the core of WSÁNEĆ society.

The reef net is called SX̱OLE in the W̱SÁNEĆ language. This word also refers to the material that the net was constructed of, the inner bark of the willow tree. The species of willow that was most likely used was the Pacific willow or the Hooker's willow, which were both prevalent in the W̱SÁNEĆ Territory.[16] Fishing with the SX̱OLE was an incredibly sophisticated technique, which required in-depth knowledge of the salmon, their habits and travel routes, the tides and currents, and of plants, among other things. To see the reef net in action in this day would amaze anybody. This fishing technique could not be successful without the W̱SÁNEĆ people's deep respect for the salmon, the earth, and each other. The principle of respect was an integral part of the W̱SÁNEĆ people's worldview.

The SX̱OLE was hand constructed from cedar and willow. The reef-net fishing apparatus consisted of a lead to guide salmon into a net suspended between two canoes.[17] The net was secured in an ideal location, such as at the mouth of a bay, for entire fishing seasons by the use of giant rock anchors.

The lead of the reef net consisted of cedar log buoys, cedar ropes to form the sides and the floor of the lead, and specially made rock weights. Dune grass was threaded through the twining of the ropes that formed the floor and the sides, which was used to fool the salmon that they were actually safely swimming near the bottom. Ropes to permanent anchors secured the front of the lead, and the rear of the lead was connected to the fishermen's canoes and to the net itself. The net was suspended between two canoes, and it would bag out with the flow of the tide. The sterns of the canoes were also secured to the bottom with ropes and anchors. When the net was hauled and fishing was stopped, the rear of the lead was tied to those rear anchors and the lead of the reef net remained in the water, usually for the duration of a season, unless repairs had to be made. This is a simple description of a very complex fishing technique.

After a school of salmon had entered the net, the captain, or CWENÁLYEN, would give the order to release the rear anchor lines and the tide would bring the canoes together. At this point, the salmon could be rolled into the canoes and brought ashore. The rear anchor lines would be attached to the rear of the lead, and the fishing location would be maintained. At the shore, the women and children would receive the salmon, again with great respect. The catch was divided among the crew and the family, and was divided in twos.[18]

To successfully catch salmon using the reef net, the WSÁNEĆ fishermen had to be aware of tidal flow and the location and habits of the salmon. The direction of tidal flow is usually the direction in which the salmon travel; it would push the salmon directly into the net. An ideal location for setting the reef net was at the mouth of a bay, with tidal flow coming out of the bay and directly into the net. Reef-net fishing locations, called SWÁLET in the WSÁNEĆ language, were the birthright of the WSÁNEĆ people and fishermen, meaning they were passed down through families from generation to generation, just as family names and history were passed down. Fishing locations were not owned; rather, the families belonged to it. In traditional WSÁNEĆ society, the extended family was considered a part of the family unit, and this was how everything was passed on, including a family's NE,HIMET (history, teachings, laws, principles). The Elder of the family was usually the captain of the fishing crew and held the knowledge and history that connected the family to that fishing location. It was their responsibility to pass on that knowledge. This is, in part, how the WSÁNEĆ governed their fishery.

The WSÁNEĆ people successfully governed their traditional fisheries for thousands of years, prior to contact. This was not just because there were laws and rules in place, and that everybody followed them, but there was also a different way of thinking about fish and fishing, which included a profound respect. At the end of the net, a ring of willow was woven into the net, which allowed some salmon to escape. This is more than just a simple act of conservation (the main priority and narrow vision of the Department of Fisheries and Oceans). It represents a profound respect for salmon. It was believed that the runs of salmon were lineages, and if some were allowed to return to their home rivers, then those lineages would always continue. The WSÁNEĆ people believe that all living things were once people, and they are respected as such. The salmon are our relatives. All things on earth are to be respected, since it is the earth that we all share. This is a teaching of the WSÁNEĆ.

Out of respect, when the first large sockeye was caught, a First Salmon Ceremony was conducted. This was the WSÁNEĆ way to greet and welcome the king of all salmon. The celebration would likely last up to ten days. All fishing stopped; not just the fishermen who caught the fish, but the whole nation of fishermen joined in on the celebration. The act of celebrating the return of this special salmon exemplifies the respect held for the salmon. I would argue that this deeply rooted respect was integral to the WSÁNEĆ people's governance of their fisheries, or, to employ a Eurocentric concept, their overall management scheme. I say this because at this time of celebration, it was likely that the peak of the salmon run was travelling through the WSÁNEĆ Territory. Taking time to celebrate allowed for a major portion of the salmon stocks to return to their rivers to spawn, and to sustain those lineages or stocks. This kind of fishing behavior is in direct contrast to the approach of Department of Fisheries and Oceans, where it is their mandate to catch as many fish as possible, while allowing a minimal number of fish to escape based on "scientific formulas."

The WSÁNEĆ reef-net fishery is a highly sophisticated fishery that was directly suited to the WSÁNEĆ people. It allowed the WSÁNEĆ to live in their lands in prosperity for thousands of years. It is more than just a fishing technique; it is a model of governance over an integral part of what it means to be a WSÁNEĆ person. Fish and fishing is the WSÁNEĆ identity. To govern ourselves as WSÁNEĆ would mean to also govern our fisheries and live and fish as we always did, with the reef net. This is what is promised in the Douglas Treaties. The WSÁNEĆ are an example of a traditional Indigenous society that had an extensive system of governance in place that allowed this society to flourish. This situation, however, could represent any traditional Indigenous society on Canada's Pacific Coast.

Treaty Protection of WSÁNEĆ Governance

According to WSÁNEĆ oral history, it is believed that, despite the signing of the treaty, WSÁNEĆ ĆELÁNEN was assumed to remain intact. Similarly, it would be safe to state that the WSÁNEĆ also believed that since there was a promise that the WSÁNEĆ would remain undisturbed in their lands, their NE,HIMET—family history and teachings —would also be protected for generations to come.

For the purposes of this chapter, the concept of NE,HIMET is important, because it includes the SX̱OLE (reef net) as a component, and it is part of the overall governance system in WSÁNEĆ, which was essentially protected by the treaties. Because the Douglas Treaties explicitly state that the WSÁNEĆ people are at liberty to carry on fisheries as formerly, then that must mean the WSÁNEĆ people are at liberty to carry on those traditional governance systems that are encompassed by the WSÁNEĆ people, NE,HIMET, and ĆELÁNEN.

A WSÁNEĆ person's NE,HIMET was passed on through family teachings, and it consisted of components such as a S,IST, SX̱OLE, SX̱IX̱ŦE, SMÍEŦ, ḰO, Á,LEN, and TENEW̱. A person's S,IST refers to what they owned, essentially all of their personal belongings. In more contemporary terms this was their collateral. The SX̱OLE is of course the reef net, and this was undoubtedly a vital possession. In conjunction with the SX̱OLE, there was also the SWÁLET, or physical fishing location. This included not just the fishing location per se, but also the camping location and the Á,LEN (longhouse), the SMÍEŦ (deer drive), and ḰO (fresh water supply).

Therefore, the NE,HIMET gave the family a right to a specific location or locations. This right was passed down in the traditional way, along with their ancient family names. It was the Elder of the family who carried the right to NE,HIMET, and he was the captain, or CWENÁLYEN, of that location. Not only was it this person's responsibility that all the fishing operations were carried out, but it was also their responsibility to ensure the transmission of all these teachings to the family.

WSÁNEĆ people's traditional governance, social organization, and use of the land and resources, including the reef-net fishery, were all intertwined. Therefore, treaty protection to "fish as formerly" means more than just a right to fish; according to WSÁNEĆ teachings, it means a right to ownership of all those fishing locations (and the whole of our traditional territory) and to the system of governance that stood in WSÁNEĆ for thousands of years or more.

Therefore, it is apparent that when the WSÁNEĆ signed a treaty with Governor James Douglas, which we believed protected our fisheries as formerly and more, it protected everything that defined the WSÁNEĆ as a distinct nation. Today, the WSÁNEĆ are controlled by the Indian Act, and WSÁNEĆ fisheries are entirely governed by the Department of Fisheries and Oceans. So, it is evident that, because of the Douglas Treaties, there is a moral and legal obligation by the Crown to respect the terms of that treaty. On the other hand, it also presents a challenge to the WSÁNEĆ to preserve and revive these ancient fisheries and systems of governance and to once again be WSÁNEĆ. Instead of living our lives in complacency under the Indian Act, the WSÁNEĆ should rebuild our WSÁNEĆ society, and reinstitute our governance systems that honour our traditions, which are protected by the Douglas Treaties signed in 1852.

AUTHOR'S NOTE: It is both an honour and a privilege to research and write about such an important and vital part of WSÁNEĆ culture and life, the reef-net fishery. I would like to acknowledge and thank my SÁĆS, my Uncle Earl, for giving the majority of this information about the WSÁNEĆ reef-net fishery. His knowledge, particularly of WSÁNEĆ language, terminology, and WSÁNEĆ beliefs, is invaluable. Without his knowledge, this paper would have been impossible and meaningless. It is my vision that this knowledge can be passed on for generations to come, and that the reef-net fishery can once again become a central part of WSÁNEĆ life.

[1] Earl Claxton Sr. and John Elliott Sr., *Reef Net Technology of the Saltwater People* (Saanich, BC: Saanich Indian School Board, 1994), 46.

[2] *Regina V. White and Bob*, 52 D.L.R. (2d) 481, <library2.usask.ca/native/cnlc/vol06/684.html>.

[3] Nicholas Claxton, "The Douglas Treaty and WSÁNEĆ Traditional Fisheries: A Model for Saanich People's Governance," Masters thesis, University of Victoria, 2003.

[4] Robin Fisher, *Contact and Conflict: Indian-European Relations in British Columbia, 1774–1890* (Vancouver: University of British Columbia Press, 1977), 42.

[5] Paul Tennant, *Aboriginal Peoples and Politics: The Indian Land Question in British Columbia, 1849–1989* (Vancouver: University of British Columbia Press, 1990), 17–25.

[6] Ibid., 18.

[7] Ibid., 30.

[8] Ibid., 20.

[9] Ibid.

[10] Ibid.

[11] James Hendrickson, *The Aboriginal Land Policy of Governor James Douglas, 1849–1864.* Paper presented at BC Studies Conference, Simon Fraser University, November 1988.

[12] Chris Arnett, *The Terror of the Coast: Land Alienation and Colonial War on Vancouver Island and the Gulf Islands, 1849–1863* (Burnaby: Talonbooks, 1999), 37.

[13] Claxton, *The Douglas Treaty and WSÁNEĆ Traditional Fisheries.*

[14] Janice Knighton, "The Oral History of the Saanich Douglas Treaty: A Treaty for Peace." Masters thesis, University of Victoria, 2004.

[15] Ibid.

[16] Nancy Turner, *Plant Technology of the First Peoples of British Columbia* (Vancouver: University of British Columbia Press, 1998).

[17] Earl Claxton Sr. and John Elliott Sr., *Reef Net Technology of the Saltwater People*, 14.

[18] "Two" was a sacred number, according to Earl Claxton Sr., personal communication, (2003).

Chapter 3

Strengthening our Relations in Gespe'gewa'gi, the Seventh District of Mi'gma'gi

FRED (GOPIT) METALLIC

"Songs are important, songs can teach you and help you stay connected and I think there's a lot to learn from the songs."

Recently, a Mi'gmaq Elder from Listuguj, Gespe'gewa'gi, Mi'gma'gi, shared her understanding of how Gtapegiaqann (songs) keep us connected with our environment, with all of Ugs'tqamu, Creation. She said:

> There's a song that I sing, of late, and there's a lot of respect that comes out of it. It's called the Mi'qmaq Honour Song, and it's not a song that you can sing at any old time. I find it's a song that promotes respect and a lot of people respect it, …you've put your drum beat 4 times and all that and people are standing there, and … that spirit is there, and it's a beautiful song. An Elder fasted for that song …[1]

In our ways, as Mi'gmaq, we often open a mawiomi (gathering), a pestie'wimg (feast), and other important events with a song. The songs welcome and honour gngi'gwinaqi'g (our ancestors) who have, and continue to, stood and fought for who we are and how we may live, as L'nnu, as Mi'gmaq.

Mi'gmaq Honour Song

Gepmite'tmej, ta'n teli Lnnu'ltigw,
Migmajtut, ge' mawita'nej
Gepmite'tmej, tan'n wetapegsulti'gw
Migmajtut, apoqonmatultinej.
Apoqonmatultinej ta'n Gisulg
Teliga'lugsi'gw, ula ugs'tqamu'g

O way o hey hi ya ha
Way o hey o hey hi ya
Way o hey hi ya ha
Way o hey hi ya
O way o hey hi ya
O way o hey hi ya ha
Way o hey hi ya hey o

Gm'tginu, Our Territory

In Mi'gmaq, our Elders tell us, "tet tle'iawultigw," that we belong to this territory. Many also say, "Ne'gaw weji'mimajultigw gmaqamigalminal," we've always lived from our lands.

By living on the territory—maqamigal (lands), samuqann (waters), ugju'snn (winds) and musigisg (sky), naguset (sun), tepgunset (moon)—we, the Mi'gmaq, practised ta'n teliangweiasultieg (ways of governing) that respected our gm'tginu. From our relationship and understanding of gm'tginu, gtplutaqann (laws) emerged to guide Mi'gmaq in our everyday lived ways of governing: on the land, with each other, and with all of Creation. These tplutaqann do not originate with the arrival of the Europeans—and their descendants—in Mi'gma'gi. Neither do the laws originate within the walls of their wi'gatignmual (written traditions): instructions by the Crown, proclamations, Imperial Orders, Orders-in-Council, for instance. Nor are Mi'gmaq laws derived solely from Canadian legislation, court decisions, and government policies.

For our People, as Mi'gmaq, the European methods of inquiry have built a very limited understanding, space, and place for our life

60

ways, knowledge systems, ta'n teliangweiasultieg (ways of governing), and gtplutaqann (laws). Our stories, Mi'gmaq ways of living, can be traced much further back than to the Europeans' arrival to our shores. Although some scientists and academics acknowledge our ways, our Elders maintain that we must continue to tell our own story by following our protocols, in our own ways and language, in this circle of life.

As L'nnu, as Mi'gmaq, we continue to learn how to speak about, and live, our life ways, negaw ta'n telmimajultieg. In Mi'gmaq, you are instructed, "Ma' gisi'siwn ugjit wen piluwei," meaning "You cannot speak for someone else." The Mi'gmaq term "netewistoq" describes the role of a particular person who is asked to speak on behalf of the community. Even then, as netewistoq, you can only speak with limited authority: "pas ta'n goqwei gisisgu'tes na ta'n wegwi'gjitigen aq pas ta'n goqwei geitun aq nemitutep."

In Mi'gmaq traditions, when you come together through a mawiomi, those participating share what they know, their experience and understanding of different teachings. There are protocols that guide you in the sharing of your story and in the exchange of knowledge and learning. Mi'gmaq ways such as tlisuti (language), atugwaqann (stories), gtepegiaqiann (songs), and ta'n telo'ltigw aq ta'n telnnu'ltigw (traditions) have sustained governing practices within our respective traditional territories for thousands of years. In Indigenous ways of knowing, teachings and traditions (songs, prayers, stories) are not treated as "sources of information" that can be accumulated for personal gain. Rather, teachings are often shared with the intent and understanding of strengthening our family systems, communities, and our nations.

As we travel along in this journey of rebuilding our nations, we often forget what our Elders have taught us, that the territory is alive and continues to provide all the necessities of life. We need to listen and hear what needs to be done in order to move forward in a healthy and respectful manner.

Gespe'gewa'gi, the Seventh District of Mi'gma'gi, is interconnected through numerous river systems. Sipul teluisgl: Listuguj, Matapegiag, Apse'tgwejg, Patapegiag, Metamgetjuig, Waqamatgug, Gesgapegia'jg, aq Winpegijuig. The river systems are important for the Mi'gmaq.

Long before the establishment of land routes, the river systems enabled Mi'gmaq to easily traverse and live on the territory. Today, Elders in the district describe the rivers as their lifelines—to their ancestors, and to the future of their children.

In the story that follows, I want to share and honour what the Listuguj Sipu and what the plamu (salmon) have taught me about how to live in a Mi'gmaq way. I am sharing this story in the context of Indigenous Peoples' struggle today to live in accordance with our cultural teachings. The Indigenous struggle is about living and respecting the teachings of our ancestors. Our struggle is to rebuild our nations out of the shadow of colonialism.

Relationship on Gm'tginu, Our Territory: Ugs'tqamu, Creation

> Wejatigemgeg wesgijinuauluteg Nnu, Mi'gmawaj, negaw gegung aq e'w'g assusuti ugjit siawi angotmenin sipu'l aq niputg'l ula tet Gespeg'awagi, iluigenegewei maqamigew Mi'gama'gig. Ula assusuti wejgieg gisulgigtug negaw maqamigew e'w'meg ta'n teliangweiasultieg.
>
> Ever since the Mi'gmaq were born, we have maintained and used our authority to continue to care for the rivers, fish, woods, animals and birds in Gespe'gwa'gi, the Seventh District of Mi'gma'gi. Our authority comes from the Creator; the land has always taken care of our People.[2]

Many Elders and language speakers attest that sites and gathering places throughout all of Gespe'gwa'gi were named, known, and used prior to the arrival of Europeans. The names of gathering sites, rivers and woods, plants and medicines are remembered in the Mi'gmaq language. "The land has always taken care of our People"—in accepting that we have always lived from our land, in accepting that the land has taken care of us, we also accept that the land is a gift given to us from the Creator. By acknowledging the land in this way, we affirm a relationship with all of its beings.

Our occupation and use of different parts of the territory, at differing times of the year, has given us understandings of the life cycles of many different beings. Ta'n teliangweiasultieg (governance) in this manner can be seen to be evolving cyclically rather than in a progressive linear path as we humans move to more complex ways of organizing. The understanding behind the cyclical journey is to build relationships along the way, thus strengthening governance capacity.

My family has always been involved with the fishery, most particularly with the salmon. Recently, I was asked: "When does the fishing season begin?" In reply, I said: "It all depends on the environment." While this answer may be short, learning to read the environment is something that requires years of observation and practice. Learning to read the environmental text is part of our Mi'gmaq way of learning. Learning in this manner is how we continue to live in accordance with the flux of Creation.

The plamu have always travelled up the sipu. Likewise, Mi'gmaq social, political, and spiritual orderings exist because of Mi'gmaq Peoples' inalienable and inherent relationship with the water, the fish, the land, and the resources. An Elder from the community of Listuguj spoke about ceremonies, and the importance of the water:

> I do ceremonies four times a year, just for the water. And, I try to follow the seasons. Like the day of the seasons, let's say the 21 of September ... the fall season; I would bring a spirit plate, what we call a spirit plate, to the direction of the south. Whatever she wants for that direction there is what I provide, whether it's rice, corn, little bit of salmon, little bit of blueberries, and tobacco and I will offer it to the four directions, I will also offer the spring water that's been blessed ... and smudged and offer it to the four directions and all that. So, four times a year you make that offering—and what you are doing is you are asking the ancestors for that protection for your community, for your families. Four times a year, you're pleasing the ancestors. So, that's what I was taught. Early on. I have learned a lot of teachings from different Elders.[3]

The water ceremony is reflective of the long-standing belief in the spirit world that is part of all life. This teaching can be understood as one of the "doorways" that opens to a lived world view in which gepmite'taqan (respect), ta'n telmi'wat'mg goqwei (giving thanks), and ta'n tel gegnu'mimajultimg (ceremony and protocol) are recognized as integral principles to the traditional Mi'gmaq ways of governing. Through ceremonies, we are reminded of our agreements with all beings—with the water, and with all the beings that depend upon the water.

In Listuguj, the salmon is one guide, which reminds us of the importance of balance and good order in our relationships with and within "Gm'tginu, our territory."

> *We know when the salmon is going to arrive by the changes in the environment. . . . We know that as soon as the ice leaves the river, the gaqpesaq will flow, then the fiddleheads will blossom, we know that the pqalmawj (black salmon) that have been here all winter spawning are on their way out [to the north Atlantic]. Even though we know that they are 'good eating fish,' we don't generally fish those because they are going out to sea, and they will have to come back home at some time. We know that not long after that the big males and females will come. We generally don't fish those because they have to spawn . . . they have to continue with their life cycle. We know that you have to pay attention to the moon, moon tides, the birds, and the wind. All of this has an effect on when the salmon decide to move up river. When the bugs are out in June, and the pugwalesg (swallows) — when they're around in the afternoon and the winds start picking up: there's certain times when you know it's good fishing, you just know. You know that's an indication: the salmon are on their way in, the salmon are coming. And when the salmon arrives, you know it's on its way back from Greenland, up in northern Atlantic, so it comes back home, when it arrives back, depending on the size of the salmon you can tell where they are in their cycle, where we are in ours.*[4]

Similarly, in what he says, and in how he conducts his affairs as Sagamaw of Gesgapegiag, San Maltan often reflects on Mi'gmaq visions of governance. In the following passage the connection between Mi'gmaq occupation and use of the territory and Mi'gmaq life ways is clear:

> Our ancestors had a great knowledge and understanding of
> their relationship with their environment and all Creation
> and it is this knowledge and understanding which gave them
> clear direction on how they should conduct themselves to
> maintain balance and good order in these relationships.[5]

Mestialsusultieg: Strengthening the Foundation of our Rights and Responsibilities

For many Mi'gmaq across Mi'gmagi, there are similarities in the stories
that we hear with regards to our rights, the historical injustices of our
people, and the struggle to arrive at a just and meaningful relationship between the Mi'gmaq and non-Mi'gmaq settler governments. For
many years, the governments (federal and provincial) have refused to
acknowledge, recognize, and respect Mi'gmaq and our long-standing
relationship—our rights and our responsibilities—on our territory.
There is no shortage of stories about the denial of our Peoples' ways.
For instance, when he spoke about his early memories of salmon fishing,
an Elder of Listuguj recalled the time when Mi'gmaq were denied access
to the rivers:

> *I remember buying salmon from the White Man: 'Peter Fish' we used to
> call him. We were barred from fishing. Powerless. Our struggle goes way
> back. We paid an awful price. But through tactics we've gained more and
> more. But we can't forget what price we paid to get to where we are.*[6]

This testimony speaks of the colonial context in which Mi'gmaq peoples have struggled in order to use and occupy their traditional territory.
Similarly, an Elder of Gesgapegiag stressed the importance of remembering Mi'gmaq history in order for change to occur:

> *Get the message out to the kids 25–30 years ago the Gesgapegiag water-
> front was all leased. We couldn't fish till 1976. Things have changed
> because people have stood up. To stand up and risk everything for some-
> thing you believe in, change happens. Stand up and do it.*[7]

Mi'gmaq resistance to colonial imposition is very much a part of
our history. Yet, I argue that the story of resistance does not go far
enough. Because "[t]o stand up and risk everything for something you

believe in, change happens" warrants the question, "as Mi'gmaq, what do we believe in?" The territory is integral to our knowledge system—our ways of knowing, perceiving, and understanding the world around us, as Mi'gmaq people. Our Elders remind us not only of the history of denial, but also the need to teach our children the importance of defending our territorial relationships. We are trying to teach our children through fishing how to be strong, and to live according to Mi'gmaq cultural teachings. Often, in our communities, we share these stories about how we have stood up and fought for what we believe in, and, in so doing, we strengthen our relationships with the salmon, the rivers, and our families.

When I reflect on my own experiences, salmon fishing with the old men, I understand that as a child, when I was out there with them (despite the colonial laws barring Mi'gmaq from the rivers), I never once felt afraid or sensed from them that I ought to be afraid:

> I remember fishing with my Uncle Danny'og, my aunt's husband Isage'jo'g, and my uncle's son Wayne'og, many of them have passed away now. But I remember going fishing and even though we knew there were wardens out there, and people out there who didn't want us to fish, we never once felt like we had to be afraid of them. I never sensed from them that we ought to be afraid, as though we were doing something wrong.

From these experiences, fishing and being on the water with my extended family, I learned about my rights and responsibilities to the fish and to the waters. These experiences formed a positive foundation on which I could base my convictions that, as Mi'gmaq, "we have a right to be doing this, that we have a right to have this relationship with the salmon, that we have the right to be here with each other."

> It's interesting, you know, because we would drag our net out in the mud and we would use rocks as anchors for the net, we would use cork floats, and when the tide would come in we would use the flat bottom boat that Danny made himself . . . we used a gi'gamgo'n, a [spruce] boat pole. . . . So when the tide was up, we used the boat that was made by Danny and the poles that somebody got in the woods. . . . When I sat there on shore, when we were on shore talking, I never once felt that they were afraid of getting caught for fishing. We've always believed that there was nothing to be afraid of.

66

In our right to be here, fishing and living from the land, it is the salmon that keeps us connected. The salmon arrives every spring and, with its arrival, we, the Mi'gmaq, continue to live according to our ways: laws and practices learned over thousands of years. Life ways, ta'n getu telmimajultieg, are taught, practised, and shared from one generation to the next.

Ta'n Telipi'taqati'gw: The First Catch and the Principle of Sharing

The rivers share the fish, the wind reminds us when to go out, and knowledge holders continue to pass on teachings about the salmon, the water, and the wind, about the many rivers and tributaries of Gespe'gewa'gi. In this way, the salmon—and many other beings of our territory—are integral to our knowledge systems and life ways.

As Mi'gmaq, we have a right to fish, yet, in exercising that right, there are obligations that need to be respected in order to maintain our relationship—in balance and good order—with the salmon.

The principle of sharing is integral to maintaining and strengthening relationships within the territory. There is an obligation to share that first catch with your family:

> *That's just the way it is. You first give it to your extended family, that's how you affirm your relationships to each other and that's how you strengthen the relationships within that family system. It's how you acknowledge and continue to support how we're all interconnected: the salmon, my uncles, my father, my first cousins and those living in our neighborhood.*

As Mi'gmaq, many of us were taught the importance of sharing, whether it is fish, moose, money, or teachings. Sharing is an integral principle of governance. Many Elders say that the principle of sharing guides our people, and our social, cultural, and spiritual ways.

> *I would ask my mother 'Wen nuta'mat plamueiwei?' 'Who needs the salmon?' I understood that we would be sharing and distributing the fish among our relatives.*

Because many of our teachings are embedded in our language, and because the language is verb-based, it is possible to concentrate on the relationships rather than on the objects of our exchanges. In Mi'gmaq, there are many ways to express and acknowledge how we share or distribute resources: Mawi'tante'gemg (to hunt together); Tpi'tenewei (how to share the resource); Netugulumgewe'l (how to distribute resource); Pestie'wimg (celebrating the resource/feast); and Mawiomi'l (affirming our ways at gatherings).

The language emphasizes relationships and the processes that are needed in order to live in and with the environment: social, political, spiritual, and physical. From our teachings, we learn to consider the many interconnected processes associated with the salmon. Through the salmon, it is possible to reconcile, strengthen, maintain, affirm, and build new relationships. Through the salmon, it possible to balance the diverse roles and responsibilities that are all necessary in order to live with, and to respect the many gifts of, Gm'tginu, our territory.

Mi'wat'mg: Offering Thanks

The sharing of salmon, the giving away of salmon to your family, the acknowledgement of the salmon, in terms of supporting your family and supporting your relationships, need to be acknowledged. Acknowledgement can be as simple as offering tobacco. Offering tobacco acknowledges the gjijaqamij of the salmon, the spirit of the salmon. In our beliefs the salmon has a life, it is not an object. When we talk about the salmon in our language we never consider the salmon as not being alive.

> In Mi'gmaq I say 'the salmon is my brother.' If the salmon is my brother, then he's no different from my uncle, my cousin, my aunt's husband who has passed away. And all these people are buried here, all these people who shared their experience and understanding of salmon fishing, they shared their experiences and knowledge of this territory. They taught my father everything that he knows about salmon fishing ... and he taught me ... we continue to give back to people through the salmon so that we can continue to acknowledge and strengthen that we are connected.

We are connected to each other. We live in and from the territory; the salmon, through the water, keeps us connected. The land and the water are no different, just as the salmon and I are no different.

Netewistoq: Speaking on Behalf of the Salmon

In Mi'gmaq ways, when we come together under the Mawiomi, a way of governing relations that has been in place for thousands of years, everybody participates in the circle. Everybody participates in the sharing and exchange of dialogue. In Gespe'gewa'gi there are many discussions about self-governance and the validity of our traditional systems of governance. There are concerns about the condition of our lands and the quality of our waters. When we think about our ancestors, and the future leaders of today, our youth, we need to reconcile the competing interests that influence decisions about how we govern within our traditional territory.

> You know the salmon influences our lives, the salmon informs us about how the water is important to the salmon, and what we know about the water. And we share all that. But, there comes a point in your life when 'You have been taught and it is time for you to speak.' It's like the circle: sometimes when you are young, you want to speak loud and you want—you're insisting—that you be heard, and maybe you are getting impatient and maybe you're sitting at the other side of the circle and you're saying 'I have something to say right now.' But, it's not your turn to say it because we're not there in the circle. And that circle, there's a protocol. You have to respect when is the time to speak.

When we speak about the salmon, and our relationship to the territory and the importance of the environment, there is a story that is not being told and it needs to be told because we are not paying attention. We need to learn to listen and pay attention to what the land is saying:

> The big salmon are not coming back in the river, the grandfathers are not coming back in, our grandmothers are not coming back in. Any time your grandfathers or grandmothers ignore you, there's a reason why they are ignoring you. It's a particular form of discipline.

When we speak about the salmon, we are talking about a relationship the Mi'gmaq have had for a long time. Despite the many colonial laws that have prevented us from accessing the rivers and the many resources of our territory, nevertheless, as a people, we've always trusted that the salmon—in following the natural cycles and seasons—would return each year. You could even say: Ap nemultes, siggw! "In the spring time I will see you back in Listuguj!"

Yet, increasingly, there are concerns. The salmon are not coming back and only the younger salmon are coming in. Those returning are not coming back in good health. Evidently, the health of the water is becoming a real issue. Often, the discussion about Indigenous rights and our responsibilities focuses on the territory. We are preoccupied with the land; however, what our Elders are starting to say is that we need to focus on the water, "respect the water, and the water will respect you." If the salmon are to have voice in the dialogue, then we would understand the direction that we need to take in order to arrive at a sustainable form of governance.

Ta'n Telwo'gmatultimg: Rebuilding Our Relations

In our communities, many are learning the ceremonies for Gm'tginu and all parts of Creation. We need to acknowledge and celebrate the knowledge that the salmon allows us to have. The salmon has taken care of us for so long; this way of life has been passed on for thousands of years. This way of life is sustainable.

There are many people who fast, sing, and pray for the salmon. If we acknowledge, honour, and celebrate those who have the knowledge about our traditional ways, then it is possible to sustain our relationships on our territory, with each other, in a good way.

In our language, there is an energy that can be felt. For instance, if you speak to those who know the songs, some will tell you: *"When you sing the songs in our language, they're even ten times stronger because of the connection that you are making with Creator."* Others may say: "When we speak, you can feel the energy coming towards you; you can feel it, I don't know why. All I know is that—you just know that they are listening."

Further, the more that we strengthen our Mi'gmaq ways—our language, practices, protocols, and traditions—then we, in fact, honour our ancestors who placed the mark of their totem on treaties signed with the newcomers. When our ancestors signed treaties of co-existence, treaties meant to protect our ways of living, they signed them with the hieroglyphic writing system of our people: Muin, Plamu, Plawej, Wapus, Gwimu, so forth. In essence, these signatures remind us of many voices of the land that sustain who we are, as L'nnu.

> *There are some simple instructions when it comes to fishing: 'Go fishing when the tide changes; go fishing when there are certain wind conditions, certain bugs, certain birds, you can follow that.' There are other teachings: 'Can you begin to follow the moon? Can you begin to read the water?' Know how alive the water is . . . where it's so alive you shouldn't be out there. So alive that—it's because of the salmon, it's alive.*

Ta'n tesit nogmaq.

---

[1] Interview with Mi'gmaq grandmother, November 14, 2005, Listuguj, Quebec.

[2] Nm'tginen: Me'mnaq Ejiglignmuetueg gis na Naqtmueg (Listuguj, Quebec: Mi'gmawei Mawiomi Secretariat, 2007).

[3] Interview with Mi'gmaq grandmother, November 14, 2005, Listuguj, Quebec.

[4] Italicized quotes represent the author's personal reflections on his own Mi'gmaq teachings.

[5] Sam Malton, Plamuwesit Mi'gmaq Salmon Curriculum Wejwapniag School, Gesgapegiag, Quebec, 2003.

[6] Wesgijua'luet Research Report (Listuguj, Quebec: Mi'gmawei Mawiomi Secretariat) Presented at the Annual Assembly in Gespeg, June 2007, forthcoming 2008.

[7] Ibid.

Chapter 4

Our Elder Brothers: The Lifeblood of Resurgence

Leanne Simpson

There is a sacred place, sitting at the eastern doorway of the Nishnaabeg Nation, where it is believed that Original Man was first lowered to the earth.[1] This place is one of the physical reminders of our original instructions, and it contains many teaching formations. One of the formations shows three pathways, nearly in the shape of an Eagle Feather: a long path veering to the right and then up; a path leading to the left and then up; and one in the middle, leading straight, but then abruptly stopping. A few years ago, an Elder explained to me the significance of these teaching rocks. He told me that one path represented the Nishnaabeg[2] way of living and being in the world, the other the white world, and that these two worlds and ways of being run in parallel to each other, until they (potentially) meet sometime in the future. The middle road, a path that mixes the two, stops abruptly and shortly after beginning. The Elder originally explained this to me in terms of identity, that "mixed blood" people must chose and commit to only one path, and that choosing a middle road results in the destruction of oneself. Pre-colonial citizenship policies reflected this belief, with "mixed blood" Nishnaabeg readily accepted into our nation if they chose to honour our relations, or they were free to seek citizenship elsewhere if that was their desire. In the context of colonialism, I have now come to understand a broader meaning. If we are to continue on an Nishnaabeg pathway, we must choose to live as Nishnaabeg, committing to mno bimaadziwin,[3] and committing to building resurgence. We have a choice, and that choice requires action, commitment, and responsibility. We are not simply born Nishnaabeg, even if we have "full blood."[4] We must commit to living the good life each day. We must act. We must live our knowledge. This ancient teaching provides us with an important template for building an Indigenous resurgence based on a common politic of decolonization and resurgence rather than continuing our divisions over blood quantum, status, and other forms of petty colonial politics.

I believe one of our most critical and immediate tasks in building an Indigenous resurgence is ensuring that the knowledge of our ancestors is taught to the coming generations. But, according to our intellectual traditions, *how* we do this is as important or perhaps more important than the product of our efforts. Nishnaabeg Knowledge Keepers believe that the processes we use for transferring that knowledge will either positively or negatively influence the outcome. So, the first thing we must recover is our own Indigenous ways of knowing, our own Indigenous ways of protecting, sharing, and transmitting knowledge, our own Indigenous intellectual traditions. And we must begin to practise and to live those traditions on our own terms. Recentreing the revitalization of Indigenous Knowledge (IK) within the knowledge systems themselves provides the only appropriate context for building an Indigenous resurgence. Indigenous Knowledge systems have always been process-oriented systems of knowledge. They have always derived their meaning from context rather than from decontextualized content. Doing things in the proper way is paramount, and Nishnaabeg Knowledge Holders have been pretty clear about what this involves.[5] They have told us repeatedly that our children must understand their languages, not in a tourist sort of way, but in a way that preserves the complexity of our highest philosophical debates. Our children must have a strong connection to land in order to be able to maintain the necessary connections with the plant and animal nations and the spirit world to nurture balance, and our children must have the skills embodied in Bzindamowinan,[6] listening, so that they can fully appreciate and synthesis knowledge from the Oral Traditions of their peoples.[7]

It is well known fact to Indigenous Peoples that Indigenous Knowledge systems are poorly understood, or entirely misunderstood, by settler governments and the Western academy.[8] Universities have historically been sites of colonization, and although individual researchers have begun to change that, the institution in its current role, as a whole, has not committed to attaining a post-colonial or de-colonial state.[9] Similarly, while settler governments have expressed an interest in learning IK to suit their agendas (climate change, for instance), and have sought to do so on their terms, they fund projects that meet their needs and not necessarily those of Indigenous Peoples.

Disconnecting ourselves from the agenda of settler governments and institutions in terms of Indigenous Knowledge is a critical first step to recentreing our collective strategies for revitalizing the base of our nations. IK is critical for resurgence. Everything that makes us Indigenous as individuals and as nations resides in our knowledge systems. For Indigenist thinkers, this is where we will find the answers to combat colonialism, to decolonize, and to re-Indigenize.

The Nishnaabeg knowledge system has always encouraged its learners to look inside themselves as individuals, as families, as communities, and as nations, and to engage in a process of restoring and maintaining balance within the cosmos. The belief is that by changing oneself, you change your reality, and by committing to a process of decolonization and Indigenizing, a collective transformation can occur. Aided by beings in the spiritual realm, our political processes shift as we decolonize our traditions, our knowledge, and begin to live our traditions as a collective. As we begin to act as strong, healthy, independent Indigenous Nations, a new political reality emerges, and a new people emerges who are equipped with the tools and strategies in the war against our territorial losses and colonial attempts to disengage us politically.

Throughout colonial history, the colonizer has thought at every stage that he was doing the "Indian" a favour by assimilating him, by eradicating his "primitive" ways, and by showing him a "better" way of life. In contemporary times, the colonizer continues to tell us that if we do not write down our knowledge, it will be lost forever. That if we do not adhere to the Western intellectual traditions to ethically conduct research in our communities, we will do our communities a disservice. That if we do not publish our theses and dissertations in written English, rather than our own languages or adhering to our oral traditions, we will not be sharing our work with the widest audience and we will not be living up to our responsibilities to share knowledge. That if we do not participate in their projects to document as much of our knowledge as possible, we will lose the knowledge forever.

All the while, settler governments continue to attack the very foundations of Indigenous Knowledge systems by promoting the destruction of the environment within our territories and by promoting cultural genocide through the education of our children in an (still) assimilative school system. While the mantra of "stay in school" is drilled into our children's heads, we are compelling them to stay within a colonial system that continues to ignore Indigenous history, values, knowledge, language, and intellectual traditions, while promoting linguistic genocide as another generation of Indigenous children grow up without their languages. If we are serious about "saving" and "protecting" Indigenous Knowledge for future generations, and if we are serious about decolonizing our political systems and governance, we must be prepared to blatantly reject the colonizer's view of our knowledge and we must embrace strategies based on our own distinctive Indigenous intellectual traditions. The basic premise of Indigenist and decolonizing theories is that we bring the knowledge of the ancient ones back into contemporary relevance by capturing the revolutionary nature of those teachings. The following represents a four-part strategy to do just that: the need to confront our own "funding" mentality; the need to confront linguistic genocide; the need to vision resurgence; and the need to awaken ancient treaty and diplomatic mechanisms for relating to, and building solidarity with, neighbouring nations.

Confront "Funding" Mentality

"Funding" is always a source of conversation in any Indigenous community—which projects need funding, which projects will get funding, and things we would love to do but which will never get funding. It is time to admit that colonizing governments and private corporate foundations are not going to fund our decolonization, because the colonial relationship serves their interests and they remain the beneficiaries of colonialism. Most projects at the local community level that address the four components of a strategy presented in this chapter are impossible to fund through governmental and non-governmental sources. Too many times, lack of funding stops the projects before they even began. Some communities are successful at manipulating funding agreements to promote their own agendas; others are not. But I am suggesting a more radical approach.

In pre-contact time, we did not rely on "funding" to support the cultural aspects of our lives. Grandparents were willing to teach their grandchildren their culture. Communities, clans, and families supported and took care of their Knowledge Holders. The beauty of our knowledge systems, even in a dominant, capitalistic, commodity-based reality, is that they do not cost capital to maintain. We do not need formalized, funded projects to link youth with our Knowledge Holders; we simply need the will.

In "modern technologically advanced" Western society, knowledge requires capital because Western society is exclusively literate, as opposed to oral (or aural). Knowledge production in Western society requires vast amounts of natural resources. Western socity requires money to produce and distribute books. It requires computers (plastic, heavy metals, dioxins, etc.) to store and retrieve information, and electricity (hydro-electric development, nuclear waste, etc.) to run the computers. The production of high-tech knowledge equipment (computers, cell phones, fax machines, printers) requires natural resources, and at the end of their short life cycle, they become highly toxic techno-trash releasing dioxins and heavy metals, including mercury and lead, into the environment.

The Oral Tradition is the ultimate in "environmentally friendly," requiring a willingness to share and a willingness to listen, in addition to the cultural skills necessary for learning knowledge. IK systems are not an "industry" reliant on "resources." Recentreing our work means forgoing the funding that supports our making digital libraries that the community cannot access, film and video production seen primarily outside the community, and engaging in the ever popular "land use studies," which the past twenty years have shown us bring no real benefit to the community, in favour of building relationships with our territories and the Keepers of our Knowledge, things we can do largely without the support of capitalism.

Confronting Linguistic Genocide

Too often I have heard academics, non-Native and Native, myself included, speak and write about the importance of language with regards to Indigenous Knowledge, only then to go on to speak or write entirely in English.[10] It is a case of acknowledging that English is inadequate to fully and correctly communicate many of the complexities and nuances of Indigenous Knowledge systems, but also a passive resignation to this fact. The reality is, of course, that if one is truly interested in fully and responsibly engaging with Indigenous Knowledge, then one needs to learn the language so one can fully and respectfully engage in relationships with Indigenous Knowledge Holders—a commitment few of us (again including myself) have made. This is the kind of work that is unpaid, unsung, and not acknowledged by the colonial standards of settler society. This is the kind of work that is ignored by hiring committees, and tenure and promotion committees. It is the behind-the-scenes nation-building work that our grassroots community workers know well. There is little recognition or glory attached to it, but without it, we will lose ourselves.

Indigenous Knowledge systems are encoded in Indigenous languages, and Knowledge Holders all over Turtle Island for the past several decades have been expressing that language is absolutely critical to understanding the true nature of Indigenous Knowledge. If we do not teach the current generation of children their mother tongues, as many as 90 to 95% of the world's spoken languages, including most Indigenous languages, may be facing extinction by the end of the present century.[11] To confront linguistic genocide, we must adopt aggressive programs to teach our peoples their languages, and we cannot rely on Native language courses in Canadian universities to accomplish this goal.

Many sites within the academy continue to actively facilitate the colonization of Indigenous Knowledge and the colonization of Indigenous Peoples. The most obvious examples of this is that our Knowledge Holders are not fully present in institutions of higher education, unless they are invited to yearly "Elders conferences" or to give "traditional teachings." Academic departments denoted as Native or Indigenous Studies are dominated by Western-trained academics who teach and conduct research heavily based on the traditions of the Western academy.[12] Indigenous Knowledge Holders are rarely given tenure-track positions, and thus do not have the power within educational institutions to ensure that the conditions are right for the protection of Indigenous Knowledge systems.[13]

Within this context, the university has, more often than not, contributed to linguistic genocide with its nearly absolute promotion of English in research, writing, and publication. For example, a few years ago, a Mi'gmaq[14] student, studying in my territory toward an MA, wanted to write and defend his thesis in Mi'gmaq. His thesis was community-based, it followed Mi'gmaq intellectual traditions, and the community wanted it published in their language, without an English translation. His research proposal adhered to his nation's community guidelines for conducting ethical research, and had been approved by a national Mi'gmaq ethics committee. Mi'gmaq Elders and community-based language experts were fully engaged in his thesis from start to finish, and felt that the student met the tests for rigour within their traditions. A prominent Mi'gmaq academic and fluent language speaker was also on the examining committee, along with two other supportive academics who did not speak Mi'gmaq.

The main argument against the student and his community's publishing the thesis only in Mi'gmaq (coming from some Indigenous academics within the Indigenous Studies Department) was that it would make the work inaccessible to those who did not speak Mi'gmaq. They felt strongly that the role of university research was to share knowledge, and, at a minimum, they believed the document should be fully translated into English, even if this occurred against the community's wishes.

Their insistence that Western intellectual traditions should take priority over Mi'gmaq intellectual traditions and the desires of the community who participated in the research is more than worrisome. In my mind, this is the problem with engaging in the politics of recognition within colonial institutions. The idea that we must first meet the needs of the university, before we can even entertain the idea of meeting the needs of our communities, makes me question whether Indigenizing the university is even desirable.

The truth of the matter is that publishing a work in English makes it inaccessible to those who do not speak English (Mi'gmaq Knowledge Holders, for instance), and the fact is that most academic work is written in a form of English that is inaccessible to most lay people. What this argument revealed to me is that *who* the work is inaccessible to is critical within the context of colonial academic institutions—it is acceptable if research is inaccessible to Indigenous People, but it is decidedly unacceptable if the work is inaccessible to English-speaking academics.[15] Universities will go to great lengths to protect these interests, as evidenced in the outcome of this situation: the student and his community were eventually allowed to proceed as planned, and he wrote and defended his thesis in Mi'gmaq without translation, but there is now a new policy in place that makes it more difficult for students to write and defend their work in Indigenous languages.[16]

The lesson here to me is that because language is so important to the transmission and continuance of Indigenous Knowledge, and because this is so widely recognized by Indigenous Knowledge Holders, Indigenous Peoples *themselves* must develop strategies with language activists to confront linguistic genocide *without* adhering to the policies, agenda, or the academic criteria of colonial academic institutions. As communities, we must support our fluent speakers and our language experts, and honour them as experts.

The Master Apprentice Language Learning Program (MALLP), developed in the 1990s to help save Indigenous languages in California, is one strategy that might help us to meet our needs. It involves pairing a fluent speaker (the master) with a language learner (apprentice). The two create an immersion setting for ten to twenty-plus hours per week.[17] The benefit of this program is that it can be done in urban or rural areas, it requires no infrastructure or curriculum support, and the apprentice can provide household support (or other kinds of help) in full or partial exchange for language instruction, thus not relying on outside funding for program support. Communities, whether they are rural or urban, could support and facilitate such arrangements by identifying language speakers willing to commit to the MALLP, and identifying students willing to participate. This can be done without trying to convince colonial institutions of the benefits of this approach.

Visioning Resurgence

Nishnaabeg Knowledge Holders know that the first step to making something happen is often a dream or a vision. Teaching a class in Sekena-Carrier Territory (Prince George, BC) for the Indigenous Governance Programs at the University of Victoria, I asked the class to come up with an alternative to the British Columbia Treaty Process, based on their own political traditions. I was concerned that although the students could provide me with a detailed, articulate, and well-founded critique of the colonial ills that plagued the process, no one had any alternatives. After a few days of work, in which many of them consulted their Knowledge Holders, they came up with a process that would take place in their own territory within their own time frame; involved appropriate ceremony, traditional leaders, Knowledge Holders, women, and children; and took place entirely in their own language. In short, they developed a process, based on their own political traditions, where they were in a position of power because they were the rightful owners of the land, and the colonizers were negotiating on the terms of the people.

The power of this exercise was that it awakened both the students and myself. It showed us clearly the work we needed to do in our communities to be able to properly support the process the students were proposing. It was a concrete way forward that strengthened the community and nation, and, I think, that brought us one step closer to resurgence. It forced them to articulate an alternative vision based on their own traditions, and laid out a long-term strategy to move forward.

The importance of visioning and dreaming a better future based on our own Indigenous traditions cannot be underestimated. But, according to our traditions, those visions or messages from our Ancestors and the Spirit World will be lost if they are not acted upon.

For the past five years, I have worked exclusively outside the academy, and grounded my research in the needs of communities. Taking a step away from the academia allowed me to recentre my work, away from the academic literature on the topic, and to ground my work within an Indigenist agenda, as articulated by Indigenous Knowledge Holders at the community level. I immediately found two things: the people did not see a need for "research"—but they did see a need for assistance in creating space and opportunity for Knowledge Holders, in this case Elders, to connect with community youth on the land and according to Nishnaabeg intellectual traditions and ways of knowing.

The best way (perhaps the only way, according to some Knowledge Holders) to preserve Indigenous Knowledge systems is to live Indigenous Knowledge systems by creating a generation fully connected to the land, our languages, and our Knowledge Holders and trained in the artistry of the oral/aural tradition. Over the past fifteen years of working with communities and Knowledge Holders, I have found that the way to accomplish this is to simply provide the space and time for youth to connect with their Elders or the Knowledge Keepers of their community. We do not need loads of cash to develop fancy curricula and learning programs; we need to provide opportunity and support, and then get out of the way.

Ningo Gikinonwin Cultural Project in Hollow Water First Nation[18] is one project aiming to do just that. The project provides opportunities for community youth and Elders to connect and develop relationships based on their own community's cultural traditions. In a sense, the project simply provides the space and opportunity for Elders and youth to be on the land together, engaging in traditional activities, arts, and ceremonies.

The youth learn directly from the Elders. There are no books, no videos, no interviews. The youth are taught how to interact with the Elders according to their own cultural traditions. They are encouraged to develop life-long relationships with their Knowledge Holders in their local community on their territory and often in their language.

Gdoo-naaganinaa, Our Dish

Within our web of liberation strategies, Indigenous Peoples need a culturally grounded way of relating to each other and building solidarity across our nations. Pre-contact treaties and international relationships among Indigenous Nations can provide us with contemporary models for Indigenous solidarity in both urban and reserve settings. Our traditional relationships with other Indigenous Nations were often formally encoded in international relationships, and many Knowledge Holders still have knowledge of the rituals, ceremonies, and traditions that nurtured these diplomatic relationships. Pre-colonial diplomacy provides contemporary Indigenous Peoples with meaningful and powerful models for international solidarity. Reviving and reliving these political traditions are a viable alternative to the state-sanctioned national Aboriginal organizations, which are struggling against a tide of criticism from the Indigenous community. They also are a viable alternative to Pan-Aboriginalism, which is so prevalent in urban Aboriginal organizations. This alternative, however, requires a deep commitment to our Knowledge Holders and our languages, and it requires a massive shift in our current political strategies (or lack thereof).

For citizens of the Nishnaabeg Nation, pre-colonial international relations were governed by the principles and values encoded in the Seven Grandfather teachings,[19] and these were formalized with neighbouring nations through the concept of "Gdoo-naaganinaa, Our Dish."[20] For instance, in what is now known as southern Ontario, Gdoo-naaganinaa acknowledged that both the Nishnaabeg and the Haudenosaunee were eating out of the same dish through shared hunting territory and the ecological connections between their territories.[21] Gdoo-naaganinaa represented the shared territory. Both parties had responsibilities to maintain the Dish according to their environmental ethics. Gdoo-naa-ganinaa did not threaten the sovereignty, independence, or freedom of either the Nishnaabeg Nation or the Haudenosaunee Confederacy. It did not give one party the right to invade, to colonize, to commit acts of genocide, or to attempt to assimilate. Both parties agreed to separate political jurisdictions, within a shared territory.

The Nishnaabeg Nation and the Haudenosaunee Confederacy related to each other through the practice of Gdoo-naaganinaa. It was not just simply agreed upon, but practiced as part of the diplomatic relations between the Nishnaabeg Nation and the Confederacy. The Oral Tradition of the Nishnaabeg also tells of a similar treaty with the Dakota, with whom we shared the western boundary of our territory.[22]

Contemporary Clan Mothers can still recall traditions regarding the Dish With One Spoon treaty and Wampum.[23] The concept behind the Dish with One Spoon Wampum reflects the principles that were given to the Haudenosaunee by the Peacemaker in the Kayaneren'kowa (Great Law of Peace).[24] Again, the dish represents shared hunting grounds. There are no knives near the bowl, only a spoon, to promote peaceful co-existence of the shared hunting territory.

Renewing our pre-colonial treaty relationships with contemporary neighbouring Indigenous Nations promotes decolonization, and peaceful co-existence, and it builds solidarity among Indigenous Nations. I believe these kinds of relationships can form a strong international Indigenous presence politically, with a base of support far larger and more powerful than current national Aboriginal organizations. It also provides us with an ancient, decolonized model for relating to other nations, even settler nations with whom we share parts of our territory. It preserves our own visions of sovereignty, self-determination, nationhood, and freedom, while showing us how to relate to other nations in a just and responsible manner.

Indigenous Knowledge systems provide us with the lifeblood of resurgence. Our Elder Brothers provide us with the sustenance for our journey. But we, as peoples, must be willing to recover the revolutionary aspects of these systems, as well. Fundamentalism, rigidity, and exclusion too often plague our efforts to revitalize our cultures. Our

Knowledge Holders teach us of a radically different way of relating to the land and of being in this world.

---

[1] This is part of one of the Nishinaabeg Creation Stories.

[2] Nishnaabeg is translated as "the people" and refers to Ojibwe, Odawa (Ottawa), Potawatomi, Mississauga, Saulteaux, and Omàmìwinini (Algonquin) Peoples. Nishnaabeg Peoples are also known as Nishnaabeg, Anishinaabeg, and Anishinaabek in adjacent dialects. All words in Nishnaabemwin (Ojibwe language) in this chapter are in the eastern Manitoulin dialect of the language.

[3] Translated as "the good life" or "continuous rebirth."

[4] Kiera Ladner reminded me that this was never the case. One could always choose to join another nation, as long as one was prepared to follow the immigration policies of that nation, in addition to the new nation's rules regarding citizenship. One was Nishnaabeg by living up to the responsibilities encoded in the Original Instructions.

[5] Leanne Simpson, "The Construction of Traditional Ecological Knowledge: Issues, Implications and Insights," PhD dissertation, University of Manitoba, 1999.

[6] Listening in this context is not just hearing, it is the ability to interpret stories and knowledge within a cultural context according to cultural traditions.

[7] Simpson, "The Construction of Traditional Ecological Knowledge."

[8] Ibid., and Leanne Simpson, "Anti-Colonial Strategies for the Recovery and Maintenance of Indigenous Knowledge," *American Indian Quarterly* 28, 3/4 (2005): 373–385.

[9] Marie Battiste, "Decolonizing the University: Ethical Guidelines for Research Involving Indigenous Populations," in *Pursuing Academic Freedom: "Free and Fearless"?*, ed. L. M. Findlay and P. M. Bidwell, (Saskatoon, SK: Purich Press, 2001), 190–203; and M. Battiste, "Enabling the Autumn Seed: Toward a Decolonized Approach Toward Aboriginal Knowledge, Language, and Education," *Canadian Journal of Native Education* 22, 1 (1998): 16–27.

[10] There are, of course, several Indigenous academics who are both Western-trained and trained in their own Indigenous intellectual traditions, just as we are lucky enough to have several Indigenous academics who are fluent in their own languages.

[11] Andrea Bear Nicholas, *Education through the Medium of the Mother-Tongue: The Single Most Important Means for Saving Indigenous Languages*, <www.nativestudies.org/works.html>, October 2005.

[12] There are several Indigenous and non-Indigenous academics within these departments who do not engage in research that colonizes, but there is no collective or formal commitment to engage in decolonizing or anti-colonial work.

[13] For example, in my own urban community, one Elder recently retired from our local university. She was a tenured full professor, based on her Nishnaabeg credentials as an Indigenous Knowledge Holder. She was not Western-trained. The university did not replace her with a similarly trained person and subsequently does

not have any core faculty capable of teaching their Native language courses. All the current faculty now have the same Western academic credentials as any other academic at the university.

[14] Note that Mi'gmaq is spelled differently across the territory. Mi'gmaq is the correct spelling in Listuguj, while, in other parts of the territory, it is spelled Mi'kmaq.

[15] In reality, because the thesis was written and submitted for a degree credit, it was accessible to academics—they could either chose to learn Mi'gmaq, as some Anthropologist have done in the past, or they could hire someone to translate it for them. Even in the hypothetical case of a young Mi'gmaq student (who only spoke English) who wanted access to the thesis, by not translating the document, one requires them to actively engage with Mi'gmaq speakers and or Elders to fully understanding the document—an activity of which I cannot see the downside. One can only imagine what the response of the academy will be when an Indigenous student submits an oral thesis in her or his language, not to be recorded or translated. The senate of York University changed their policy in the spring of 2008 to allow theses and dissertations to be submitted in First Nations/Aboriginal languages of North America subject to certain conditions.

[16] This section has been approved by Fred Metallic, who is now writing his PhD dissertation in Mi'gmaq at a different university.

[17] Wasiyatawin Angela Wilson, "Defying Colonization Through Language Survival," in *For Indigenous Eyes Only: A Decolonization Handbook*, ed. Wasiyatawin Angela Wilson and Michael Yellow Bird, (Santa Fe: School of American Research, 2005), 109–127.

[18] This paragraph has been approved for publication by Norbert Hardisty, Project Coordinator of the Ningo Gikinonwin Cultural Project at Hollow Water First Nation.

[19] Paula Sherman, *Indawendiwin: Spiritual Ecology as the Foundation of Omàmìwinini Relations*, Unpublished PhD dissertation, (Peterborough, ON: Department of Indigenous Studies, Trent University, 2007).

[20] According to Alan Corbiere, Project Coordinator of Kinoomaadoog at M'Chigeeng First Nation (personal communication May 4, 2007), this treaty between the Nishnaabeg Nation and the Haudenosaunee Confederacy is called "Gdoo-naagani-naa" by the Nishnaabeg in both historical documents written in Nishnaabemwn, and in our Oral Tradition. It means "Our Dish." This is the inclusive form, as opposed to the ndoo-naaganinaa "our dish (but not yours)." Victor P. Lytwyn's research shows that historical documents containing the concept also use the term "Kidonaganina," Gdoo-naaganinaa is the correct spelling in the Fiero orthography eastern Ojibwe dialect. See Victor P. Lytwyn's "A Dish with One Spoon: The Shared Hunting Grounds Agreement in the Great Lakes and St., Lawrence Valley Region," *Papers of the 28th Algonquian Conference*, ed. David H. Pentland (Winnipeg: University of Manitoba Press, 1997), 210–227.

[21] For a detailed historical discussion of Kidonaganina based on archival documents from the seventeenth, eighteenth, and ninetheenth centuries, see Lytwyn, "A Dish With One Spoon."

[22] This is a traditional story, which, in short, tells of how the Big Drum was given to the Nishnaabeg to stop fighting with the Dakota and as a symbol and reminder to maintain peace and goodwill between the two nations.

[23] The Dish Wampum Belt is currently housed at the Royal Ontario Museum.

[24] For discussions of the treaty from an Haudenosaunee perspective, see Barbara Gray's "The Effects of the Fur Trade on Peace: A Haudenosaunee Woman's Perspective," in *Aboriginal People and the Fur Trade: Proceedings of the 8th North American Fur Trade Conferences*, ed. Louise Johnson (Akwesasne Mohawk Territory: Dollco Printing, 2001); J.A. Gibson, *Concerning the League: The Iroquois League Tradition as Dictated in Onondaga*, ed. H. Woodbury, R. Henry and H. Webster, *Algonquian and Iroquoian Linguistics Memoir* 9 (1991); A.C. Parker, *Parker on the Iroquois: Iroquois Uses of Maize and Other Food Plants: The Code of Handsome Lake, the Seneca Prophet: The Constitution of the Five Nations* (New York: State University of New York, 1992). Note that the Dish with One Spoon was also a treaty and way of relating among the Five Nations of the Haudenosaunee.

Chapter 5

Keepers of the Water: Nishnaabe-kwewag Speaking for the Water

Renée Elizabeth Mzinegiizhigo-kwe Bédard

Nishnaabe-kwewag and also all women across the continent
of North and South America, we have a great responsibility
as women to carry that work as light keepers, carriers of the
water, carriers of light.[1]

Nishnaabeg people have always lived along the water of the Great Lakes.[2]
The ziibii'ganan (rivers), zaagiganan (lakes), bog'tingoon (rapids), wiik-
wedoon (bays), dkibiin (natural springs), biitooshk-biisenyin (swamps),
and ziigiinsan[3] (streams) have sustained the Nishnaabe people on these
traditional territorial lands for thousands of years. Water has been, and
continues to be, critical to the health, politics, spirituality, culture, and
economy of Nishnaabeg communities. Nishnaabeg people have picked
medicine like wiingaash[4] (sweetgrass) and food like nishnaabe-mnoom-
in[5] (wild rice) along the shores of the waterways. They have cooked their
food using the waters they pull from the streams and natural springs.
Babies and children have always been washed in the waters of our rivers
and lakes. Spiritually, it is the women who are responsible for praying
to the water and caring for the water during ceremonies, and, as we near
the end of the first decade of the twenty-first century, it is not surpris-
ing that Nishnaabeg women are standing up to protect the water. They

want cleaner, non-exploited and healthy water on the Great Lakes for their children, grandchildren, and all future generations.

In this chapter, I seek to understand the historical and contemporary significance of water to Nishnaabeg people, especially to our women. I do so by engaging with the words and wisdom of Nishnaabe-kwewag Elders Shirley Williams of Wikiwemikong Unceded First Nation and Josephine Mandamin of Thunder Bay, Ontario. I will discuss traditional Nishnaabeg knowledge about water, and the responsibilities of women in protecting water. Also, I will highlight some of the current grassroots work by the Mother Earth Water Walkers. The Water Walkers are a group of Nishnaabeg women who are carrying water taken from the Great Lakes region as they walk around each of the Great Lakes in order to advocate for protection of the environment and Indigenous rights to clean water. It is my hope that this chapter will reinforce the importance of water to the health and well-being of Nishnaabeg people and all Indigenous Peoples across North America.

French River Girl

> We are the wives, the mothers, daughters and sisters, the grandmothers, the aunties and the nieces of our community. We speak for the children and grandchildren of today, and for those yet unborn.[6]

I offer this passage because it best describes the role of Nishnaabeg women in speaking out for their responsibilities to the future generations. First and foremost, there is our responsibility to protect water and ensure that water is there for future generations. I am aware as I write this paper of my place in "all of Creation"—as an Nishnaabe-kwe. I gladly advocate for clean water and environmental awareness, because I grew up along the waters of the French River, calling myself a "French River Girl." This topic, the articulation of Nishnaabeg women's responsibilities to water and the safe-guarding of clean water for those "children and grandchildren of today and for those yet unborn"[7] is the core of my identity. As a French River Girl, I see the water as the lifeblood of my Mother the Earth.

I am a member of Dokis First Nation, in northern Ontario, along the French River. The French River has always been a highway of water travel and fur trading for the Nishnaabeg from the interior of northern Ontario, into the Great Lakes and beyond. The history of the French River is rich, including numerous First Nations cultures: Ojibwe, Nipissing, and Omàmìwinini (Algonquin). Many French settlements and fur-trading posts were established along the edges of the waterways (rivers and lakes). Mining, lumbering, ice cutting, fishing, and hunting brought many surveyors, explorers, and industries to the region. The railroad led to the development of new towns, villages, and the future city of North Bay. Steady development of this water highway brought newcomers to the region, forever interweaving the cultures and heritage of both First Nations and settler peoples. Treaties constructed the current Indian Bands of Nipissing First Nations Reserve, Garden River First Nations Reserve, and Dokis First Nations Reserve along the connected Nipissing Lake and French River area. Together, these Nishnaabeg communities formed a tight network of families, political alliances, and shared common cultural similarities defined by living on the water's edge.

The French River contains vast stretches of islands and is surrounded by diverse watersheds of marshes, forest, sand beaches, and rocky granite shorelines. I spent my childhood catching frogs, fishing, or picking blueberries along the water's edge of the many islands that dot the French River. When I dream, I dream of the water along the French River. When I think of my ancestors, my thoughts include stories that always involve the French River. When I think of politics, it always includes the river, its people, and its history. When I think of culture and spirituality, they are grounded in traditions and teachings of that dynamic relationship that we have as Nishnaabeg people who have lived along the water's edge of the French River. The waters of the French River and Dokis First Nation represent an intimate and critical aspect of my identity as an Nishnaabekwe. Without water and watersheds like the French River, Nishnaabeg individuals like myself would experience a fundamental disconnect with who we are as Nishnaabeg people. The water, along with the land, defines our identities, sustains our families and communities, and provides us with the knowledge of how to live as Nishnaabeg people.

Along the French River there are rapids. These are spaces where the waters from different channels meet and literally dance together in converging currents. The water moves forward and backward, upward and downward, and from side to side. Twisting and swirling together, these converging currents are spaces where the river speaks to the world in a thundering voice to all who come across its presence. Several years ago, I wrote in my Master's thesis: "The rapids seem like a dangerous place and they most definitely are, but they are also a place of life, cleansing, freedom undeterred and where the life of the River is heard above all other sounds."[8] The song of the rapids is a cleansing song, speaking of regeneration, transformation, and the health of both the water and the land. The ability to cleanse the land and river waters has always been the role of the rapids.

I am reminded of the words of (Nishnaabe) Odawa Elder Shirley Ida Williams, where she describes the cleansing power of the waters in lakes and rivers. She said to me:

> I know that the water cleans itself. When we were growing up my father used to say 'It will take at least over a hundred years for the water to clean itself....There are natural deposits in the water to help to clean itself. It's just like soap when you wash your body,' he said. There are things under the water to clean itself, to purify the water itself. And, because we are putting too much dirt and other things in the water it doesn't have enough time to clean itself out, so it gets polluted. So it will take a longer time to clean itself out.[9]

Shirley's words remind me of when I was a child and we used to go to the Dokis reserve marina to do our laundry in a little shack that acted as a laundromat. I remember the sounds of the churning water in the giant metal washing machines and the smell of Sunlight soap perfuming the air. My mother, aunts, cousins, and I would spend hours at that tiny shack doing load after load of dirty laundry. I also remember the times when we used to go fishing and have afternoon shore lunches along the mouth of the rapids. The water of the rapids could be heard from far away and the smell of the water hung in the air—sunshine, pines, blueberries, and the hot granite rocks. The rapids always reminded me of the washing machine at the Dokis marina laundromat-shack. Like a washing machine, the rapids pull water into its grip and cause it to bubble and froth with oxygen, as if to clean the water and breathe life into it again. Then out the water goes, back into the river.

Similarly, the rapids are also like the heart and lungs of the human body. A heart pumps blood in; the lungs fill the blood with oxygen and cleanse the blood. Next, the heart sends that blood back out through the body, delivering essential elements to the body, while working also to remove harmful wastes. The rapids work in a similar fashion, both cleansing and feeding the river. But pollution in the waters of the French River has interfered with this sacred role. The amount of pollution being created is too much for the river waters to clean. Like a smoker or alcoholic who puts toxins into the body faster than the body can cleanse itself, the waters of our landscapes are made more unclean every year by the people living on them. As Shirley Williams warns, the increasing pollution people are putting into the water of rivers and lakes leaves no time for the water to cleanse itself.

Nishnaabeg women have always been strong proponents for the movement to clean and protect the water around the Great Lakes region. Our children have to drink the water, we bathe our babies in those waters. As well, we feed the children wild meat and medicine taken from lands contaminated by corporate development, human refuse, and garbage. I remember a time when our women—our mothers and aunties—would take their babies down to the shoreline at sunset to wash them in the waters of the river. These beautiful women would chat about the day's goings-on, socialize, and share stories. Now, children are washed in water that has to be heated or is filled with chemicals like chlorine to kill any parasitic bacteria. Water is now bought and trucked in from outside sources, and state-of-the-art filtration technology is used to purify the water. The water is then cleaned of everything, including all lifeforms.

Sacred Medicine or Poison?

All that we drink and eat is stored in our bodies and can either heal or harm us. Over time, our bodies can build up both nutrients and toxins from the food and water that we ingest, in a process that is known as bioaccumulation. To the Nishnaabeg people, this means that all that we eat or drink is stored in our organs, tissues, and cells for as long as we live. For those who live a traditional lifestyle of harvesting fish, animals, and water from the rivers, lakes, and streams in Nishnaabeg territories, the danger can come in mercury poisoning, bacterial infections, and other harmful pollutants. If the deer or fish the hunter kills and consumes is tainted with toxins, then the hunter and his family will absorb those toxins into their bodies. The harmful chemicals ingested by fish, animals, plants, and birds move through the food chain until they reaches people. Nishnaabekwe scholar Winona LaDuke explains this phenomenon by relating it to the sturgeon fish in the rivers of the Great Lakes:

> To the Nishnaabeg, bioaccumulation means that whatever toxins the fish has swallowed and stored in its flesh will come to be stored in our flesh as we participate in our traditional way of life based on harvesting from our lakes and streams. The disaster of mercury contamination has already impacted tribal communities throughout North America.[10]

In the past, the water we drank was considered medicine, but now it is hard to say whether it is a medicine or possibly poison we are putting in our bodies.

Now that the water in the lakes, streams, rivers, and water tables is no good to drink, Nishnaabeg people are being forced to buy water. Odawa Elder Shirley Ida Williams recalls the vision her father saw for her in the future about her having to buy water one day. She tells it this way:

> When I was growing up in 1950s, my father noticed that the water wasn't as clear as it's used to be. He was already aware that the water was not very clean. He said that before that you could see everything.... And he said at that time

'In your time you probably will see that the water is not going to be very clean and unhealthy to drink. And you will see the day where you will have to buy water.' I think I was working in St. Catherines in 1984 and I didn't like the taste of water over there. So, I thought, 'I saw bottled water in the grocery store. I think I better go get one.' When I bought it a voice came into my head that said, 'You are going to be buying bottle water in the future.' And I thought, 'Oh, how did my father know that?' And here I am I'm buying water. I was paying for the water at the cash register."[11]

Shirley's reserve of Wikwemikong Unceded First Nation now has water delivered to the homes in the community. Natural water from the rivers and lakes is no longer relied upon as a pure source of drinking water. Companies that supply water are trucking water into the community for local residents to purchase and use in their everyday lives. She adds, "When I go home the water now is being delivered to homes. Even that water doesn't taste that good. My sister, the one I stay with when I go home, she buys water. Periodically, I think many of the women boil water that they are going to drink." Due to the poor quality of water on her reserve (and on the many other reserves and reservations on both sides of the border), community members are now often opting to buy water that has been "cleaned" or "purified" by water treatment or filtration systems.

Shirley Williams worries about whether it is healthy for her community to buy water that is bottled or imported by truck to people's homes. She says, "I am concerned because when they deliver the water, how clean is the water in the water truck that is being delivered to the home? And the children drink it." Our children, who are referred to as our "future," are ingesting chemicals such as chlorine, fluoride, and the residue from the disposable plastic bottles used to store water. During a workshop at Trent University, to an audience of women, Josephine Mandamin warned about the dangers of water in the plastic bottles the women in the audience were drinking. She said:

> When I talk about the bottled water, I always think about this Elder.... I started to learn about my traditional ways when I was about twenty-seven years old. I started waking up from

my deep sleep of not knowing who I was an Nishnaabekwe.
I had this cedar in a plastic bag and I put that down beside
her. I had my little cedar and I put it down beside me. She
pointed at it and said, 'How long would you last if you
slept in a plastic bag?' I said, 'Not very long.' 'Well the same
thing is going to happen with your medicine. It is not going
to last very long.' Sure enough, I didn't take my cedar out of
the bag. Two days later, it started turning brown and then
the next day it started to get mouldy. It was decaying, it was
dying. It was actually dying in the plastic bag! The water
that you're drinking is about the same way. It is mouldy.[12]

We should be asking ourselves: Where does the water we are buying come from? Is it treated with chemicals to clean it? What is the
impact of bottling water in plastic containers made of chemicals? In
the end, buying water becomes a band-aid on a wound that is festering
beneath. Buying water does not solve the problem of a polluted environment. The land, plants, birds, and animals cannot buy "clean" water, so
what do they do?

Mide-Waaboo

Traditionally, the Nishnaabeg people consider water to be our relative.
Nishnaabeg believe that "all my family" includes not just our human family, but the animals, plants, birds, fish, the water, air, and the earth, which
all form part of the great interdependent web of life. Even the things that
are considered inanimate, we call our relatives. We call the Earth "our
real Mother," the land as our "Mother's lap," and water the blood of this
Mother the Earth. The calling of all Creation (including the sky, water,
lands, animals, fish, and birds) into our family describes a relationship of
trust, love, and faithfulness between human beings and the natural world.

Whereas colonial society views the environment as separate, the
earth consisting of raw material resources to use, exploit, and deplete,
Nishnaabeg people view the land, water, plants, animals, and sky world
as one unified and interdependent living system that works to sustain
us all. As the land, water, sky, plants, and animals are connected, so
is every aspect of life. The sacredness of water is not separate from

human beings. Therefore, every act, whether throwing a Pop can in a river or using chemical detergents to wash our laundry, interferes with that sacred relationship between the water and humanity. Everything has its respective place in this web of Creation, and interference with any component, no matter how small, will eventually have repercussions on all the other components.

Our traditional stories tell us that in the web of Creation, water is a sacred medicine. Shirley Williams shares that:

> From stories that I have heard they say that there is water up in the sky world somewhere in the land of plenty and that when we leave this world, this physical world and when you go into that spiritual world that there is water up there. But that there is a special place up there somewhere in the sky world where there is what they call the holy water.[13]

She explains that, according to the traditional teachings of the Midewiwin, they refer to this water as the mide-waaboo, which is similar to holy water. In the Midewiwin, they also have songs for water. There are songs in particular that are given to women to sing when you pray to the water or for the water in thanksgiving for what it does."[14] She explains that because women are given these sacred prayers and songs to sing for that sacred medicine, we therefore must speak out on the water's behalf.

The Elders use water as a medicine in ceremony to both nourish and cleanse our bodies, minds, and spirits. When we come out of our fasting lodges, it is water that is there to greet us, to bring us back to the world of the living and cleanse the way for us. Water is a great gift that sustains and transforms. Water can bring life into the world, make rivers, or break the great rocks over time. Water teaches us strength, the ability to endure, and patience. If water can take thousands of years to wear down, transform, and break through a rock, then we too can have the patience to do anything. Josephine Mandamin argues that water is a precious resource.

> Because water is so precious, that the only time I drink water is in the morning. First thing in the morning, that is my first drink, is that water. And I hold it up to the Creator. I hold it up to the Spirit, the Woman-Spirit who

> waters that water in that Third-Realm. I hold it up to her.
> I ask her to bring the mide-waaboo that I am going to put
> into my body. And I ask for blessings and I raise it four
> times and then I offer it to the ground or out the window
> or whenever I am and then I drink the water. That's the
> first drink. That is the most powerful drink, that is that
> first drink of water in the morning. Because it is that Spirit
> that you have called on to come to that water that you are
> holding in your hand, in that glass of water.[15]

The sacredness of water means that the water should be viewed as more than a mere commodity to be bought and sold. As Josephine describes, the very act of drinking water can be a ceremony that connects an individual to our relation—the water.

Water does not exist solely for use by human beings. All of life has access rights to the use of the water and its gifts. Exploiting the water to human ends will ultimately mean the break with the relationships to other parts of Creation: the animals, the land, plants, the birds, land, and sky. The women of Bkejwanong Territory remind us:

> We understand that the Creator Grandfather, made all that
> there is and breathed life into it. He made the land and the
> water to be pure....Our teachings say these waters must be
> kept absolutely pure because these river waters are our Holy
> Water. By taking even the minutest chance of contaminat-
> ing it, you are desecrating all that is sacred to us.[16]

The water is the birthright and a source of sustenance for our people. Each of us, therefore, has a great responsibility to protect and care for it. People were created by the Creator to act as "caretakers of the land" and all that is here. Therefore, humans should not let water be exploited, destroyed, or sold.

Keepers of the Water

Women are particularly connected to water in Nishnaabeg culture. Nishnaabeg women are often referred to as "The Keepers of the Water."[17] Josephine Mandamin calls Nishnaabe women the "carriers of the water." She says,

> As women, we are carriers of life. Our bodies are built that way. Men are not built that way. We are special. We are very special and unique in how our bodies are made that way. And the water that we carry, is that water of unity, that unites all of us. It unites all women. It unites all men. It unites all families, all nations all across the world. That little drop of water.[18]

Women have an intimate connection with water because of their ability to bring forth life. Shirley explains, "And because we are women we are the life-givers and when we have children, when it is birthing time it is the water that comes out first."[19] The birth of children marks a spiritual relationship from the time of pre-conception to birth where the waters of the woman's womb burst forth to cleanse the way for that new life to come forth into the world. Women are therefore held in high regard for these life-giving responsibilities and carriers of that sacred water.

Shirley Williams teaches younger women to respect their roles as lifegivers, and warns that it is up to women to maintain their responsibilities to the water. She believes that all women have to protect the water as the lifeblood of Mother Earth. She supplies this perspective on the matter:

> woman is given the responsibility of looking after the water because it is the mother earth, it is the woman. The woman is the mother earth and through the mother earth she has the rivers and the lakes, that's her bloodline. We in turn because we are women we are given that responsibility to help her, to clean her by praying and singing and to help her to clean herself.[20]

Josephine Mandamin says that "the main message is to walk the talk. To do what needs to be done for our Mother the Earth. She needs us!" If we are going to say we have responsibilities to water, then we have to act to carry on those traditions and fix the damage already done to the waters of our lands, lakes, and rivers.

Women's cycles, or blood time, are considered very powerful medicine for women. It is during the moon-time when women release that blood from their bodies that is most sacred. Bringing back the ceremonies of Berry Fasting and First Blood for the young girls involving their moon-time bleeding is critical to restoring the relationships and responsibilities of women to Mother the Earth as "Keepers of the Water." Those ceremonies have become a way to resist the Western culture that does not respect the sacredness of water and women's moon-time. Josephine Mandamin feels that it is important to instil knowledge in the minds and hearts of young girls about the importance of that water we carry in us.

> Women, especially girls who are just starting their moon-time. That is the time when Mother the Earth needs that blood. She is the blood. She gives us her blood in that water. And we as women have to give her our blood, which is our precious blood. And that first blood of our young children is what she needs. So we are teaching our young girls, young women that when they first give off of their blood, give to Mother the Earth. We ask them to, don't put your blood in the sewer, don't put your blood in the garbage can. Put it in a paper bag and when you're done your first blood we'll go put it out in the bush and we'll bury it, and Mother will use that. And don't use the toilet when you're first showing your blood. Use a plastic pail or a little pail and go there. Put that water on the Earth, she needs that. Because she gives up her water, we as women have to give back the water. I remember when my grandmother used to say when somebody was on her moon-time. That very first time she would say... now she is medicine! A woman is carrying medicine in her body, that is that powerful medicine—is her blood.[21]

As Josephine teaches in the above quote, a woman's body carries powerful medicine. During their moon-time, women's menstrual cycles are connected to the movements of Mother the Earth, but also to the moon and all Creation. Women have biological reminders of that connection with water every month when the moon-time arrives. Again, Josephine illustrates this connection:

> And when your moon-time comes, also, that is the most strongest time of your month, is when you're having your period. You can actually feel the pull of the moon in your moon-time. You can actually feel in your womb, that pull when you are on your moon-time, with Mother the Earth.[22]

As Josephine describes, the moon, described as Grandmother Moon or Nokomis in Nishnaabemwin, is seen as a force that guides not just our water or our blood during moon-time, but also various other aspects of water in nature.

The moon controls the waters of lakes, rivers, oceans, and the seas. Levels of water in lakes and rivers go up and down, currents change directions and cause storms to occur. Mother the Earth goes through cycles, just as women do. Throughout a month, weather shifts and changes just as women's bodies make ready and cleanse the womb for new life. Josephine articulates that Mother Earth goes through the same process as women:

> It's the same way when our Mother the Earth feels that full moon on Mother the Earth. If you look at the difference of the water during different times of the full moon and how that water reacts to the pull of the moon. It could be violent, it could be very gentle, it could be very peaceful, it could be all things if you watch very carefully how that water moves with the full moon. It's the same way with us women when we are in our moon-time. We go through the same cycle. We go through the same feelings. Our emotions are violent sometimes, peaceful, crying. There are different emotions we go through. Our Mother Earth goes through the same thing with her water during different times of the month. So we are told by our grandmothers when you are in your moon-time that's the most strongest time. Pray hard. Go and sit somewhere, peaceful and be with Mother Earth. And just pray for people at that time.[23]

Moon-time represents not just a reminder of a woman's responsibility to water, but of her water or blood as sacred medicine, and a time when she should think of others besides herself. Therefore, the water in nature and the water that women carry in the vessels of our wombs connects us to all of Creation—all our relations. All female creatures that live and breathe have cycles and carry that life-giving water. In this water, all female beings throughout the world, whether human, four-legged, those that fly or those that swim, all experience the pull of the water and the drive to carry life in their wombs.

Because women have this intimate relationship with water as a sacred medicine, it makes it more tragic that the water that we should pray for, drink, and birth our babies in is now threatened. Nishnaabeg women across Nishnaabeg Territory need to stand up for our rights to clean water and to protect our traditions, culture, and identities. We are now hearing the warnings prophesized by our Elders come true. We are now forced to buy water, to watch our Mother Earth become sick with toxins, and see our four-legged animal relatives suffer or even die due to polluted water. Shirley Williams warns us all to act now before it is too late.

> We once lived in water and we are born in water. And because we have not been taught to respect our own bodies and also respect that water and what it does for us, that is why we are in this predicament today! Many women are now beginning to realize that we have to do something about the water and the pollution in water because if we don't, all of us are going to be sick at some point.[24]

Mother Earth Water Walkers

> When we hear of prophecies, we listen to those prophecies and sometimes those prophecies hit us just like that, hits you right in the heart. In the year 2000, when I was at a Sundance and an Elder was taking about the prophecy about the water. He said, 'Thirty years from now ounce-per-ounce of that water is going to cost $300 per an ounce of water within the 25 years or sooner.' He talked about the roles of women. How they have to start picking up their work, picking up their bundle and doing what needs to be done about the water. And how he talked about how the Elders long time ago talked about how that water was going to be poisoned. How that beautiful water, he never believed it as a child when he heard those things. When he finished talking he looked at the crowd and said, 'What are you going to do about it?' What are you going to do about it, hit me right in the heart. It seemed like he was looking straight at me when he said that. For a year-and-a-half that burned in my heart. I talked to other women about it, that

we need to do something. What can we do? What are we going to do about it?[25]

The above quote by Josephine Mandamin comes from a workshop held at the Indigenous Women's Symposium at Trent University in Peterborough, Ontario, in March of 2007. Josephine shared with the audience how the Mother Earth Water Walkers formed. The Water Walkers are a group of First Nations women (Nishnaabeg women and some men) who are taking action to focus public attention on the growing problems facing this world's most precious resource—water, the lifeblood of Mother Earth. So far the Water Walkers have walked around most of the Great Lakes and have only Lake Erie to complete the circle of their journey.[26]

Josephine describes how the Water Walkers began in the winter of 2002. A group of women were sitting around, talking about traditional teachings, roles of women, and water songs.[27] She says they asked themselves the question: "What can we do to bring out, to tell people of our responsibilities as women, as keepers of life and the water, to respect our bodies as Nishnaabe-kwewag, as women?"[28] As they discussed what to do, the idea for the walk just came to them. Someone in the group simply commented:

> Well, you know we could walk around with the water and raise awareness? And somebody else said, 'Yeah! A Pail of water, lets walk around with a pail of water.' And somebody said, 'Lake Superior.' I, myself live about a fifteen-minute walk from Lake Superior where we live. Then somebody else said, 'I can just see Josephine walking around Lake Superior with a pail of water. And I said, 'Seriously let's do it!' And they said, 'Sure, okay let's do it!' So that's how we talked about it and talked to other women that we met. So, we did it! It's just one of those things that when the Spirit moves you, when you know that something has to be done, you don't question the Spirit, you just do it. And, that's what we did. We just did it![29]

From there, in 2003, Josephine Mandamin and other Nishnaabeg women began the circle of their journey with around the entire perimeter of Lake Superior. To date, they have travelled around the perimeter of Lake Huron, Lake Ontario, Lake Michigan, and Lake Superior. Their ultimate goal has been to raise awareness of the need to protect water, the lifeblood of Mother Earth.

According to Josephine Mandamin, the Water Walk has been a "spiritual walk."[30] It has brought together women from different clans and areas surrounding the Great Lakes in both Canada and the United States, and women and men from different backgrounds. The accomplishment of the Water Walkers lies not just in their ability to raise awareness about the state of water, but also to draw women, men, children, and community together as one voice for change. The women carried water from each of the Great Lakes in a copper pot, saying prayers and singing songs of the water along the route. Josephine writes, "The water we carried in our copper pail, always reminded us of our womanly responsibilities as givers of life as Mother Earth gives us, her children."[31] The action of walking is a movement toward change for the present and the future. For many of the women participating in the Water Walk, the walk represents a chance to make a difference. In their call for the 2007 Water Walk, the organizers said: "Please join in this great and wonderful event, through walking, assisting, donating, accommodating, feasting, providing security, hosting events, and spreading the word— everything helps us all."[32] Everything does help us all when it comes to taking action to save the world's most precious resources—Nibi/water.

As one of the organizers of the Water Walk, Josephine has written in her journal log:

> This journey with the pail of water that we carry is our way of Walking the Talk. We really don't have to say anything. Just seeing us walk is enough to make a person realize that, yes, we are carriers of the water. We are carrying the water for the generations to come. Our great grandchildren and the next generation will be able to say, yes, our grandmothers and grandfathers kept this water for us!![33]

The Water Walk has enabled First Nations women from various communities to be a part of the decision-making process to protect water. In spite of a history of being exploited by government and organizations,

First Nations people are working together in grassroots movements like the Water Walkers in order to empower their people. By just walking for the right to clean water, the Mother Earth Water Walkers are empowering themselves, rather than waiting for either the government or organizations to handle the problems.

This grassroots initiative has not been funded by any government agency or organization, but by the donations of supporters along the route, fundraising efforts at local events, and the money of the Walkers themselves. Josephine notes, "We didn't have any money. We had two vehicles. We had a truck and an old Chevy Lumina that we used for the light that went around to warn people of people walking. And so we started off with donations people gathered at the ceremonies that were at the 'Send Off.'"[34] Through the help of people living along the route, friends, and family, the Water Walkers were given food, water, and support carrying the water. The overall goal has been to gather more numbers, with support from persons, groups, and organizations to participate in the regional walks. With more walkers, both women and men, the Water Walkers' message becomes stronger and louder, more publicity is raised, and more First Nations women are aware of their responsibilities to the water.

Josephine has described this walk as a calling, not just for herself, but for all women. She talks about being called upon by not just her Grand Chief of the Midewiwin Lodge, but Mother the Earth herself, to take up the Water Walk around the Great Lakes. There is a spiritual calling to take action in this walk. Josephine writes in her trip journals:

> We are guided by vision and dreams, but most of all we are guided by our Spirit and Spirit Helpers. The journey with the water has become a lifetime experience, in that, the work is year round. More women and young girls are hungering for women teachings. We must feed their hunger. Elders have given advice/direction on how to proceed further. There is a concern by the Elders that First Nations in Canada are not getting the message about our concern for the water. It has been foreseen that I must walk to all the First Nation communities (reservations) along Lake

Superior. How this is to be done, I cannot fathom when and how. Only the spirit will guide that journey.[35]

Josephine suggests in her logs that the message the Water Walkers are spreading through their trek around the Great Lakes is not just for First Nations women and their partners, but for all peoples in the region.[36]

The Walker Walkers were on their last walk around Lake Erie in April 2007.[37] The conclusion of walk itself does not conclude the issues raised by the women like Josephine Mandamin. The message and increased awareness of their concerns for the state of water on the Great Lakes has now been passed on to countless grandmothers, aunties, mothers, and daughters of the Nishnaabeg Nation, and to many peoples living in the region. As women, we have a great responsibility to the water if we plan to continue to drink and eat the foods supported by the water of the Great Lakes region. Mother the Earth and her mother, Grandmother Moon, count on us to help the water and restore balance to water—to make it clean again for the future generations.

I leave off this section with a quote by Josephine Mandamin, reporting on the Water Walks trek around the Lake Superior region. She writes this in her journal log at the end of her first walk in 2003. The quote encapsulates our responsibilities as women to Earth our Mother and, in a way, it is a vision of the role we as women must fulfil:

> The wonders of miracles and the sheer impact of what inno-
> cent prayer can bring melted our hearts and quietly marveled
> at the reality of what we asked for when we wished for ful-
> fillment of our needs. Needs not wants. The wonderment
> of coming together of Grandmother Moon with her daugh-
> ter Aki Kwe, our mother, or as science calls it, the eclipse.
> In this union, I was awestruck and was held in suspension
> with tobacco in hand as I listened to our Mother speak to
> her Mother about her hurts, her pains, and that she is hurt-
> ing so much, that she can hardly sustain herself to provide
> for her children. She was telling our Grandmother how we
> are causing her slow destruction and causing her great pain
> and many illnesses. On and on she spoke, in much the same
> way we have spoken to our mothers when we were hurting
> or when we were telling on someone. Grandmother listened

to all her daughter was telling her and spoke, 'It's okay my girl, I will look after all things for you. There are those who are still following the teachings, doing their work, those who still keep their stories, their songs, will be recognized and acknowledged when the time comes.'[38]

This quote represents a call to action for Nishnaabeg women and all women around the world. The grassroots work of the Water Walkers is an initiative that teaches us that we do not need lots of money, the government, or organizations to make change in our own communities as First Nations women and men. All we need is an idea, the strength to carry through, and the support of community. The message I take away from the Water Walkers is that we all have our own individual responsibilities as women and men to protect Mother our Earth, not just for us, but out of respect for our ancestors and those generations yet to come.

Nishnaabe-kwewag, Keepers of the Water

I offer some brief concluding thoughts. It is my hope that Nishnaabeg women, First Nations women, and women in general, will hear the call to action in the words offered by the Elders and by myself. Since we all need water to survive, is it not up to all of us to protect it? I ask that the thoughts, ideas, and words expressed here are passed on to others, so that the message of protecting this world's most precious resource—water—will reach many ears.

To finish this chapter, I wish to pass on a poem that inspired me to write this paper. The power comes from a position paper called "Minobimaatisiiwin—We Are to Care for Her" by the Women of Bkejwanong Territory (Walpole Island Unceded First Nation). The poem is named "Nibi" and goes as follows:

Nibi

Nishnaabekwe, the Daughters,
You are the keepers of the water.
I am Nibi ... water ... the sacred source,
the blood of Aki, Mother Earth,
the force, filling dry seeds to green bursting.
I am the womb's cradle.
I purify.
Nibi, the lifegiver ...
forever the Circle's charge.
I have coursed through our Mothers veins.
Now hear my sorrow and my pain
in the rivers rush, the rain ...
I am your grandchildren's drink.
Listen, Daughters, always,
You are keepers of the water.
Hear my cry,
For the springs flow darkly now
through the heart of Aki ... Miigwetch/ We thank you.[39]

---

[1] Josephine Mandamin, Deb McGregor, and First Nations Youth, "Women, Traditional Knowledge, and Responsibilities to Water," Workshop presented at Indigenous Women: "Celebrating Our Diversity," 8th Annual Indigenous Women's Symposium, Peterborough, ON: Trent University, March 16–18, 2007.

[2] The Great Lakes consist of Lake Superior, Lake Michigan, Lake Huron, Lake Erie and Lake Ontario. They sit in the eastern portion of the North American continent and straddle the border of what is now known as Canada and the United States.

[3] These terms are from Shirley Ida Williams, *Gdi-nweninaa Our Sound, Our Voice* (Peterborough, ON: Neganigwane Company, 2002), pp. 13–21.

[4] Shirley Ida Williams, Native Studies 390: Immersion Spring/Summer Course, Nishinaabe-naadiwiziwin, Trent University, 2004.

[5] Williams, Gdi-nweninaa, 310.

[6] Women of Bkejwanong (Walpole Island) First Nation, "Position Paper, Minobimaatisiiwin, We Are to Care for Here, Bkejwanong—Where the waters divide," in Nin.Da.Waab.Jib, General Files, Walpole Island Unceded First Nation.

[7] Ibid., I.

[8] Renée Elizabeth Bédard, "An Nishnaabekwe Writes History: An Alternative Understanding of Indigenous Intellectual and Historical Traditions," MA thesis, Frost Centre for Canadian and Native Studies, Trent University, 2004, p. 65.

[9] Interview with Shirley Ida Williams, March 7, 2007, Peterborough, ON.

[10] Winona LaDuke, *Recovering the Sacred: The Power of Naming and Claiming* (Toronto, ON: Between the Lines, 2005), 234–235.

[11] Ibid., 234–235.

[12] Mandamin et al., "Women, Traditional Knowledge."

[13] Interview with Shirley Williams.

[14] Ibid.

[15] Mandamin et al., "Women, Traditional Knowledge."

[16] "Women of Bkejwanong," Position Paper, 2.

[17] Lynn Gehl, "Science Measures, But Doesn't Prevent Water Pollution," *Anishinabek News* (October 2006): 17.

[18] Mandamin et al., "Women, Traditional Knowledge."

[19] Interview with Shirley Williams.

[20] Ibid.

[21] Mandamin et al., "Women, Traditional Knowledge."

[22] Ibid.

[23] Ibid.

[24] Interview with Shirley Williams.

[25] Mandamin et al., "Women, Traditional Knowledge."

[26] "Aki/The Land," *Anishinabek News* (September 2006):7; "Lake Ontario 'pitiful': Walkers," *Anishinabek News* (July/August 2006): 23; "Nbi/Water: Lifeblood of Mother Earth," in *Anishinabek News* (April 2007): 11; "Walkers Raising Awareness About Water Issues," *Anishinabek News* (May 2005): 17; "Water Protection Spiritual," *Anishinabek News* (October 2006): 17; "Women Carry Copper Pail Around Lake Michigan to Create Awareness," *Anishinabek News* (June 2004): 17.

[27] Mandamin et al., "Women, Traditional Knowledge."

[28] Ibid.

[29] Ibid.

[30] Josephine Mandamin, Mother Earth Water Walk, Journal Entry 1, <www.motherearthwaterwalk.com/lakeHuron.html#m3>, 2005.

[31] Ibid.

[32] "Nbi/Water: Lifeblood of Mother Earth," 1.

[33] Mandamin, Journal Entry.

[34] Ibid.

[35] Ibid.

[36] Ibid.

[37] *Anishinabek News* (April 2007): 1.

[38] Mandamin, Journal Entry.

[39] "Women of Bkejwanong," Position Paper, 5.

Chapter 6

The Friendship Wampum: Maintaining Traditional Practices in
Our Contemporary Interactions in the Valley of the Kiji Sìbì

PAULA SHERMAN

Over the past 400 years, Omàmìwinini (Algonquin) people have struggled to maintain our long-standing relationships within the valley of the
Kiji Sìbì (Ottawa River) as a result of French, English, and Canadian
colonialism and the implementation of foreign social and political
structures. These structures have led to policies that enabled Europeans
to profit from our lands and resources while economically and politically marginalizing us to the fringes of our own territory. These policies
not only worked to jeopardize our autonomy and jurisdiction, they also
attempted to colonize our minds and transform our perceptions of our
relationships with the land and even with each other. The contemporary "land claim" is one example of those processes, as are our current
interactions with the Ministry of Natural Resources (MNR), cottagers,
and township municipalities who have established themselves within the
boundaries of our traditional territory.

This chapter will explore those interactions, their impacts on our
lives, and the ways in which Omàmìwinini people within the Ardoch community are reviving traditional practices and protocols as a mechanism to
resist colonialism and restore our relationships with the Natural World.
The use of long-standing traditional practices in all our interactions will

111

not only strengthen the community's position with respect to our deal-ings with the MNR, municipalities, and the Canadian government, but those traditional practices will also secure our continued survival as distinct peoples by providing the cultural, spiritual, and linguistic foundation necessary to carry us forward into the future. With a solid grounding in that foundation we will once again possess the knowl-edge we need to mould our young people into leaders who will not only recognize the importance of our relationships with the land for the articulation of our autonomy, but who will actually see it as imperative to our physical and cognitive survival.

Ardoch Algonquin First Nation is a confederation of Omàmìwinini families whose ancestors lived along the tributaries of the Kiji Sìbì from Lake of the Two Mountains to Lake Nipissing, in what is now known as Ontario. While it is not ethically possible to provide detailed maps or descriptions of the traditional lands utilized by contemporary people in the Ardoch community, it is acceptable to reveal that the land and waterscapes in that section of the territory continue to be under the autonomy and jurisdiction of these families and the community as a collective entity. No part of Omàmìwinini Territory was ever surren-dered or sold to the Crown, in spite of the fact that both the federal and provincial governments operate out of our territory on a daily basis.

Ardoch Algonquin First Nation also maintains a traditional coun-cil called Ka-pishkawandemin, which meets on a regular basis to deal with internal and external issues of importance to the community. The council works to reach balanced decisions through careful discussion and dialogue in which all families participate through the Family Heads they have appointed to represent them. The council is currently composed of nine men and women who range in age from thirty-five to eighty years old. As a governance system, Ka-pishkawandemin enables all community members to have a voice in the issues affecting the community and there-fore a stake in striving to reach consensus on difficult issues.

Ardoch, as an Omàmìwinini community, certainly seems to have a lot going for it—our autonomy and jurisdiction are still intact, and we continue to maintain a traditional governance system long after most other Omàmìwinini communities in Ontario misplaced theirs. Indeed, we are lucky that those things have not been lost and owe much to our ancestors for maintaining what they could of an original ontology against sometimes impossible odds. While acknowledging those achievements, and their important contribution to our understanding of ourselves as Indigenous people, we cannot escape the fact that our territory was invaded and continues to be occupied. We have been forced to endure wave after wave of colonial policies that were designed to eliminate us from the consciousness of Canada while also appropriating our lands and resources for the sole use of settler societies. This dispossession happened in spite of the fact that neither the French nor British ever acquired those lands legally.

These policies have had an impact on our psyches and our ability to resist colonialism, for while we recognize in our minds that we have relationships with the land,[1] we do not always feel that connection in our hearts, and, as a result, we often lack confidence in ourselves to collectively assert our inherent rights to relate to the land and waterscapes in ways that are culturally appropriate. One need look no further than our current struggles with the MNR, North Frontenac Township, and the cottage association, which developed out of our decision to build a cultural heritage centre on traditional land at Pine Lake. As a site of important cultural significance, the community felt strongly about locating the centre there with adjoining grounds for gatherings and outdoor teaching space.

Community plans to build the centre continue to be undermined by the MNR, who have taken the position that they have the responsibility to manage the site as Crown land.[2] Cognizant of the contemporary land-claim process, and the undeniable fact that the land in question sits within the established boundaries of traditional Omàmìwinini Territory, the MNR has tried on various occasions to manipulate the community into a position that could jeopardize our autonomy or jurisdiction. One of the most disturbing instances involved an attempt on the part of the MNR to issue the community a land-use permit wherein they stated they would "give back" the land to the community.[3] In this instance, the MNR representative in Bancroft assured us that this was their process through the law to give the land back to us and that there was no attempt to compromise our assertions of inherent rights to the land.[4]

There were many discussions about this offer from the MNR within the community and some Council members, acting on existing cultural protocols for relating with others,[5] felt it would be appropriate to work with the MNR to get the land back. Other Council members felt that working at all with the MNR was a mistake that could compromise the autonomy of the entire community. They felt that any sort of agreement between the MNR and the Council would jeopardize the active stance the community had taken. Elders on the Council, such as Harold and Neil Perry, went further to say that "we could not allow the MNR to give us land that had never been surrendered or sold to the Crown."[6] In the end, consensus was reached by the council and the decision was made not to enter into any agreement with the Ministry of Natural Resources.

While this decision was proactive and allowed the Council to stand its ground and not accept ownership for the land at Pine Lake, it did not settle the ultimate issue of jurisdiction. Consequently, the MNR stepped up their campaign of interference and applied it on many levels. As expected, officials from Bancroft suggested that they could lay charges and get an injunction to stop the work that was underway on the site. One of the more subtle approaches attempted by the MNR during this period was an offer of a free culvert for seepage, and truckloads of logs for the centre, valued at over $10,000. On the surface, this gesture was interpreted as a sign of good faith by community members who wanted to heal the rift in the relationship. Other community members doubted the sincerity of the MNR and came to the conclusion that the gifts were probably contingent on recognizing MNR jurisdiction, policy, and process. For them, the gifts were nothing more than carrots that were being dangled out in front of us to lure us in, creating a false sense of security and trust.

In retrospect, almost every action on the part of the MNR has probably been the result of concise use of government scenarios that test various responses to Aboriginal blockades and protests. Such scenarios have existed for years and were even discussed as part of the testimony at the Ipperwash Inquiry in 2005. Some of those scenarios could have been developed by the *Interministerial Committee on Aboriginal Emergencies.*[7] Known as the "blockade or barricade committee" among government officials, membership in the committee fluctuated depending on the location and particulars of each situation involving Aboriginal peoples.[8]

Talking about this committee in November of 2005, Jeffrey Bangs, executive assistant to Christopher Hodgson, implied that the interministerial committee was only a "clearing house or information gathering body that created options or made recommendations to the government"[9] with respect to dealing with Aboriginal protests. Minister Hodgson offered a different perspective in his testimony in January of 2006, stating that the committee played a much more important role than that and was actually "in control, or overseeing the situation around Ipperwash."[10] There was, in fact, a policy document that had been distributed to various ministries, including the MNR, entitled "Guidelines for Responding to Aboriginal Emergencies" which existed prior to 1995.[11] While Ipperwash is not the subject of this chapter, it is important to point out that the MNR had access to scenarios and actually participated in the discussions surrounding Ipperwash and the further development of mechanisms for responding to Aboriginal protests and blockades. It is, therefore, not a stretch of the imagination to suggest that some of those developments could have influenced the ways in which MNR officials attempted to deal with Ardoch Algonquin people and the situation at Pine Lake.

The point emphasized here is that the community realized that the MNR could not be trusted to put Algonquin interests before those of the Crown. Gifts are among the many avenues employed by the MNR to assert influence over the collective lives of Algonquin people. As gifts, the culvert and logs were nothing more than a ploy to extend the control of the province onto Algonquin land at Pine Lake. Fortunately, the community came together in time and was able to present a united front against that particular ploy. We have not been as lucky with respect to the application of our *Principles of Development*[12] to the environmental assessment process normally employed by the MNR.

Prior to any work being done on the site, the Council considered possible risks and directed two Elders with extensive experience of the site to carry out an assessment of potential risk, which they did over a period of a year. They examined the site in all its cycles to measure

115

possible impacts but none were revealed to them. In addition, ceremonies were performed on the site to ask for spiritual guidance, and the site was discussed in Council meetings on a monthly basis. It was through this lengthy process that the community determined that the site was the appropriate one for the centre and would provide a safe cultural space for community members and off-reserve people to come together for the programs and services that would be offered there.

Confident in the decision to build the centre there, the community began the process of developing a site plan and drafting possible designs for the building that would complement the site. Trees were cleared from the immediate area where the building would be located and the adjoining powwow grounds. The removal of trees from the site, however, drew shocked responses from some of the cottagers who had purchased lots around the lake from the Township of North Frontenac. Not aware of the complicated history of the area, or underlying Omàmìwinini title and jurisdiction, the cottagers assumed that they had the right to interfere with community plans for the site because the site is adjacent to a public boat launch.

While Omàmìwinini people had been visible to cottagers prior to this action, many actually lived outside the region and stayed in their cottages only in the summer months. Most of the cottages were in fact vacant by the time the Manomiin Celebration happened in September of 2003 to honour the community's twenty-five-year victory over commercial harvesters. Undoubtedly, while many of these same cottagers passed Omàmìwinini people on the highway driving to and from their cottages or walked past them in local stores and restaurants, we had no real economic or social impact on their lives and thus we did not exist.

When Omàmìwinini people began to clear away the trees and prepare the land for the building and powwow grounds in the height of their summer holiday, however, the cottagers suddenly recognized that we were there. They protested our actions and demanded consultation on our plans for Pine Lake. While the community rejected the idea that they had to consult the descendants of settlers who had appropriated the land in the first place, there were those individuals who reminded everyone of the responsibilities that we had to maintain our relationships. As a result, the community did hold an initial meeting with local residents and concerned cottagers to reveal the site plan and building design, and to answer questions.

The attitude and behaviour of certain people led to blatant remarks and statements that were racist and discriminatory. While a few individuals were supportive of the project, other people stated with outright anger and hostility that they did not intend to spend their summers or holidays listening to "wild Indians banging on drums" or "singing and dancing around campfires." A threat was even issued by a man who said he could withhold fire services because he was not required to extend those services to Omàmìwinini people at Pine Lake. It appeared to the Omàmìwinini people in attendance that the majority of the cottagers felt that we were squatters who had no right to build anything at Pine Lake. Even the attempts by Omàmìwinini representatives to remind those in attendance that the lands in question had been taken from us illegally fell on deaf ears. Our presentation of the historical facts was met with sharp resentment by the cottagers, who said that our claims were worthless because we had been "conquered long ago."[13]

Even though the meeting went terribly wrong and created a deep division between Ardoch Omàmìwinini people and the surrounding cottagers, those in attendance came back to the community and shared their experiences with the Council. This resulted in the decision to avoid further meetings because of the racism and discrimination that accompanied that engagement. The cottagers, for their part, were upset that the community refused to meet with them and formed a cottage association to take their complaints to the MNR and the Township of North Frontenac. The MNR used the cottagers in an attempt to assert their own jurisdiction over Pine Lake. The complaints made by the cottagers were used by the MNR to justify their demands that the community follow an environmental assessment process that would be under the direction of the Ministry.[14]

The mayor of the Township of North Frontenac, who initially supported the project, was pushed by his council into openly opposing the centre. This opposition materialized in the request that the community secure building permits from the township for all proposed construction.

The community did not share this assessment and responded to the mayor that there would be "no permits taken out to build on land that was already under Omàmìwinini jurisdiction."[15] This enraged the cottagers, who appointed a lawyer from Toronto to represent their interests. This lawyer pleaded their case once again to the MNR, insisting that the MNR take charge of the situation. The MNR used this turn of events to pressure the community once again into complying with the MNR environmental assessment.

The majority of the Family Head's Council felt that the environmental assessment required under MNR policy was another mechanism that was being invoked by Ministry officials to interfere with Omàmìwinini jurisdiction on Omàmìwinini land. There was general confusion on the best course of action to follow, however, and some community members came forward to articulate a position in favour of working with the MNR, the township, and the cottagers to resolve the issue so the centre could be completed. The confusion and conflicting perspectives led to heated debates within the Council. The nature of the debates reduced the Council to unpleasant disarray that further fuelled the animosity developing between people on the Council. Much of the tension sprang from the fact that the MNR had deemed Omàmìwinini principles for evaluating human development irrelevant to the environmental assessment and wanted the emphasis the community placed on those principles minimized in favour of a scientific model of assessment.

This division and conflict, although not absent from Indigenous communities, was not a regular component of Ardoch Omàmìwinini governance. The conflict took on a life of its own and led people away from the Seven Grandfather Teachings that normally provided guidance and balance within the Council. Some individuals pushed for the Council to follow their process and work with the MNR to resolve the issue with the cottagers. These individuals maintained that this option was not out of character, as we were supposed to maintain relationships at all costs with our neighbours. Others felt strongly that allowing the MNR to take charge of the assessment would imply that the MNR had jurisdiction, when it did not. Then there were those people in the community who just felt that the MNR would take advantage of the situation and grind the process to a halt or extend it for years that would seriously jeopardize the project.

Unfortunately, at that time, very few people commented on the potential danger to the community should we not follow through with the traditional principles for development that had already begun. Those principles caution us that "altering the land requires conscious and moral decisions that recognize in practice responsibility for the spirit of the land and the future generations who will also be dependent on it."[16] The *Principles of Development* goes on to say:

> Algonquin people are the first people of the Kiji Síbí water-shed and therefore have a special responsibility to ensure that the land is cared for. Algonquin people can look to no other place in the world to find their origins. Kijimanitò created Omámíwinini (Algonquin) in this valley to give them life and purpose. The creatures with whom we share this valley are our closest relatives. All that is Algonquin, our culture, spiritual practices, language, governance, hon-our and relationships is the 'story' of this land.[17]

Likewise, the responsibility for protecting and preserving our homeland is still a greater part of Algonquin culture and values. In fact, Canadian law provides constitutional protection of our Aboriginal Rights and Title as defined historically by the Crown in its own laws and decla-rations.[18] As Omàmìwinini people, we have never ceded or sold our Aboriginal Rights and Title. We therefore enjoy the relationship of trust and protection offered by the Crown in the Royal Proclamation of 1763, trade conference promises, historical documents, and the *Constitution Act* 1982.[19] However, it is important to recognize that the laws of Canada do not supersede the intention of the Creator in placing Omàmìwinini people here and giving us a way of living and a sacred responsibility to this land. It is this relationship that is the highest authority and from which all Omàmìwinini people must take guidance.[20]

The lack of understanding about our relationships with the land and waterways within our own territory speaks to the larger issue of cultural and linguistic loss that plagues this community and many others as a result of colonialism and Canadian policies of assimilation and elimination. It also speaks to the difficulty of finding solutions that meet our specific needs in the present and future. We are not working to find our way back to what we once were in the past, but are, instead, diligently struggling to bring forward those teachings, ceremonies, practices, and ways of relating that can help to rebuild a strong cultural base from which to resist contemporary colonialism and the cognitive elimination that accompanies the physical changes to our territories and bodies. The process of redefining ourselves within the contemporary world is being challenged and constantly interfered with by forces outside the community, such as the MNR and cottage association, but we are also our own worst enemy when it comes to having confidence in ourselves and articulating our autonomy without fear of reprisal by those forces who want to see us disappear from the land and waterscapes in our own territory.

The Ministry of Natural Resources, as a provincial entity, has no real physical power over us, yet we struggle to find the words to remind them of the relationships we share and the principles that were embedded in the wampum belts that were exchanged with the British in the eighteenth century. Likewise, the Township of North Frontenac, as a municipality that is operating out of our lands, has no authority to force us to acquire building permits or consent to inspections to ascertain our compliance with the Ontario building code. We are the ones ultimately responsible under Omàmìwinini Law, which is why we undertook our own community environmental process. In spite of this powerful symbol of autonomy, however, we fell back on our old insecurities and actually considered the MNR's request. Although much confusion exists about what should be done in situations such as this, acknowledging the MNR process is disrespectful to those Elders who worked to complete the community evaluation and it devalues their knowledge and their hard work.

In the end, opposition to the MNR environmental assessment prevailed, but the determination to keep the MNR and the cottagers out of the process created animosity where there was none before. The Council did reach a resolution of sorts by hiring a biologist who would work under the direction of the community and not the MNR. Her work would expand on the assessment completed by the Elders, but it would not replace their work. This compromise allowed for raw feelings to be put aside, but tension remained between particular individuals who felt strongly about their positions. Since the situation is so volatile and we still carry those insecurities about ourselves, the tension that still exists between particular individuals could escalate once again and explode as new issues emerge with respect to the site.

This struggle to restore confidence in ourselves is imperative because we desperately need to come together in a culturally significant way to secure our survival as distinct people. Traditional governance and title to our territory are important but they are not sufficient to combat the cognitive colonialism that continues to imprison our minds, spirits, and bodies. In this assimilated state it is difficult to recognize our true selves and next to impossible to comprehend the necessity of maintaining spiritual connections with the land. Without that connection, we lack confidence in our collective identity as Omàmìwinini people, which in turn affects the decisions that we make and the ways in which we carry out our lives.

It is really a matter of confidence, of understanding our relationships with the land and then acting on that knowledge and understanding for the benefit of future generations and also the Natural World. The sacredness of the land is reflected in the *Principles of Development*, yet I am not convinced that we feel that sacredness in our hearts or emulate it in our behaviour or interactions with the MNR or the township. How else could we consider devaluing those principles in favour of an MNR assessment or township building permits? We have the responsibility as Omàmìwinini people under Omàmìwinini law to articulate our relationships within the land in ways that promote the balance and survival of the Natural World and all living entities. Since Omàmìwinini people are components of the land and Natural World, it could be the case that our survival is dependent on the continued use of the land in culturally appropriate ways. Thus, allowing the MNR or the township to dictate and guide our interactions with the land is not culturally sustainable and could jeopardize our survival. Therefore, that interference should be limited if not stopped altogether.

These principles for relating are all around us in cultural documents such as wampum belts that were passed between Omàmìwinini people and the French and English, linking them in relationships that had corresponding responsibilities. The Friendship Belt, for instance, under the care of Omàmìwinini Elder William Commanda, dates back to 1700 and contains three figures, representing the French on one end, the English on the other, and Omàmìwinini people in the centre. The placement of Indigenous Peoples in the centre of the belt represents the special position that Indigenous Peoples have as central figures of autonomy within the landscape of North America.[21] This belt not only carries forward the relationships between Omàmìwinini people and children of the British who inhabit our lands today, it also carries forward the spiritual nature of Omàmìwinini relationships with the land.

The belt reminds us that we have responsibilities to maintain those relationships through the use of lands and resources in ways that are culturally appropriate so as to promote balance and sustainability for all living entities. This includes securing the cultural futures of our children and grandchildren. There is a significant need for the cultural heritage centre in the Ardoch community as a place of safety where community members can come together to celebrate that relationship with the land. Centring the programs and services in this space can facilitate the growth of culture and language among community members that will help Ardoch Omàmìwinini people to truly feel and experience their relationship with the land and waterscapes and not merely theorize it in their minds. The purpose of the centre, with its indoor and outdoor cultural space, is not to appease or annoy the MNR, cottagers, or the municipality; its true purpose is to provide the cultural and spiritual space necessary to heal the multigenerational trauma of colonization caused by the last 400 years of colonialism in the valley of the Kiji Sìbì. The centre will be a significant tool in coaxing Omàmìwinini people from the margins where we remain cognitively colonized and unsure of ourselves and our relationships with the land.

The only thing standing in our way of seeing this vision fulfilled is the lack of confidence that we have in ourselves. The greatest defence that we have against the MNR, cottagers, and township is the fact that we are Omàmìwinini people and we were created as part of the Kiji Sìbì. We exist as human beings because the four elements of Creation came together with the breath of life from the Creator. Our connection to the land goes back that far into the past. Our authority to build a cultural centre at Pine Lake therefore cannot come from the MNR, the cottagers, or the municipality, nor can it come from Ontario or Canada. That authority can only come from the Creator, and through Omàmìwinini Law, which evolved out of our relationships with the land over thousands of years. We followed the proper cultural protocols as we understand them for assessing potential risk to the land and Natural World, and are not required to follow those of Ontario or Canada.

We took ownership of the project by hiring a biologist who would work under the direction of Elders and the Family Head's Council, and whose work would enhance what was already completed. Instead of an MNR-controlled assessment, the work by the biologist would become a component of the community environmental assessment, thus leaving the autonomy within the community where it belongs. The issue with the cottagers has not gone away but has been mediated away from the community to the architect who is overseeing the construction so that legitimate questions can be addressed and not lost in the racist barrages that have passed for concern on the part of the cottagers. This allows the community to move forward with less anger and despair, which has had an impact on the wampum belt held up exclusively by Omàmìwinini people at this point.

Is it time for us to drop our side of the belt, given the fact that our shoulders are hanging down from the weight? Probably, but the teachings that still remain in the community will not allow that to happen. In good conscience, we could not continue on as Omàmìwinini people if we abandoned our side of the belt. What we can no longer manage, however, is to carry the weight of the children of the newcomers on our back; it is time that they stood up and grabbed the other side of that belt. Whether they manage to do this cannot deter us from the important work we have to do to prevent colonialism from claiming any more of our distinct identity as people than has already happened. Their lack of respect for the principles embedded in those wampum belts cannot be allowed to harm our children and grand children any further, and we must restore what has been stolen from us so that we can maintain our relationships with the land and with each other.

The fact that we have been cognitively colonized to live in the shadows of our former selves goes without saying; the ability to recognize the fact that we are colonized and in need of cultural and linguistic retraining is the first step down the path to making that happen. That path will always be filled with obstacles, but they do not have to be insurmountable if we can gain enough confidence in ourselves to carry us through. The culture and language embedded in the programming to be offered in the centre at Pine Lake will not only allow Ardoch Omàmìwinini people to recognize the relationship that we have with the land, it will make it possible for us to actually come to know that that relationship is one of spirituality, which must emulate from the depths of our hearts and not just our mind.

Author's Note: This chapter was submitted to Ka-Pishkawandemin, the Family Head's Council, for ethical approval prior to its inclusion in this publication. This is in keeping with the Ardoch Omàmìwinini community ethics process that requires academics and researchers to work with the community on all scholarship and to submit that scholarship to the Council for final approval.

[1] The point being made here is that there is a difference between knowing the land intellectually within your mind and feeling the history of that connection in your heart. The knowledge that one develops over time from that historical connection within the land and waterscapes results in positive identity development as Omàmìwinini people. Solid identity makes it possible to fully understand the importance of maintaining Omàmìwinini relations, which is in keeping with traditional Omàmìwinini ontology.

[2] The site is not part of a reserve, but is traditional Omàmìwinini land that was never sold, ceded, or surrendered to the Crown.

[3] Ministry of Natural Resources, E-mail Communication to Chief Randy Cota, 2005.

[4] Ibid.

[5] The historical precedence for maintaining balanced relationships with the Natural World and other peoples stretches back into the ancient world and the teachings of Creation. For a historical look at the importance of relationships for Omàmìwinini people, see Paula Sherman, "Indawendiwin: Spiritual Ecology as the Foundation of Omàmìwinini Relations," PhD dissertation, Department of Indigenous Studies, Trent University, 2007.

[6] Harold Perry, Council Meeting, Ardoch Algonquin First Nation, July 31, 2005.

[7] Ipperwash Public Inquiry: Testimony of Jeff Bangs, Executive Assistant to Christopher Hodgson, November 3, 2005.

[8] Ibid.

[9] Ibid.

[10] Ipperwash Public Inquiry: Testimony of Christopher Hodgson, January 12, 2006.

[11] Ibid.

[12] *Principles of Development* are those protocols within Omàmìwinini tradition that provide guidance to individuals and communities when contemplating decisions that can alter the landscape. While council members approach this responsibility differently, many prepare for meetings and discussions about development by asking for guidance from the ancestors. In many situations, ceremonies are required to determine possible impacts of human activities on the land. These protocols are based upon the fact that Omàmìwinini people were brought into an ecosystem that was already complete before our arrival. We are therefore required to adjust our attitude and behaviour toward the Natural World so that we make the least footprint possible. That is our responsibility as human beings who were created in this place. We have relationships that emerged from Creation, which demand respect and reciprocity. The *Principles of Development* are a cultural mechanism that reminds us of those relationships and responsibilities.

[13] Meeting with Cottagers and Residents of the Township of North Frontenac, October 5, 2005.

[14] Ministry of Natural Resources, E-mail Communication.

[15] Ardoch Algonquin First Nation, Correspondence to the Township of North Frontenac, November 2005.

[16] Ardoch Algonquin First Nation, *Principles for Development*.

[17] Ibid.

[18] Robert Lovelace, Contributions to the Principles of Development.

[19] Ibid.

[20] Ardoch Algonquin First Nation, *Principles for Development*.

[21] Paula Sherman, *Indawendiwin*.

Chapter 7

Living Inuit Governance in Nunavut

JACKIE PRICE

In *Nunavut*,[1] Inuit homeland, big changes are coming and their impacts will be great. Climate change and resource development are changing the land physically, and this is changing the relationship Inuit have with the land. It is important to acknowledge that these new changes are in addition to challenges Inuit continue to experience as a result of being forcefully removed from living their independent and subsistent lives on the land. New political strategies are needed in order to strengthen the relationship Inuit have with each other, and with the land. In this chapter, I argue that by respecting the principles of Inuit governance, Inuit will have the means to work through the challenges of the past and can begin actively strategizing for the future.

For Inuit, winter is central to identity, as it is both a physical and conceptual experience. The relationship between the physical and conceptual experience is also central to Inuit being. Inuit as Indigenous Peoples understand the fluidity between these two spaces, and it is this fluidity that guides individual and collective logic while also inspiring the practices of Indigenous pedagogy, spirituality, and political systems. Yet, climate change is challenging this foundation. Climate change has resulted in erratic weather patterns, thinning ice, and melting permafrost, all of which is challenging Inuit means of predicting and navigating the weather, land, and animals. While many Inuit are responding to these physical changes through adaptive land and hunting strategies, the conceptual environment in and around Nunavut is not adapting as quickly. Nunavut's conceptual environment continues to focus on identifying and documenting the technicalities of these physical changes. Collective strategies seem left for the future, and the absence of these strategies support a gap between the Inuit physical and conceptual experiences.

This gap is further supported by spin-off challenges resulting from climate change, such as the opening of the Northwest Passage. This waterway stretches across the arctic and is heralded as the next big shortcut by the naval world. This shortcut would mean a new influx of non-Inuit people into the north, individuals who have a different relationship with the waters from that which Inuit have. This new group is in addition to the other wave of peoples into Inuit homeland, specifically researchers and scientists participating in the International Polar Year (IPY). IPY is a concentrated, international campaign that endorses physical and social research in 2007/08 at both poles. It is calling researchers and scientists to the north, armed with methodological and ethical logics that are not of Nunavut, not the Inuit way.

Like climate change, resource development is widening the gap between Inuit physical and conceptual experiences and has also resulted in direct and spin-off challenges. Although Inuit have always understood the land to be resourceful, this new campaign understands Nunavut's resourcefulness in a different way. Resource development is now faster and concentrated, and its goal is maximum economic benefit through massive extraction. Nunavut and Inuit economic prosperity and future well-being is linked directly with mining. This new way does not respect the Inuit principle of subsistence living. This view of resources and the need for economic prosperity has encouraged many Inuit to consider prospecting in Nunavut, but, more seriously, this mentality beckons developmental businesses and corporations into Nunavut. Diamond and uranium mining are currently the focus in Nunavut, and Nunavut political organizations chant that *Nunavut* is "open for business."

Political support for mining and resource development flows from the Nunavut Land Claims Agreement (NLCA). The NLCA states that "Inuit shall receive defined rights and benefits in exchange for surrender of any claim, rights, title and interests based on their assertion of Aboriginal Title."[2] In signing the NLCA, Inuit surrendered their rights to their homeland, and, in return, the Inuit of Nunavut received a financial compensation package, the right to establish a territorial government, and a defined territory boundary. Although the NLCA is often presented and celebrated as a means for strengthening Inuit and Canada's relations, it is important to acknowledge that in signing the NLCA, the Canadian federal government secured legal right and title to over 83% of Nunavut's land mass. This means that the majority of Inuit homeland is now federal Crown land. This reality is exacerbated by Nunavut's sheer geographical size—it spans approximately 2.1 million square kilometres, an area one-fifth of Canada's total size. The NLCA also provides Nunavut with a governing framework. It contains many articles specifically on land use and planning, and resource development, and outlines the administrative and legal responsibilities for defined political players. These responsibilities are legally expressed and expected.

Climate change and resource development, the establishment of political structures with specified legal and administrative duties, and the influx of people armed with new methodologies and ethical processes have created a new chaos in *Nunavut*. This chaos further exacerbates the challenges that continue to exist in *Nunavut* resulting from the last sixty years of change. New ways of practising spirituality, justice, community governance, child rearing, and interacting with family and the community have become the norm in the north. These new ways have required time, energy, and focus, and this has meant that Inuit rules, supports, and expectations are left behind to support these new systems. Inuit are not privileging the Inuit way of doing thing. This reality must cease. To recover from the challenges of the earlier generation, and in order to prepare for the future challenges, I argue Inuit must look back to Inuit knowledge systems in order to imagine a time where Inuit are able to rise above the colonial chaos. Inuit must remember the lessons that come from interacting with the land.

Inuit Homeland: *Nunavut*

Indigenous ways of being recognize the land as the source of all existence. Marino Aupilaarjuk, an Inuk Elder whom I deeply respect, argues: "The living person and the land are actually tied up together, because without one the other doesn't survive and vice versa."[3] In recognizing the influence of, and responsibility to, the land, the governance of a specific area must begin by respecting its geographical reality. In *Nunavut*, the land and weather are extreme. People not of *Nunavut* use the word "harsh" to express *Nunavut's* environment, as it is a challenging landscape that both deserves and commands respect. It is a territory that sits north of the treeline, and this reality often inspires the comment that in *Nunavut* there exists a stronger sense of distance. Everything is open, and, as you travel the land, you notice all changes, whether they be subtle or dramatic. For Inuit, this reality is what makes *Nunavut* so beautiful. This openness reminds individuals that there is no hiding, and that change is obvious. Living and learning from the land means individuals must remember that honesty is necessary, because truth is always around you, and, just as the land continues, knowledge also continues. Inuit have also understood that the land belongs to no one, as it was free to be respectfully used by all people. This requires that all actions, whether individual or collective, be accounted for. This respect for the land is obvious when hearing Inuit describe *Nunavut*, as Rosa Paulla does: "The land is so beautiful with its high rivers and lakes waiting to be fished. It has great mountains and images form as if you could be caribou among them."[4] For Inuit, *Nunavut* is beautiful and full of resources and potential.

Inuit also respect the patterns and realities of *Nunavut*, demonstrated by their collective memory and continuing presence of traditional survival skills. Knowledge exists within the rhythm and realities of the land. This knowledge has also influenced and inspired Inuit political systems, or Inuit governance. Each community lives its governance, and this was supported through knowledge and relationships, which serve as the foundational structures in Inuit governance.

Inuit Governance

Nunavut is a metaphysical force that influences Inuit life and it is a force that cannot be manipulated. Inuit have constantly interacted with and studied the land, and this has guided the formulation of Inuit survival knowledge. Maligait is an example of such knowledge. Maligait has a number of translations. In its literal form, and within the context of Canadian colonial authority, maligait translates to law, "customary law," specifically, Canadian law. This is not the context in which Inuit understand this term and does not express its depth and range of authority. For Inuit, this term means "things that had to be done" and represents the force by which Inuit lived. Marino Aupilaarjuk of Rankin Inlet explains:

> When I think of paper I think you can tear it up and the laws are gone. The maligait of the Inuit are not on paper. They are inside people's heads and they will not disappear or be torn to pieces. Even if a person dies, the maligait will not disappear.[5]

Maligait are rules that govern Inuit in their relationships within the metaphysical world. Respecting maligait is a requirement that flows from traditional Inuit spirituality, which recognizes the constant presence of spirits and respects the authority of spirits to challenge Inuit physical survival. Spiritual authority exists within an intrinsic spiritual network of relationships that guides Inuit existence, which included Inuit, the land, weather, and the animals. Therefore, any individual who disrespects maligait affects the spiritual balance of these relationships, challenging individual and community well-being. For example, not respecting maligait led to negative consequences, such as constant extreme weather or the absence of animals;[6] in fact, many Inuit Elders advise that not respecting maligait will shorten one's life.[7] Therefore, maligait demands respect.[8]

Respecting maligait requires individuals to be constantly aware of their surroundings and actions, and, when necessary, to be critical of their own conduct. This awareness was not only held at a theoretical level, it was practically applied. For example, if a known maligait was not followed, and hardship was being experienced, it was the responsibility of the individual to confess their wrongdoing. The likelihood of a public confession increased with the assistance of an angakkuq (shaman), as the angakkuq had the ability to identify what wrong had been committed by whom. Yet, it is important to recognize that an angakkuq could amend the spiritual upset only once a confession was made. An angakkuq did not just "fix" the problem; an individual had to first admit their wrongdoing to the broader community.

Maligait reminds Inuit that through discipline and the structure and support of the family, Inuit are able to live within the extreme land and weather. But physical survival is not the only goal for Inuit. Inuit expect life with metaphysical forces to be harmonious, an expectation that also requires Inuit collective life to be harmonious.

Inuit governance supports various leadership roles simultaneously. To understand the role of leadership within Inuit governance, it is necessary to first understand leadership within the family. While relationships are the foundational structure of Inuit governance, the central relationship is the family. Leadership within the family is shared amongst the older generations—the "grandparents" and "parents."[9] Sharing leadership is successful and effective as it is supported by constant interaction, an understanding of each member's strengths within various fields of responsibility, an appreciation and recognition of each other's experience, a sense of responsibility and commitment to the family, and, of course, a strong relationship foundation. To ensure all members of the family become independent and productive individuals, family leadership commits to sharing accumulated experience with those with less experience, and this sharing is supported through child rearing. In essence, family leadership works to ensure all family members become leaders in their own right.[10] As children mature and represent their growth through experience, family members also begin respecting individual discretion, as expressed by Zipporah Piungittuq Inuksuk: "People left all the major decisions to their parents and the Elders, but they had a lot of freedom to do as they pleased."[11] The freedom given to family members is respected in a manner similar to maligait. As the experience of others can only guide and not direct individuals, if an individual chooses not to follow direction, then they are responsible for accepting and addressing the consequences of their actions.

The roles and responsibilities of familial leadership are also reproduced within the broader community through leadership roles such as camp leader, Elder, and angakkuq, or shaman. All leadership roles support the community in their own way, and are both supported and supplemented by local individuals recognized for their expertise in particular fields such as child birth, health matters, or weather prediction. Although each leader practises their role, their authority as leaders is not exclusive. A leader's authority is upheld for as long as the community continues to respect and recognize the leader, and a leader's direction is respected as long as it falls within the leader's area of expertise. For example, Zipporah Piungittuq Inuksuk explains, "the only decisions the (camp) leader had to make concerned moving families to the seasonal hunting grounds."[12] Community leaders interact amongst each other respectfully, and in a manner not based on hierarchy. Camp leaders take advice from Elders, and, like angakkuq, Elders can sense when a taboo or maligait has been broken. It is an angakkuq's responsibility to interact with spirits when a wrongdoing occurs, and it is the responsibility of the Elder and camp leader to instil the importance of not breaking maligait or taboo. Elders look to camp leaders for food and shelter, while a camp leader can go to an angakkuq to help determine the cause for extreme weather or to find animals. Leaders are also free to approach another leader if a mistake had been made. Lucassie Nutaraaluk explains: "If the Elders disagreed with what the leader was deciding, they could say anything they wanted to him. The Elders would not be afraid to speak to the leader and point out what they disagreed with."[13] Community leaders also interact with their community constantly, which ensures accountability, as expressed by Imaruittuq:

> In the old days, when we were totally dependent on wildlife, I would make the decisions concerning hunting. Hunting decisions were not my wife's responsibility, but if she knew I was making a bad decision, she had the obligation to tell me…. If a person who is older is making a decision and you think it is wrong, you have the obligation to tell them.[14]

Leaders have many similar traits. Leaders are modest, disciplined, and trustworthy, and respect experience. In understanding leadership within Inuit governance, however, it is not the identification of traits that is important; instead, it is the reasoning behind the traits. For example, modesty requires and supports a particular style of confidence. A modest individual has the ability to be proud of their accomplishments without needing recognition. This is not to discredit the importance of mutual support and recognition within a group, but, instead, modesty represents a confidence that signifies individual meaning and the recognition of authorities more significant than the leader. Being thankful is necessary because in Nunavut individuals are vulnerable to natural forces. It is a vulnerability that inspires learning and creative design, as well as skill improvement. To learn and to be creative, individuals need a strong social network, meaningful interaction, and an internal discipline.

Bringing Inuit Governance Back to Today

The authority of the land is central to the function of Inuit governance. To exist alongside this authority, Inuit organized themselves within a structure of relationships in order to share experience and knowledge. Interaction and gathering were key processes that supported and maintained relationships. Through gathering, Inuit shared experiences and learned from each other. By reflecting on experience, individuals grow intellectually and emotionally. The word "isuma" represents the strength and discipline of an individual's emotions and mind. Individual growth is determined by the development of isuma, and a respected individual is an individual with a strong mind and solid reasoning. In his book *The Other Side of Eden*, Hugh Brody explains isuma as "the capacity for sense and reason that grows as part of becoming an adult."[15] Individually, gathering is also a time for individual accountability,[16] as social and collective responsibility are reaffirmed, providing individuals with the guidance to conduct themselves with awareness and confidence. Collectively, gathering provides families with the opportunity to become comfortable with each other. Consistently interacting allows community members to understand each other's pattern of behaviour, and to accumulate their own knowledge of how the community interacts.

How can this discipline and responsibility be supported in Nunavut's current context? I argue this can be supported within the forum of political consultation, a popular political process in Nunavut. For political organizations, consultation offers the opportunity to gather community knowledge, experience, and perspective. For communities, consultation provides them with the opportunity to share their expectation of political organization and instruments such as law, policy, or capital projects.

Although political consultation is held in high regard, my own understanding of the process reveals a gap between its intent and how it is supported. In Nunavut, consultation is driven by political organizations. It is the political organization who organizes the consultation's logistics, they travel to the community to gather information, they direct the dialogue, transcribe it, translate it, and own it once it is complete. Political organizations also determine how the information will be used in implementation strategies.

Imagine what political consultation would look like if it was guided by an expectation that comes from Inuit governance. Political consultation would be treated as a site where community members gather to share experiences, and time, energy, and focus are directed to the community. Gathering and sharing experiences would allow communities to create their own knowledge methodology—their own way of understanding themselves. In doing this, communities will have direct access to their own information and needs, allowing the community to create its own knowledge base, which grows each time the community initiates and participates in consultation tours. Consultation inspired by Inuit governance would support community history, while at the same time building a collective community vision for the future.

A community knowledgeable of its own history and vision for the future has greater potential to create active solutions, much more so if this responsibility is left with a single, territorial-wide, political organization whose administrative and legal responsibilities are absolute, and whose systems are privileged in communities. In response to this potential, I have designed one solution to support Inuit communities. The Kitchen

Consultation Model (KCM) is a community-based consultation model that privileges individual community methodology and voice.

The Kitchen Consultation Model

The KCM provides Inuit communities with infrastructure to support responsible community consultation. This model recognizes the ability of individual communities to engage in political dialogue in their community. It removes the authority of political organizations from the practice of consultation and places this responsibility within the community. Communities can begin to explore the principles for supporting political discussions, while also directing action stemming from discussions. Also, in supporting and directing the logistics of consultation, the community retains its authority over the information shared and compiled. This means communities retain authority over their own experience and perspective. The communities can then determine how their own knowledge will be used, and by whom—different government departments, other political organizations, and even other communities. This is different from the current practice, in which communities often wait to hear the results of their own consultation participation. Also, the KCM will provide a forum where different aspects and perspectives are respected. Communities become their own strongest resource.

The practicalities of the KCM are straightforward. Communities will have a core, representative community group that will be the main contact for "outside political organizations" interested in initiating the consultation process, such as the territorial or federal governments. Contacting the core community group will be the first step in this process, and this group will be responsible for providing leadership to the community in its consultation. The manner in which this leadership is practised will depend on the style and politics of the individual community. Once the community group has agreed to consult on a particular topic, it will work with other community groups and members to support three streams of interaction: public meetings, group meetings, and kitchen table meetings. Each community will likely use different modes of communication, including the local radio stations, CB (short wave) radio, and, where possible, the local community television channel, to support these interactions. All logistical and staff support, such as facilitators, translators, interpreters, and transcribers, will be community based. The outside political organization will have limited responsibility for, or participation in, the logistics of the community interactions.

The three streams of interaction will be used to communicate and interact with community members. Each will occur at different times throughout the consultation process and, generally, they will stand on their own, though each process does support the other. Each stream can be used more than once and some streams may be implemented at the same time as others. Once interactions with community members have begun, facilitators in these meetings will be responsible for compiling the different perspectives in partnership with the core community group. This process will allow the community to retain the raw information shared amongst community members, both in content and in process. Using different streams creates the opportunity for different experiences to be heard and shared. It builds a collective trust and expectation, and it creates positive involvement based on experience. It is a system in which Inuit communities once again can use and privilege Inuit knowledge systems and governance.

AUTHOR'S NOTE: This chapter is an excerpt from the author's Master's thesis, "Tukisivallialiqtakka: The Things I Have Now Begun to Understand: Inuit governance, Nunavut and the Kitchen Consultation Model," MA thesis, Indigenous Governance Programs, University of Victoria, 2007.

[1] *Nunavut*, when italicized, refers to the Inuktitut use of the word, our land or Inuit land. Nunavut, when not italicized, refers to the territorial jurisdiction within Canada.

[2] *Nunavut Land Claim Agreement*, I, <www.nucj.ca/library/bar_ads_mat/Nunavut_Land_Claims_Agreement.pdf>.

[3] John Bennett and Susan Rowley, eds., *Uqalurait* (Montreal and Kingston: McGill-Queen's University Press, 2004), 118.

[4] Ibid.

[5] Ibid., 14.

[6] For example, as remembered by Aupilaarjuk: "We have always been told not to abuse wildlife because we believe this causes hardship to the animals. We were told not to make fun of wildlife so we and our children would have a good life. We were constantly told this." See Janich Oosten, Frederic Laugrand, and Wil Rasing, eds., *Interviewing Inuit Elders: Perspectives on Traditional Law* (Iqaluit: Nunavut Arctic College, 1999), 33.

[7] Oosten, Laugrand and Rasing, *Interviewing Inuit Elders*, 13.

[8] Respecting maligait increased the likelihood of favourable conditions. For example, as remembered by Frank Analok, "Before [cutting] up a seal, Inuit would get a handful of drink water from [their] mouth and pour it in the seal's snout.... It was done to be thankful for a catch, because in the future the seal would be coming back again.... In this way the seal would be renewed." See Bennett and Rowley, *Uqalurait*, 54. Also, respecting maligait increased the likelihood an individual would live a long life.

[9] Understanding leadership from a family dynamic makes sense, as families who had the skills to live independently did so. This is remembered by George Agiaq Kappianaq: "We lived on our own because my father did not like to live among other people. Because he was a skilled hunter, we were able to do so. After he became less able to hunt, we started living with others. After my brothers and I started hunting, we went back to living on our own, and my father didn't need to hunt anymore." See Jarich Oosten and Frederic Laugrand, eds., *Inuit Perspectives on the 20ᵗʰ Century: Travelling and Surviving on Our Land* (Iqaluit: Nunavut Arctic College, 2001), 20.

[10] Child rearing was approached with clarity of purpose and vision, as argued by Uqsuralik Ottokie: "If the child clearly knows that he is loved, he will listen to you because he hears that he is a nice person and that he is a very good child.... You have to balance discipline and love when raising them." See Jean Briggs, ed., *Interviewing Inuit Elders: Childrearing Practices* (Iqaluit: Nunavut Arctic College, 2000), 53. This was supported through practical action. Children were in constant close physical proximity to family, and family members constantly interacted with the child. This proximity encouraged children to mimic the roles of their family, and this was how children played. Family members constantly observed the actions of children, allowing family members to determine when play transitioned to small chores and responsibilities. Although the actions changed, the principles the child learned remained the same. For example, "selfishness was not tolerated, and young hunters were taught to take care of all camp members," as expressed in Bennett and Rowley, *Uqalurait*, 87. Interacting with children this way allowed them to practise and gain experience.

[11] Bennett and Rowley, *Uqalurait*, 96.

[12] Ibid., 96.

[13] Oosten, Laugrand and Raising, *Inuit Perspectives*, 121.

[14] Ibid., 50.

[15] Hugh Brody, *The Other Side of Eden: Hunters, Farmers, and the Shaping of the World* (New York: North Point Press, 2000), 44.

[16] For example, the knowledge surrounding, and gained from, maligait was shared with the broader community to ensure the community benefited from the experience and to prevent additional hardships.

Chapter 8

Ooshkahneekwayweuk, Living What I Love Most

JOCELYN CHEECHOO

For as long as I can remember, my freedom and my community's freedom have been threatened by industrial development. My love and respect for the land, water, trees, animals, air, fish, and birds are something I want to share and experience with those I love. My early passion for the land has created a lifelong engagement and commitment to protecting what was given to the Ehlileweuk, the people of the land, from the Creator.

My career and educational choices have revolved around what the dominant society would deem as the environmental sector, but my choices were not made to "preserve" and "conserve" the "resources" of my territory. For me, it is not about turning my territory into "parks" and "reserves" for the recreational enjoyment of southerners. It is about ensuring that my territory is intact and thriving to teach future generations of Cree about their land, history, and the responsibilities, identity, and the practices of their people. It is about continuing to practise our responsibilities as Ehlileweuk.

In this chapter, I assert that our youth are going to need a whole new set of skills and strategies to protect our territories, identities, and freedoms in the future. Throughout the seasons, young people will still need to learn from their grandparents, parents, and traditional teachers, but they will also need new skills to complement our traditional ways. By sharing my life stories, I illustrate my personal responsibilities in contributing to cultural sustainability through undertaking a unique approach to land guardianship, rooted in a strong foundational love for the land and all it has to offer the Ehlileweuk. This foundation has empowered my voice on the resource development issues facing my community and has also resulted in my participation and observation of alliances between groups and Indigenous communities.

Relating to this Work

I am a proud member of Moose Cree First Nation and I was born and raised on the island of Moose Factory, Ontario, located a few kilometres south of James Bay. I am now twenty-six years old and, in the last ten years, have periodically lived in my community. When I am living away from home, I return for holidays and important events. My time in the community is shaped by the Cree activities my family participates in, such as hunting, fishing, gathering, cooking, camping, and storytelling. Academically, I have a BSc in Environmental Resource Science and I am now completing my MA at the University of Manitoba in Native Studies. Professionally, I have worked for my community, Moose Cree First Nation, in various capacities. Currently, I am working in San Francisco for the Rainforest Action Network on their Old Growth campaign.

I approach these issues as an Ehlileweuscho (Cree woman) who has practised my right to hunt, fish, and gather on my family's harvesting areas for as long as I can remember. I also come from a family who exercises their harvesting and gathering rights on a seasonal basis, which is more often than I can. I am not a fluent speaker of my Cree language, and this has limited what I am able to learn, and I do not claim to be an expert in any way related to the land. Within the past years, I have been learning how research, community consciousness, community resistance, youth empowerment, messaging, and market strategies can contribute to keeping the territory thriving and intact for future generations. The opinions and perspectives expressed in this chapter are mine and I take full responsibility for them.

Building My Foundation: The Birth of a Warrior

As soon as my brother and I were old enough, our entire family would go out in the bush for two to three weeks in April for the annual Canada goose harvest. The first ten years we went on the harvest, my maternal grandparents would stay with my parents, my brother, and me in our cabin. These harvests were some of the happiest times of my youth and upbringing. I would spend hours with my grandparents, parents, aunts, and cousins where there were no telephones, television, or electricity. This period really fostered strong relationships within our family. One of my fondest memories of the harvest was at bedtime, when we would turn off the gas lamp and tell stories or recapture the highlights of the day. I remember often falling asleep with a smile on my face. Those were the moments I felt closest to the members of my family.

Those hours spent in the camp, the hunting blind, and on the land with my family provide the foundation of my values and perspectives on the land. I learned that the law of the land is greater than any human-made law. I learned to respect the land and all that it has to offer by taking only what I need and by showing thanks for what I have been given. The land taught me how fragile life is and how dependent we are on it for our survival.

I remember returning to the spring harvest after my grandfather had passed on, the previous fall. Being out on the land was a time for my family to heal and honour my grandfather. At times, it would be sad and at other times laughter would be shared. It was a time and place of healing and honouring for my family. Even today, being out on the land is a time for reflection and observation. The past two spring harvests, I was faced with some major career choices, and being in the bush gave me time, space, and clarity to ponder and make those decisions.

I draw a lot of strength from harvesting and providing for my family. At a young age, my parents would encourage me to join my father and brother when they went hunting and fishing. I would often go and they would patiently answer my harvest-related questions. Through my participation I learned to respect the land and to feel empowered because I was able to fulfil what is seen by dominant society as a masculine role.

Sharing is another important part of harvesting that I learned when I was young. Usually whatever is harvested is given to family members, friends, and Elders.

Today, a hunter's first harvested goose is a milestone in a young (or old!) hunter's life. I clearly remember the day I got my first goose. It was my tenth year on the hunt (I was sixteen years old) and it was warm and sunny, and most of the snow had melted. It was not my first time shooting geese; I had done it a few times. That evening, back at the camp, it was big news that I got my first goose and I learned that when a hunter harvests their first goose, it is a time for praise and storytelling. This past spring I heard a father proudly telling his family that his daughter got her first goose that afternoon. When my brother Dan and my cousin Brennan got their first geese, the whole camp was happy for them and asked to hear their stories.

Recently, my brother has not been able to attend and contribute to our family's harvest. A couple of years ago, I returned for the harvest and my brother was not there. My dad asked me to hunt more than I usually do. As a result, I was hunting on my own for the first time, and it was an empowering and spiritual experience. Sure, I missed and made some mistakes, but I learned that there was more to the harvest than a goose call, a gun, a blind, and decoys. There was a spiritual connection, something greater than just the physical outcome of the harvest.

Finding My Voice

The first challenge to my family and community's harvesting practices I encountered came from the province in the form of a hydroelectric development proposal. When I was ten years old, I was wondering what topic I should tackle for the public-speaking unit of my class. The leading candidate on my list was endangered species and, one evening after dinner, I bounced this idea off my parents. At that time I had been hearing about more hydroelectric dams being built in the river system our community is located on, but I did not know what a hydroelectric dam was. My parents' reaction to my speech topic was not as I had hoped: they did not seem very excited. My mom suggested that I should speak about the hydroelectric project and I asked, "Why?" Her response was, "You know,

Joce, if they build these dams on the river, we won't be able to go spring hunting anymore." The thought of not being able to go spring hunting really made me sad and angry that something could affect my family's life on such an enormous level. I was really sad that I would not be able to spend that time at the camp with my grandmother. At ten years of age, I learned that the cost of development would be paid by the people who were closest to the land, and the benefit of more electricity would end up in a far-off city in the south, which most people here might never visit. From that revelation I wrote the speech "Will it Be Worth Living?":

> If the dams are allowed to be built it will affect our people
> by polluting the fish, air, flooding traplines, hunting and
> camping grounds, the rivers will run dry.... If the dams are
> built I wonder if we can still go fishing, hunting, trapping,
> camping or even just getting fresh air? I doubt it! If you are
> against building dams in our area you can do your share
> to stop it, by using energy wisely, looking at other ways to
> produce more energy and by asking the government not to
> destroy our lives. To finish off my speech, I can't see any
> good things coming out of this hydro project. If dams are
> built we will probably be asking ourselves what my granny
> said … WILL IT BE WORTH LIVING??

I did not make it very far in the public-speaking contest, but I did present the speech to the environmental assessment panel that came to my community in the fall of 1991, along with a poem I had written for the hearings. The majority of the community came together to host the panel and show them how much the river meant to the Ehlileweuk. The panel heard our concerns with the project at the community hall and the community hall was packed! The morning after the hearing, my poem was broadcast on CBC Radio. The environmental assessment panel recommended that the project not move forward and the project was halted. This was a defining moment in my life and heavily influenced my career path. Looking back on this event, I recognize that the threat of the hydroelectric development project brought our community together to protect our relationship to our territory. Our resistance united our voices, and our collective strength stopped the damming of our rivers. We had successfully defended and protected the land given to the Ehlileweuk by the Creator.

143

Another experience that has been instrumental in shaping my perspective was a summer placement with Moose Cree First Nation's Lands and Resources. Through studying the province's forestry "consultation" process for First Nations, I became more informed of my Aboriginal Rights, Treaty Rights, and Inherent Rights to the land. I learned from the staff of the department and also from the members of the Lands and Resources Secretariat about Ehlileweuk responsibilities, and our vision and concerns about our territory. A clear defining moment of my placement happened when I saw a map of Moose Cree's territory. There were small Post-it notes all over the map used to mark mining exploration—there were over 100 on this map! I asked if Moose Cree knew who had staked the claims. My answer was that not only did the Moose Cree not know the companies prospecting, but also that we had never given our consent for them to do so on our territory. This is a pattern that repeats itself over and over again in my territory—whether it is mining, forestry, or hydroelectric development. No one asks our permission. Recently, DeBeers, the giant international diamond mine company, signed an Impacts and Benefits Agreement with Attawapiskat First Nation, a community in my tribal council area, to mine for diamonds on their territory. A diamond mine has never been operated in this type of ecosystem before and it will be difficult, if not impossible, to predict the impacts this extraction will have on the land and the people. This mine is not in my community's territory but it is already starting to have impacts through increase in traffic in our communities on the winter road, and disruptions and delays in our rail and air transportation. These are only some of the immediate impacts on my community. The long-term social and environmental impacts will inevitably mirror the impacts of past resource-extraction industries in Indigenous territories.

The Changing Land and Community Engagement

Even though I have spent only a relatively short amount of time on the land compared to our Elders, I have noticed some significant changes in the land. The last few springs I have gone out on the harvest, I have noticed that the spring is a lot shorter. We would usually get our water from the snow, but now the snow melts before the end of the harvest. Along with this early melt, ice conditions deteriorate quickly and make hunting unsafe in certain areas. We used to go ice fishing for trout at the beginning of our harvest, before the geese started to fly. In the past few years, ice fishing was not an option because of poor ice conditions. We have also noticed changes in polar bears in our hunting area. More polar bears have been sighted and are entering our camps and the camps around us, resulting in a couple of incidents where polar bears were going to attack people and had to be shot. The Ontario Ministry of Natural Resources' position was that the polar bears were following their food and staying on the shrinking ice on James Bay, but our Elders believe that this change in behaviour is a direct result of climate change. The polar bears feel threatened because of the loss of their habitat. I have witnessed changes in weather, precipitation patterns, and animal behaviour in my short lifetime, and these changes will only become more severe, affecting our culture and our relationship with our territory if we do not address the growing threat of human-induced climate change.

In addition to all these threats, I also worry about our forests. Deforestation has already severely affected the Ehlileweuk's southern territorial regions. Forestry has been a threat to Ehlileweuk practices and our territory for the past two decades. The province's "consultation" process is simply a process by which the province tells us how many trees will be cut and where. Yet again, the community has not given them our consent to engage in forestry on our territory.

Alliance Building with Environmental Non-Governmental Organizations and Groups

As Indigenous Nations find their voices, assert their freedoms, and begin their resurgence, they may find it necessary to enter into alliances with other interest and support groups in order to advance their agendas. There are many challenges and rewards for Indigenous communities working with allies. I have had the opportunity to work alongside several non-indigenous organizations and individuals on health and resource-development issues. During most of these experiences there was a difference in how we perceived the issues. It was difficult to explain to our non-Indigenous partners the importance of our Aboriginal Rights, Treaty Rights, and our Inherent Right to the land. We framed issues about the land differently, and therefore saw strategies and resolutions differently as well. I have seen allies come close to understanding our perspective only by spending months with the people in Indigenous communities and on Indigenous territories. This experience allowed them to understand the cultural context of the environment and the colonial context in which we are forced to live. Most of our allies came from an "environmental" background, which is often in conflict with Indigenous Peoples' lifestyles and interests. As a result, I sometimes sensed that some allies were going along with what was asked and not really understanding why—other times they wanted to be the ones making the decisions. An ally relationship between an environmental non-governmental organization (ENGO) and an Indigenous group can be tricky to navigate, but if the responsibilities and roles are clearly defined from the outset, then the relationship can have varying degrees of success. If an ENGO knows what they can offer to a community and are transparent about their agendas and resources, a working relationship between an ENGO and an Indigenous nation can be built on trust and respect.

The relationship between a non-Indigenous group and an Indigenous community is most successful when the non-Indigenous ally acts as a resource in various capacities such as media writing, media outreach, fundraising, networking, and providing access to a wider skill network. The decision making must be left up to the Indigenous community. The ENGO needs to understand that what an Indigenous community wants in resolving their struggle may not align with the ENGO's interests.

Looking to Strengthen my Base

I take my responsibilities to my community and my territory as a Cree woman very seriously. I choose to take on a territory guardianship role through a solid cultural foundation based on my Cree traditions and a combination of several other strategies and skills. Going on harvests and spending time on the land have built my Cree understandings of freedom, identity, and values. To complement and support this foundation, I have studied the "environment" at university, learned how to conduct "research," and am now learning the skills of corporate campaigning from the Rainforest Action Network. I have had several amazing teachers and mentors from Indigenous communities across the country. I have come to realize that there are no easy solutions to resisting the ongoing "progress" and "development" from the dominant Canadian and international corporations and governments. To continue to live by Cree teachings and to practise what I love the most on the territory that I grew up on, I have taken on the responsibility to provide my community with strategies and tactics to ensure that the health of the people and land can continue for the coming generations. This is what it means to be Ehlileweuk, the people of the land.

AUTHOR'S NOTE: Ooshkahneekwayweuk, from the title, is a Cree L dialect term for all young people.

Chapter 9

The Environment of Indigenous Economies:
Honouring the Three Sisters and Recentreing Haudenosaunee Ways of Life

Laura Hall

Pathways of resistance are always visible to those who can see through the fog and mist of the colonial mind.[1] Original ways of life are constantly in a process of renewal, despite centuries of colonial ignorance and deliberate interferences. The Three Sisters (corn, beans, and squash), or Dyonhe'hgo (our sustenance),[2] holds teachings that provide some of these pathways. Beginning with the culture in this way means revitalizing a whole interconnected way of life, from reinvigorating the leadership of women in our communities, to addressing a range of environmental needs. The Three Sisters provide an intellectual, physical, and spiritual guide for understanding interconnection, balance, and the lessons inherent to Haudenosaunee ways of seeing.

This paper is an outcome of new ways of organizing my thoughts after a summer of renewal. This renewal happened for me in the form of a Three Sisters garden that I grew with family in the backyard of our home in Toronto. Renewal also happened in a very big way with the reclamation of land by the people of the Six Nations Territory near Caledonia. In-between visits to Kanenhstaton (The Protected Place) and tending to the garden, I travelled home to Sudbury, Ontario, where my mother presented me with a drum she had made. These processes reminded me of why I was doing this work on traditional economy, land rights, and the independence of the Haudenosaunee. I had recently completed a Master's degree on the idea of appropriate economy and Haudenosaunee independence. Exhausted and somewhat tired of the sound of my own voice, I was shown this past summer what is important about this work: renewing relationships, giving thanks to Creation, and preparing for future generations. These concerns are at the heart of the questions I ask. Growing the Three Sisters brought me closer to understanding why the true language for this sacred food refers to sustenance, and why thanksgiving is inherent to nurturing and receiving these gifts.[3] Physically, watching the Three Sisters grow meant watching the actualization of Indigenous scientific understandings—the abilities of these plants to nurture one another, to grow intertwined, was astounding. The Three Sisters taught me to truly understand thinking Seven Generations ahead. As I began to gather seeds and to put my energy into healing the soil of my garden (through planting companion plants that are meant to cleanse the soil of toxins), I had a real sense of responsibility for perhaps one of the first times in my life—I felt certain that I am truly responsible for thinking and acting in a good way for the generations not yet seen.

The Three Sisters economy was, and continues to be, a part of a sustainable way of life that the Haudenosaunee were given with Creation and as a gift from Skywoman and her daughter. In her far-reaching and in-depth treatment of Haudenosaunee knowledge, Barbara Alice Mann writes in *Iroquoian Women* about the Three Sisters within a number of traditions and within the original language itself. Going back to Creation, the Three Sisters can be found in Sky World narratives, as Mann writes:

> One day, due to the dishonest machinations of her husband, the Ancient One, who was jealous of her shamanic abilities, Sky Woman—variously called Awenhai (Fertile Earth), Ataensic (Mature Flowers), Otsitsa (Corn) and, eventually, Iagentci (Ancient One, or Grandmother)—fell or was pushed to earth through a hole in Sky World that had been created.... As she disappeared through the hole

in Sky World, Sky Woman grabbed at the roots of the felled Tree, wishing for sustenance. Because it was the roots she gripped, the Tree gave her seeds: In her right hand, she grasped the Three Sisters, and in her left, Tobacco.[4]

The Three Sisters are understood through a number of stories, each of which changes with the speaker of the story, and therefore constitutes more than just a healthy food and lifestyle choice. Rather, the original foods and medicines connect Onkwehonwe to relationships, interconnections, between Earth and Sky, Human and Creation.

Learning what it means to be Indigenous, to be Onkwehonwe, has been a beautiful and, at times, difficult, process. My mother's father had left his community of Kahnawake after residential school. He married my grandmother, whose First Nations heritage on both sides of her family was subsumed by shame and fear, and that side of the family now proudly claims Métis status. We were raised to be proudly Mohawk, but knowing what that means has evolved and deepened with time, especially as I have learned the importance of using our original words for our nations.[5] My grandfather had charged his family with the task of maintaining those ties and so I grew up knowing that certain things made us distinct, certain responsibilities were important. Fishing and blueberry picking on the territory of the Nishnaabeg Nation were family activities to which we felt deeply connected. As I moved south, for the first time living on the territory of the Haudenosaunee, I began to learn about the responsibilities that women hold for agriculture. I also began to learn about the degree to which land loss and environmental degradation have undermined the agricultural tradition of Haudenosaunee women.

I was also drawn, this summer and fall as I harvested the Three Sisters, back to thinking about the work that is ongoing in the community of my grandfather, Kahnawake. The Kahnawake Environment Office[6] has provided a way of understanding how Traditional Knowledge can be brought into contemporary contexts of reduced land holdings and even of toxified soil and water that do not allow agriculture to flourish.[7] The Kahnawake Environment Office has created a series of what *A Basic Call to Consciousness* calls "liberation technologies."[8] These are technologies that allow Indigenous communities freedom from being plugged into environmentally harmful and culturally limiting technologies.[9] Kahnawake has thus hosted a sustainable and culturally appropriate housing venture called the Kanata Healthy Home, demonstrating their commitment to liberation technologies. I have continually asked questions about the far-reaching relevance of this organization's efforts, and have remained astounded at the ability of these projects to deal with a range of interconnected issues. The Three Sisters are a framework for understanding my responsibilities, while the Kahnawake Environment Protection Office and the women who sustain and create the good projects in that organization actualize those understandings of Seven Generation thinking, of interconnection, and of sustainability from a culturally grounded and spiritual perspective.

These understandings of Onkwehonwe, or original ways of life, are being renewed in the work of contemporary Haudenosaunee theorists. In Carol Cornelius's interview with Kanienkehaka midwife Katsi Cook, Katsi Cook tells a powerful story of the learning that she underwent when she first grew the Corn, reconnecting with the power of Haudenosaunee women through the process.[10] Katsi Cook's good words remind us of the responsibilities of women for cultivating the Corn, and the leadership that flows from those responsibilities. Haudenosaunee scholars Susan Hill and Barbara Alice Mann also remind us that most of the territory lay within the jurisdiction of Clan Mothers, who maintained sustainable and spiritually connected agricultural processes.[11]

Productivity, as Barbara Alice Mann found in her work on traditional Haudenosaunee economy, was consistently high, and the Haudenosaunee operated from an idea of abundance rather than scarcity. At the same time, abundance did not entail overconsumption and the limits of the land were, and are, always at the forefront of thinking about sustaining the people.[12]

Haudenosaunee Creation, Skywoman, was the first of a series of creators—the world began with her and her daughter's works.[13] The Three Sisters continue to connect the Haudenosaunee with this line of women, just as Skywoman continues her relationship with her daughter the Earth. Haudenosaunee economic relationships are only one way in which the teachings of Creation have been central. Mann writes of Creation:

> These traditions of Sky Woman and her Daughter, the
> First Women of the First Family, created strong prec-
> edents regarding the female ownership and cultivation of
> the earth, precedents with sweeping implications for the
> way Iroquoian society set up economic production and
> distribution.[14]

Focusing on the Three Sisters means revitalizing our understandings of men's responsibilities as well—responsibilities that include nurturing and cultivating the woods.[15] Male hunting parties nurtured each other in ways that mainstream machismo does not encourage. Tom Porter reminds us that men traditionally nurture one another's behaviour, as a part of the larger democratic principle of accountability and as part of leadership.[16]

And yet, ideological barriers to this understanding persist. The paradigm of Eurocentricism, described by James Sákéj Youngblood Henderson, constructs Indigenous Peoples as a savage prototype of the more advanced European.[17] Proof that this paradigm is still entrenched in many intellectual circles can be seen by a recent essay that charac-terized "Iroquoian" peoples as unproductive, sloth-like, and ineffective prior to colonization's efforts to wipe out their ways of life.[18] While pro-ductivity should not be defined in terms that encourage overconsump-tion, and while sloths are rather likable beings, the points made in the article that describes the essay are, at the very least, a perpetuation of the idea that Haudenosaunee ways of life are not viable and not preferable to the current economic status quo. Eurocentricism erases the importance of land for Indigenous Peoples and blames a lack of "success" in eco-nomic terms on racist notions of our peoples' very natures.

The processes of consumption and domination are deeply gendered as well. Cherokee scholar Andrea Smith makes the point that "the first peoples targeted for destruction in Native communities were those who did not neatly fit into western gender categories."[19] Residential schools, intended for the project of assimilation, did far-reaching damage to the generations who were forced into their confines. Sexual shame and abuse went hand in hand with teaching Native children about their "proper roles" as boys and girls.[20] These kinds of genocidal practices coincided with socializing Native people into roles as low-level workers in the capitalist system.[21] Another example of the gendered process of domination is that, in a colonial society, "breadwinners" are made to feel insecure and to take their insecurities out on the women who depend on them for economic security.[22] In *Wasáse*, Taiaiake Alfred writes about the power of Reason, kanikonriio or reasonableness, the power of the free and good mind.[23] One of the most damaging (and strategic) ways in which colonialism affects the good mind is through imparting gender divides and patriarchy.[24] Haudenosaunee scholar Dawn Martin-Hill reminds us of the complexities of gender-related oppression as it interconnects with the larger colonial project:

> Within our own communities, the loss of our Clan mothers' authority is said to have begun with the Code of Handsome Lake.... It is important to remember that this was an era marked by the severe erosion of our land base, economic wealth, social structures of matrilineal extended families and, most significantly, our spirituality, which is the foundation of our power and our knowledge. All of these early attempts to erode our society by the Western settlers supported patriarchy and male dominance. The traditional respect for women, which was structurally supported through the Great Law and which had established mechanisms of democracy and matrilinealism, was severely undermined.[25]

Addressing the patriarchal nature of colonization is possible through a focus and grounding in our traditional cultures. The memory of living well with Creation—and of living in a balanced and harmonious way as humans with all our differences and commonalities—is contained in the stories and processes of learning within the Oral Tradition.

The philosophical problems of dominant economic thought are compounded by very real practices of colonialism, or of economic protectionism for the colonial elite. If Indigenous ways of life really were so inferior that they would naturally have fluttered away in the wake of European genius, we will never know. Progress has looked more like self-rationalization: "we took what you had because you would have lost it anyway." Indigenous Nations' economies have been damaged by loss of land and resources, not because of inferiority or lack of drive. The incredible environment damages which have been wrought by industrial development (and the location of these projects at the very edge of reserve communities) are impossible to overlook. Winona LaDuke writes of the Mohawk community of Akwesasne and the pollution of the St. Lawrence River:

> There is, through all of this, very little land left for the Mohawks and the Haudenosaunee. The St. Lawrence River, called Kaniatarowaneneh, which means 'Majestic River' in Mohawk, has been the wellspring for much of Mohawk life. It has also been the target for much of the industrialism in the region. In 1903, the Aluminum Company of America (ALCOA) established a factory a few miles west of Akwesasne. Less than 30 years later, a biological survey noted serious local pollution problems. That was just the beginning.[26]

The actions of General Motors (which later compounded the problems LaDuke describes) around Akwesasne, the damming of the St. Lawrence River, and the toxification of soil, water, and air throughout the territory, tell a story of deliberate tactics, which are now refered to as Environmental Racism.[27] Drive, productivity, progress, and development are all terms that belong to an economy which necessitates the theft of Indigenous land so that colonial governments can thrive. If we continue on the trajectory of buying into these beliefs and the paradigm of which they are a part, we are headed down a road whose consequences are already evident.

Solutions flowing from the culture include varied and multi-faceted approaches. The Three Sisters provide a precedent for gendered balance, for ecological sustainability, and for culturally appropriate economic renewal. As I've come to understand, the road toward reclaiming Indigenous economies in a context of colonialism is not straight and narrow. Nor is there a prescriptive element to providing alternative visions to the status quo. Debates resound over economic initiatives such as gaming, to name only one example.[28] Yet there are ways of going about maintaining jurisdiction (a central issue to the gaming debates),

155

and of incorporating cultural and environmental wellness at the centre of economic initiatives. Oren Lyons speaks of travelling this road and avoiding the shortcuts, that, "If you really want to provide something for your people, you are going to have to provide a solid base for the next generation and the next seven generations up."[29]

> Seven generations thinking is at the heart of the work of the Kahnawake Environment Protection Office. The teachings of interconnectedness and sustainability, so central to The Three Sisters, are put into practice: commitment to creating security and wellness for future generations is at the center of the work being done by the Kahnawake Environment Office in the Mohawk community of Kahnawake. The strategies of the Kahnawake Environment Office, the work of creating sustainable and healthy housing, food production, and energy sources, can be looked to as an amazing example of creating solutions for the economic woes of our people. Sorting through the needs of Onkwehonwe, consulting widely, and allowing communities to formulate their own plans, was the first step of the Environment Office, rather than a top-down approach.[30]

The Kahnawake Environment Office has undertaken a range of projects, but perhaps the most impressive of these is the Kanata Healthy Home. Housing is a symbolic as well as practical issue for the Haudenosaunee. Longhouses were ecologically sustainable, and allowed large extended families to live together in mutually supportive ways. Longhouses were also the property of the Clan Mothers, the Elder women of each house, which is unlike the male-dominated private-property regimes of colonial states. Producing this form of housing was a communal affair, and drew from the land in sustainable ways.[31] In other words, the traditional housing of First Nations was always suited to the environment from which it came.[32] This scenario changed drastically as the Haudenosaunee land was taken and as missionaries and colonial governments pushed for nuclear-family-based individual houses.[33] The health effects of mainstream housing were researched by the Kahnawake Environment Office, and the first steps toward creating more sustainable and culturally appropriate houses were taken. Sustainable development is being reclaimed by nations who have understood such practices for tens of thousands of years on this continent.[34]

Greater steps forward will occur when resources are tunnelled into further initiatives such as these. The Kahnawake Environment Office is also partnering with the Department for Economic Development to look into using wind power in the community.[35] This work can also be done by Indigenous people who are accessing resources off the territory, or in urban spaces on the territory. Potential also exists for urban initiatives that address poor housing, environmental illness, and cultural issues with respect to those Indigenous people who are struggling with the economic challenges of the city.[36] Kanienkehaka scholar Taiaiake Alfred challenges Indigenous Peoples to live according to our truth:

> Decolonization ... is a process of discovering the truth in a world created out of lies. It is thinking through what we think we know to what is actually true but is obscured by knowledge derived from our experiences as colonized peoples.[37]

Funnelling more financial resources into those activities will allow us to reclaim life on Turtle Island, the needs of the land, of Creation, of our own people. In these ways, our Nations are addressing a myriad of issues, ranging from health, income disparity, and job creation, to energy creation and food security. We are again able to return to our traditional knowledge: at the heart of this, and at the heart of the Three Sisters, is that understanding of relationship, of interconnection between all of life.

Re-visioning the Three Sisters amounts to re-visioning what is deemed to be *possible*. In his last book before passing to the spirit world, Vine Deloria Jr. warned that Indigenous Peoples have been led to a place where we may not really believe in the power of our own traditions. Deloria reminds us:

> This uncritical acceptance of modernism has prevented us from seeing that higher spiritual powers are still active in the world ... We need to glimpse the old spiritual world that helped, healed, and honoured us with its presence and companionship. We need to see where we have been before

we see where we should go, we need to know how to get there, and we need to have help on our journey.[38]

We are charged with the task of renewing what we are told is impossible to renew: original foods, languages, and ways of life will sustain and nurture Indigenous Peoples and allow us to work for future generations. Reclaiming and revitalizing Indigenous ways of knowing and of living will create profound change for more than only our own people. What I know as a young woman is that beginning with our rights and responsibilities, as our Knowledge Keepers understand them, is a necessary start. The projects of community-based organizations such as the Kahnawake Environment Office should inspire great confidence in the viability and sustainability of Indigenous ways of life. The renewal of the territory by Haudenosaunee should inspire the knowledge that peaceful solutions to difficult problems are possible.[39]

---

[1] Among the people who have most influenced this idea of resistance, Patricia Monture's work was the first source I turned to as a young Mohawk learner, and it is work that I return to again and again. In particular, see Patricia Monture-Angus, *Journeying Forward: Dreaming First Nations' Independence* (Halifax: Fernwood Publishing, 2003).

[2] In this case, I am using Barbara Alice Mann's translation, provided in Barbara Alice Mann, *Iroquoian Women: The Gantowisas* (New York: Peter Lang, 2000).

[3] Haudenosaunee Task Force on the Environment, *The Words that Come Before All Else*, n.d.

[4] Mann, *Iroquoian Women*, 32.

[5] Kanienkehaka, meaning People of the Flint, evokes a land-based, territory-specific understanding of identity, and is the original word for the Mohawk Nation.

[6] I would especially like to thank Eva Johnson and Lynn Jacobs for taking time over the years to talk and to tell me about the office's ongoing work.

[7] For more on the connections between Indigenous Knowledge and contemporary pressures in the form of environmental degradation, see Leanne Simpson, "Listening to Our Ancestors: Rebuilding Indigenous Nations in the Face of Environmental Destruction," in *Every Grain of Sand: Canadian Perspectives on Ecology and Environment*, ed. J.A. Wainwright (Waterloo, ON: Wilfrid Laurier Press, 2004), 121–135.

[8] "A Basic Call to Consiousness," *Akwesasne Notes* (2005): 114.

[9] Ibid.

[10] See Interview of Katsi Cook, June 6, 1992, in Carol Cornelius's *Iroquois Corn in a Culture-Based Curriculum, A Framework for Respectfully Teaching about Cultures* (1999),

253–262. Katsi Cook also credits John Mohawk with having carried forward traditions regarding women's power as organizers and keepers of the land holdings of the Haudenosaunee.

[11] See Susan Hill, "The Clay We Are Made Of: An Examination of Haudenosaunee Land Tenure on the Grand River Territory," PhD dissertation, Department of Indigenous Studies, Trent University, 2005.

[12] Mann, *Iroquoian Women*, 186.

[13] Ibid., 303.

[14] Ibid., 186.

[15] Dan Roronhiake: wen Longboat has spoken eloquently in teachings and workshops on this responsibility, and on the ways in which Haudenosaunee men learn in non-sexist, non-hierarchal ways.

[16] Tom Porter, "Traditions of the Constitution of the Six Nations," in *Pathways to Self-Determination. Canadian Indians and the Canadian State*, ed. Leroy Little Bear, Menno Boldt, and J. Anthony Long (Toronto, University of Toronto Press, 1984), 14–26.

[17] See James Sákéj Youngblood Henderson, "The Context of the State of Nature," in *Reclaiming Indigenous Voice and Vision*, ed. Marie Battiste (Vancouver: UBC Press, 2000). See also J.M. Blaut, *The Colonizer's Model of the World: Geographical Diffusionism and Eurocentric History* (New York: Guilford Press, 1993).

[18] See Frances Widdowson, "Separate but Unequal: The Political Economy of Aboriginal Dependency," <www.cpsa-acsp.ca/paper-2003/widdowson.pdf>, (2003).

[19] Andrea Smith, *Conquest: Sexual Violence and American Indian Genocide* (Cambridge: South End Press, 2005), 178.

[20] Ibid., 176–178.

[21] Ibid., 37.

[22] Mann. *Iroquoian Women*.

[23] Taiaiake Alfred, *Wasáse: Indigenous Pathways of Action and Freedom* (Peterborough: Broadview Press, 2005).

[24] See Leanne Simpson, "Birthing an Indigenous Resurgence. Decolonizing Our Pregnancy and Birthing Ceremonies," in *Until Our Hearts are on the Ground:' Aboriginal Mothering, Oppression, Resistance and Rebirth*, ed. Memee Lavell-Harvard and Jeannette Corbiere Lavell (Toronto: Demeter Press, 2006), 25–33.

[25] Dawn Martin-Hill, "She No Speaks and Other Colonial Constructs of 'The Traditional Woman'" *Strong Women Stories: Native Vision and Community Survival*, ed. Kim Anderson and Bonita Lawrence (Toronto: Sumach Press, 2003), 110–111.

[26] LaDuke, *All Our Relations* (1999), 14–15.

[27] See Robert Bullard, *The Quest for Environmental Justice, Human Rights and the Politics of Pollution*, (San Francisco: Sierra Club Books, 2005), 19–42.

[28] For a particularly stunning treatment of this debate, see Oren Lyons's take on the casino started by Ray Halbritter in Alfred, *Wasáse*, 212–222.

[29] Oren Lyons in Alfred, *Wasáse*, 242.

[30] See Lynn Katsitsaronkwas Jacobs, "A Commentary on Sustainable Development," *Journal of Aboriginal Economic Development*, 3, 1, (2002): 4–5.

[31] Mann, *Iroquoian Women*, 207, 211.

[32] See, for example, Winona LaDuke, *Recovering the Sacred: The Power of Naming and Claiming* (Cambridge: South End Press, 2005).

[33] Barbara Alice Mann describes the problems that Haudenosaunee (in particular the women) faced with Quaker missionaries on these issues. See Mann, *Iroquoian Women*, 153–155, 189, 190.

[34] Jacobs, *A Commentary on Sustainable Development*, 4.

[35] Eva Johnson in L. Hall, "Decolonizing Development: Haudenosaunee Approaches to 'Appropriate Economy,'" MA thesis, Frost Centre for Native and Canadian Studies, Trent University, 2005, pp. 57–68.

[36] Land loss for those who are forced away from their communities (though many maintain varying degrees of ties) is also ongoing. See Bonita Lawrence, *"Real" Indians and Others: Mixed-Blood Urban Native Peoples and Indigenous Nationhood* (Vancouver: UBC Press, 2004).

[37] Alfred, *Wasáse*, 280.

[38] Vine Deloria Jr., *The World We Used To Live In* (Golden: Fulcrum Publishing, 2006), xvii.

[39] For further examples of the effectiveness of Indigenous land reclamation strategies, see Winona LaDuke, "Building with Reservations," in *The Winona LaDuke Reader: A Collection of Essential Writings* (Penticon: Theytus Books, 2000), 44–45.

Chapter 10

Bimaadziwin Oodenaang: A Pathway to Urban Nishnaabe Resurgence

Brock Pitawanakwat

The trouble with being (almost) assimilated is that I know something is missing but I am not sure what. The possibilities seem endless: A proud identity? An ancestral language? Connection to clan, community, and kin? Ceremonies and customs? Hunting and gathering skills? A sense of humour? All of the above? For those who are alienated from Nishnaabeg ways, it can be difficult to know what is missing, let alone calculate the costs.[1] I have lived most of my life in the city and my childhood was typically North American: too much junk food, too much television, and a formal education that instilled obedience instead of creativity. Yet one distinguishing feature for both my sister and me was that we were brown while our classmates were overwhelmingly not.

Authoritative Voice and the "Urban Mixed-Blood"

Colonization and colonial policy continue to have a profound impact on the collective and individual identities of Indigenous peoples and on our ability to determine citizenship within our own nations. In an academic setting, self-disclosure as being both urban and of mixed ancestry contextualizes my writing and opens it to immediate criticism as assimilated, acculturated, and colonized, regardless of my cultural background, connection to Indigenous communities, and commitment to decolonizing politics. Respected East Washington professor, author, and editor Elizabeth Cook-Lynn, who is Crow Creek Sioux, has identified "Urban mixed-blood" discourse as its own literary genre. This "mixed-blood literature is characterized by excesses of individualism" that she caricatures as "The 'I,' the 'me' story ... [which is] hardly an intellectual movement that can claim a continuation of the tribal communal story or an ongoing tribal literary tradition."[2] It arises from identity insecurities and "is not generated from the inside of tribal culture since many of the practitioners admit they have been removed from cultural influence through urbanization and academic professionalization or even, they suggest, through biology and intermarriage."[3] Cook-Lynn concludes that "mixed-blood visions have little or nothing to do with what may be defined as Native intellectualism."[4] She calls for "Scholars in Native intellectual circles ... [to] defend freedom, refute rejection from various power enclaves, [and] resist the superficiality that is so much the part of the modern/urban voice."[5]

Although Cook-Lynn writes primarily for a US audience, her prominence in Indigenous scholarship carries her words beyond its borders. Cook-Lynn's characterization of this mixed-blood discourse can be interpreted as both a critique of the discourse itself and a critique of those with mixed ancestry. The *discourse* critique has merit because it brings into focus the self-serving nature of much Indigenous scholarship that is of little or no benefit to Indigenous Nations. Cook-Lynn also points out how the identity *discourse* becomes a distraction from the urgent task of restoring the intergenerational transmission of Indigenous knowledge.

I agree with Cook-Lynn on both these points but the extension of her critique to *people of mixed-blood ancestry* is problematic. Cook-Lynn accuses urban mixed-bloods of individualism but it is precisely this sense of colonial alienation that is its root cause. Cook-Lynn doubts that "urban mixed-bloods" have anything to contribute to Indigenous scholarship or Native intellectualism.[6] The ironic result is that alienated Indigenous peoples are criticized by their kin for being alienated— an analysis that obscures rather than reveals the genocidal impact of colonization. These authoritative and often essentialist tensions that are prevalent in Indigenous scholarship are also, I would argue, identity distractions that Indigenous intellectuals, academics, knowledge holders, and activists can ill afford. After all, the responsibility for intergenerational transmission rests not only with the "full-bloods" who reside on the reserve.

By reconnecting with our Indigenous roots, we benefit not only as individuals, but also as nations; the individual tree grows and the whole forest grows with it. In *"Real" Indians and Others—Mixed-Blood Urban Native Peoples and Indigenous Nationhood,* author Bonita Lawrence illustrates that the personal narrative and a commitment to Indigenous Nation-building can be complementary rather than conflicting processes. Lawrence argues that being Indigenous is not about place of residence, status, band membership, appearance, or language.

> [M]ixed-blood urban Native people are Native people for one clear reason: they come from Native families, that is from families that carry specific histories, Native histories. In urban contexts, where other bonds of identity (language, band, territory, or clan) may no longer apply, family becomes all the more important for grounding a person as Aboriginal.[7]

Although the responsibilities I have to my Nishnaabeg family and community are often unclear, I refuse to succumb to a century of assimilation policy that has almost succeeded. It would be unconscionable to relinquish millennia of accumulated wisdom that our ancestors have handed down to us by abandoning our ceremonies, communities, land, and language. These derelictions arrogantly and shamefully indicate to our ancestors "that we know better than they do."[8] In truth, I am Nishnaabe, Canadian, and neither all at the same time. I often feel both labels are just as awkward to wear as "urban mixed-blood." This twilight zone between being Indigenous and being Canadian is an uncomfortable place.

There is an obvious irony in writing another "The 'I,' the 'Me,' story" already scorned by Cook-Lynn, but I am not writing this essay for her; I am writing to encourage others, like me, who have experienced colonial alienation to reconnect with ancestral ways, regardless of our blood quantum or where we live. My parents are Mary Pitawanakwat (Nishnaabe-kwe from Whitefish River First Nation in Birch Island, Ontario) and Greg Darjes (Canadian settler of Norwegian and Scottish ancestry). Both my parents nurtured my Indigenous identity in a prairie city that was and remains notoriously racist: Regina, Saskatchewan. As a child, I dreamed of winning everyone over by starring for the hometown Saskatchewan Roughriders of the Canadian Football League. This fantasy emerged from my understanding that people loved the Riders although they did not care so much for Indians. As a football star, I would prove that Indians were worthy of the same adoration the Riders received. It was a subconscious but foolproof plan that was thwarted by an unspectacular high school football career. Without the anticipated athletic scholarship to continue playing football, I was fortunate to be sponsored by my mother's band to embark on an academic journey that continues today.

Urban Communities & Indigenous Higher Education Institutions

My connection to the Saskatchewan Indian Federated College (SIFC, now First Nations University of Canada or FNUNIV) stretches back over three decades.[9] My mother, Mary Pitawanakwat, then a full-time student and single parent, would bring my sister and me along to cultural events and, occasionally, to classes when she could not afford or arrange child care. Visits back to the reserve were rare and the Indigenous community that I felt most connected with was an informal one centred on SIFC. Growing up "Indian" in the city is often an alienating experience because, as Nishnaabe scholar Leanne Simpson explains, "being out on the land strengthens our relationship to our extended families and deepens our spiritual understanding of life and our place in it."[10] Yet maintaining these relationships was difficult because our reserve is 2200 km from Regina. As a result, the cultural reinforcement from SIFC was crucial. When it was time for me to attend university, my mother already knew she was dying of cancer. She prepared me as best she could by introducing me to SIFC's instructors and academic advisors. Her death during my first year at SIFC was personally devastating and it has taken years to comprehend the cultural impact. Because my mother was our family's last fluent speaker of Nishnaabemwin, the language of the Nishnaabeg, her death severed a connection that stretched back hundreds of generations and thousands of years. Her loss has been incalculable, not only for her children, but also for her grandson and future grandchildren.

Part of what helped me through this time was the opportunity to attend SIFC. It was a life-changing experience because it was the first time since I was six years old that I had Indigenous instructors and classmates. It was here, at the age of twenty-two, after already learning French in school and Spanish while interning and studying in Mexico, that I began learning the plains dialect of Nishnaabemwin. This journey continues and, although I can never recover what it means to be a fluent first-language speaker, I have chosen to become as proficient as possible to restore this connection so that future generations of our family will know Nishnaabemwin.

After graduating from SIFC in 2000, I enrolled in a Master's degree program with the Indigenous Governance programs (IGOV) at the University of Victoria in British Columbia. It was here that I began to develop the intellectual tools to comprehend the breadth and depth of colonization upon Indigenous Peoples. My first two years with IGOV also enabled me to compare my undergraduate education at SIFC to another Indigenous program at a mainstream university. I realized that Indigenous higher education is a tremendous forum for dialogue on what Indigenous Peoples are doing to decolonize. When I was offered a teaching position at the newly named First Nations University of Canada, I quickly accepted and eagerly awaited the opportunity to work with Indigenous colleagues and students.

When FNUNIV opened its doors in June 2003, it was positioned to be a national leader in Indigenous higher education.[11] Yet, the building and the institution it houses are fascinating contradictions. The building's construction was intended to bring the disparate departments of the FNUNIV under one roof. However, the Department of Indian and Northern Affairs Canada (INAC) now occupies the top two and a half floors of this majestic building. FNUNIV students rarely attend classes in the new building because of insufficient classroom space after INAC reneged on a promised funding grant and imposed a lease arrangement.[12] Not only is our physical space compromised, but there are other serious inconsistencies in our institution. FNUNIV has made compromises in its attempt to achieve equality with other post-secondary institutions. The case of Indigenous language use at Regina campus is most telling: all instruction is carried out in English, with the exception of Indigenous language courses; all meetings and official correspondence are in English; and, perhaps most regretfully, students cannot submit their coursework in Indigenous languages. Such is the fate of pan-Indian institutions where English becomes the default language.

Many urban Indigenous communities face similar "multinational" challenges that are rare in reserve-based communities. What happens when we have several Indigenous Nations sharing a single institution? Can Dakota, Dene, Nehiyawak, Nahkawewak, and Nakota co-exist without sacrificing their distinctiveness? One disconcerting result is that many pan-Indigenous organizations adopt the working language and practices of the settler society: English language and *Robert's Rules of Order*. These compromises are troubling because FNUNIV is one of the largest employers of Indigenous people in Saskatchewan. If language is the medium by which culture is transmitted, then how can we justly consider FNUNIV to be an Indigenous institution when we fail to use our languages in the workplace? The painful question we must ask is whether we ourselves have bought into the colonial lie that our languages and the Indigenous knowledge encoded within them are obsolete. Are we contributing to the problem of cultural disintegration? If we do not honour our ways by speaking our languages and practising our customs in our institutions, then FNUNIV is a failure.

Yet, there is cause for hope. Universities are themselves communities, and the creative energy that they contain can catalyze the regeneration of Indigenous Nations. FNUNIV holds great promise as a protector of Indigenous knowledge. Indigenous staff and students work in an environment where Elders are venerated and the centre of our building is a dedicated space for pipe ceremonies. Students can study several Indigenous languages and take courses with an Indigenous focus in administration, arts, education, languages, media studies, social work, and the natural sciences. Important advances have been made in Indigenous higher education and mine was possible because of determined resistance to assimilation by Indigenous Peoples. I owe a tremendous debt to the original visionaries who identified the need for urban institutions that reflected Indigenous values. Repaying this debt means supporting existing and future efforts to build strong Indigenous communities both on- and off-reserve.

Bimadziwin Oodenaang—Living a Good Life in the City

How can city dwellers lead a good life that honours our ancestors? I believe that assimilation into settler society must be continually thwarted by creating spaces where we can live according to Nishnaabe principles. Higher education programs are one example described above. However, the example of FNUNIV suggests that more is required if our ancestral languages are to be revitalized in urban areas. Canada's assimilationist residential and public school education systems cannot be depended upon to teach our children what it means to be Nishnaabe, let alone do so in Nishnaabemwin. The answer lies in taking responsibility for cultural revitalization. We need families to organize themselves and ensure that intergenerational transfer of language occurs in the home. We can adopt the successful language nests of the Maori in New Zealand and the Kanaka Maoli of Hawai'i by establishing daycares or preschools with immersion in Indigenous languages. A language nest is a practical but powerful example of how intergenerational transfer of Indigenous knowledge can be restored. A language speaker, a child, and a home are all that is necessary to start a language nest. These measures are already underway in several Indigenous communities because one does not need major infrastructure or financial resources. However, reversing language shift away from colonizing languages remains an enormous and increasingly urgent task as the number of fluent speakers continues to decline.

Living honourably also requires that we uphold our responsibilities to our home communities. We cannot ignore the continued exploitation of Indigenous Peoples and our lands by settler society, its representatives, or Indigenous people who have surrendered and now collaborate with an unjust system.[13] Canada has frequently resorted to "divide and conquer" tactics. Urban Indigenous peoples must realize that our presence as large, urban, Indigenous populations is already being used as yet another excuse to deny the just resolution of Indigenous land claims.[14] Urban Indigenous peoples must continue to strive for the increased independence of all Indigenous communities from colonial interference by the federal, provincial, and territorial governments.

We are also responsible to Creation. The natural checks and balances that exist in local ecosystems are frequently obscured in an urban setting. We ignore restraint in our resource consumption because we can draw on others' resources after we have exhausted our local supply. This disconnection between us and our local habitat is increasingly true even on reserves where harvesting local foods has been eroded by pollution and encroachment by settler communities and industries. Indigenous peoples have become complicit in harmful economic activities and a prominent example is our dependence on fossil fuels. We exploit Indigenous territories when we use fossil fuels to power our vehicles and furnaces, because oil and gas development have devastated Indigenous lands in Alberta and Saskatchewan. Our dependence on electricity also fuels the hydro developments that have flooded Indigenous lands throughout Canada. The environmental movement's mantra to "think globally and act locally" warrants thoughtful application to our lifestyles because, every time we engage in economic transactions, we need to think of their consequences. A passionate discourse is already exploring how we can live genuine Indigenous lives in a colonized setting and remain faithful to our ancestral ways while rejecting the seduction of settler society.[15] Our responsibility is to be attuned to, and join, this discourse and strive for a sustainable economic future beyond gaming and gas stations.

Urban Indigenous Resurgence

The phrases "urban native" and "urban Indian" are finally shedding the false notion that "Indigenous" and "urban" were mutually exclusive. This incongruity existed in the minds of settlers because of their own artificial attempts to remove Indigenous people from lands desired for European settlement.[16] Many Canadian cities were founded on Indigenous village sites whose inhabitants were removed to make way for settlers. Similar removals occurred in the prairie provinces when Indian reserves in close proximity to settler communities were relocated. The false dichotomy between "urban" and "Indigenous" has been difficult to dispel.

Until 1951, the federal government's infamous pass system prevented status Indians from leaving their reserves without the written permission of the local Indian agents. Even with the removal of this legislative obstacle, there was no immediate migratory surge into Canadian cities until the 1960s and 1970s when the post-World War II baby boom in Indigenous communities soon outstripped the available resources to support their growing populations. The first generation of Nishnaabeg who moved into Canadian cities faced many obstacles, some of which still exist today. Social and cultural isolation often occur when people move from small communities where almost every face is a familiar one to the relative anonymity of city life. Urban alienation is magnified for Indigenous Peoples because the opportunity to participate in ceremonies and social events have generally been rare or none.

Fortunately, the growing urban Nishnaabeg populations in Canadian cities have been actively promoting the creation of their own institutions such as Friendship Centres, as well as cultural activities such as round dances, powwows, and pipe and sweat lodge ceremonies. The Indigenous presence in Canadian cities promises to become increasingly visible. For example, in December 2006, the Canadian Broadcasting Corporation described local Indigenous efforts to develop a "spiritual park" in Winnipeg, Manitoba. Two urban organizations, the Inner City Aboriginal Neighbours and the Spence Neighbourhood Association, proposed that medicinal plants would be grown and ceremonies conducted in the proposed park.[17]

A similar economic revitalization process is also underway as Indigenous Peoples become increasingly involved in the urban labour force. One unique example of the continued connection between urban residents and the reserves is the Saskatchewan phenomenon of urban reserve creation. Saskatchewan bands have been purchasing plots of land in urban centres throughout the province and entering into municipal agreements for services while having the lands transferred to reserve status. Urban reserves have been created exclusively for economic reasons with none currently zoned for residential areas. The potential for urban residential reserves raises interesting social possibilities. Such a scenario would see urban reserves become important centres not only for investments and jobs, but also as community centres for urban residents.

A more controversial proposal that has yet to be attempted is the creation of entirely new bands for those who reside in the city. The creation of "urban tribes" has been underway for a long time but has yet to be officially recognized by Canada or the USA:

> One of the ideas that is being considered in one urban community is that of tribalizing the community. By this we mean that the many tribes represented in that community would become part of an urban tribe that would function and provide a tribal structure to that community. The tribe would have a council of elders that would set standards of accepted behaviour and norms for the community.... The urban tribe would have to develop quickly in the area of initiation ceremonies. Instead of allowing urban gangs and other unhealthy elements to initiate our youth, the urban tribal community would prescribe ceremonies that would initiate the youth. Warrior societies, peace keepers, and other traditional and new roles will have to be invented in order to fit the needs of a new tribe of indigenous people.[18]

Cities such as Winnipeg or Toronto have Indigenous populations large enough for several "urban tribes" representing distinct Indigenous Nations. Although there would be administrative advantages to having federal, provincial, and municipal recognition as Indigenous governments, some Indigenous Peoples may be reluctant to expand the *Indian Act's* powers to new geographical areas. After all, many migrate to urban areas to escape the frustrations of living in a band council-governed jurisdiction.[19] Amalgamation would also risk the promulgation of pan-Indian approaches that erase rather than revitalize Nishnaabeg ways. Despite these risks, it is a proposal that warrants further consideration as a community solution to the urban alienation of Indigenous Peoples.

Final Words

Belonging to an Indigenous community is more complex than our blood quantum or whether we live on- or off-reserve. In spite of Cook-Lynn's cited contempt for the individualism of "mixed-blood visions," I have shared mine. I envision a vibrant community of healthy Nishnaabeg where children grow up surrounded by our ancestral language; our presence is respected throughout our traditional territory; our economies are sustainable and honour our relationship with all of Creation; our social and political institutions meet our needs and reflect our values; and we interact within Canadian society without fear of being subsumed intellectually, linguistically, physically, and spiritually.

Nishnaabeg oral history describes a long western migration from the salt water to the Great Lakes and beyond. As our people moved, we renewed our relationship to the land to create a new bond between the people and their environment. This relationship between the people and their natural landscape is at the core of Indigenous epistemologies. Honouring our ancestors means that we carry our language and customs with us wherever we go. As urban Nishnaabeg, our ancestral legacy is to reconnect with the natural landscape and live honourably and sustainably—wherever we reside.

Author's Note: Whitefish River First Nation is located within the eastern Ojibwe Manitoulin dialect of Nishnaabemwin, the Ojibwe language.

[1] I realize that I live on the edge of Nishnaabeg oblivion, since I was not raised on my reserve nor do I speak Nishnaabemwin as my first language. I have much to learn about Nishnaabeg ways but I do know that Nishnaabeg custom tells us that we should introduce ourselves by revealing the clan to which we belong. The reality is that I cannot because I do not know the answer. Three Nishnaabeg who are my mentors and teachers have given me three different answers and I am at a loss as to know which one is correct. Indeed, loss is a common theme for those of us who

reflect on the conditions of any Indigenous people in terms of territory, language, history, and ceremonies.

[2] Devon A. Mihesuah, *Natives and Academics: Researching and Writing about American Indians* (Lincoln: University of Nebraska Press, 1998), 128.

[3] Ibid., 129.

[4] Ibid., 135.

[5] Ibid., 137.

[6] Ibid., 42.

[7] Bonita Lawrence, *"Real" Indians and Others: Mixed-Blood Urban Native Peoples and Indigenous Nationhood* (Vancouver: UBC Press, 2004), xv.

[8] I acknowledge and thank Brad Young (Opaskwayak Cree Nation) for this stark statement on the significance of our failure.

[9] Several authors have identified the importance of Indigenous institutions for urban communities and their observations validate my own experience. See Kim Anderson, *A Recognition of Being: Reconstructing Native Womanhood* (Toronto: Second Story Press, 2000); Deborah Davis Jackson, *Our Elders Lived It: American Indian Identity in the City* (DeKalb: Northern Illinois University Press, 2002); and Jim Silver, *In Their Own Voices: Building Urban Aboriginal Communities* (Halifax: Fernwood, 2006).

[10] Leanne Simpson, "Toxic Contamination Undermining Indigenous Food Systems and Indigenous Sovereignty," *Pimatiziwin: A Journal of Aboriginal and Indigenous Community Health* 1, 2 (2003): 130.

[11] There are other examples of important urban institutions for Indigenous Peoples but I have chosen to focus on the one I know best. Other important urban educational centres in Regina are the Saskatchewan Indian Institute of Technology (SIIT) and the Gabriel Dumont Institute (GDI). Outside higher education, one can also look at how the development of Friendship Centres after the 1950s created a hub around which urban Indigenous communities could coalesce.

[12] Blair Stonechild, *The New Buffalo: The Struggle for First Nations Higher Education* (Winnipeg: University of Manitoba Press, 2006), 127. First Nations University pays the price for Indian and Northern Affairs Canada (INAC)'s duplicity, yet does so in silence because funds required for the university's operations flow through INAC. Since becoming an instructor, I have taught fewer than 50 of my approximately 520 students in our building. Why? Because INAC occupies half our building and our classrooms are, as a result, too small to accommodate classes of more than forty students. Moreover, most of our staff work in windowless offices and cubicles in the basement and mezzanine while INAC's colonial bureaucrats occupy the penthouse. The symbolism is not lost on many of us who work here: Canada's colonial office and its predecessors brought us residential schools, among many other assimilative policies. Now, INAC has manipulated its funding agreement with FNUNIV to entrench its presence on our campus. Chronic underfunding and Canada's continued abrogation of its Treaty relationship with the First Nations of the northern plains have made it exceedingly difficult for FNUNIV to realize its full potential.

[13] Many Indigenous Peoples have long recognized our responsibility to maintain and enhance our independence. Unfortunately, such efforts have been obscured and often betrayed by those who claim to represent us: *Indian Act* chiefs and leaders of lobby organizations such as the Assembly of First Nations. Howard Adams, *Prison of Grass: Canada from a Native Point of View*, rev.ed. (Saskatoon: Fifth House Publishers, 1989), 155–159.

[14] Katherine Walker, *Mind shift or policy change? Government's new focus on off-reserve economic development nothing new for natives*, Canadian Broadcasting Corporation <www.cbc.ca/news/viewpoint/vp_walker/20071220.html>.

[15] Gregory Cajete, in *Native Science: Natural Laws of Interdependence* 1ˢᵗ ed. (Santa Fe: Clear Light Publishers, 2000), calls for a new cosmology and world view that draws upon the wisdom inherent in Indigenous societies. Other important recent contributions to this discourse include Taiaiake Alfred, *Wasáse: Indigenous Pathways of Action and Freedom* (Peterborough, ON: Broadview Press, 2005), 313; Marie Battiste, "Maintaining Aboriginal Identity, Language, and Culture in Modern Society," in *Reclaiming Indigenous Voice and Vision*, ed. Marie Battiste (Vancouver: UBC Press, 2000); Jackson, *Our Elders Lived It*; Patricia Monture-Angus, *Journeying Forward: Dreaming First Nations' Independence* (Halifax, NS: Fernwood, 1999); D'Arcy Rheault, *Anishinaabe Mino-Bimaadiziwin: The Way of a Good Life* (Peterborough, ON: Debwewin Press, 1999), 185; Silver, *In Their Own Voices*; ed. Waziyatawin Angela Wilson and Michael Yellow Bird, *For Indigenous Eyes Only: A Decolonization Handbook* (Santa Fe: School of American Research, 2005); Mary Isabelle Young, *Pimatisiwin: Walking in a Good Way—A Narrative Inquiry Into Language as Identity*, (Winnipeg: Pemmican Publications, 2005).

[16] Indigenous Peoples in the Americas have lived in cities for centuries before the arrival of Europeans in our hemisphere. Massive settlements, each with tens or even hundreds of thousands of inhabitants, existed in what is now North America.

[17] Unknown author, *Aboriginal Spiritual Park in the Works*, Canadian Broadcasting Corporation <www.cbc.ca/canada/manitoba/story/2006/12/15/spiritual-park.html>.

[18] Eduardo and Bonnie Duran, *Native American Postcolonial Psychology* (Albany: State University of New York Press, 1995), 207.

[19] The point is probably moot since the Canadian government is unlikely to adopt policies that serve to perpetuate status Indians whose existence is seen as a financial burden for the Crown.

Chapter 11

The Colonization and Decolonization of Indigenous Diversity

ISABEL ALTAMIRANO-JIMÉNEZ

Contemporary North America is a contested geographical construction, deeply embedded in the politics of Othering and of disrupting ancient Indigenous territories. Although an ancient notion of North America encompassing Canada, the United States, and Mexico existed, colonial and national state discourses redefined the boundaries of the region by emphasizing difference and focusing on the two English-speaking countries. Since then, social scientists and particularly political scientists have continued to emphasize the predominance of these two countries by applying dichotomies such as First/Third World, North America/Latin America, and global North/global South to the political science field. From this perspective, the notion of North America as a region limited to Canada and the United States has taken root in academic and political discourses. However, the increasing trend toward globalization has been accompanied by some attempts to conceptualize North America as a region characterized by the kind of general dynamics that affect and shape economic integration. While economic integration is taking place, this region was not created with the North American Free Trade Agreement. Before Europeans came to the continent, many Indigenous Peoples shared a spatial notion of Turtle Island, a vast territory roughly encompassing contemporary US, Canada, and Mexico. Later, colonial enterprises in North America were entangled processes that influenced each other's development.

In this chapter, I discuss the extent to which colonial and postcolonial political strategies have undermined North American entangled histories in favour of national geographies, which tend to emphasize fixed borders.[1] I argue that through the redefinition of borders, the construction of colonial societies, and the homogenization/division of what is "Indigenous" and who is and is not part of the "national" geographical spaces, the efforts to disentangled North American histories have undermined Indigenous diversity and interconnections, and promoted a racially divided conception of North America. This process has, in turn, created asymmetrical relationships among Indigenous Peoples, who, ironically, have reproduced Indigenous north/south relationships in North America.

I begin by exploring an Indigenous view of North America. Second, I discuss how colonization disrupted/domesticated Indigenous North America and its consequences for Indigenous transnationalism. Finally, I briefly elaborate on how this process can be decolonized.

A Continent of Diverse Islands

"Turtle Island" was the old name for the continent that included Canada, the United States, and Mexico, and had its origins in the many creation myths of the people who have lived here for millennia. Turtle Island, then, is North America, not present-day North America, but the continent of the past and its great diversity. Although limited to Canada and the United States, Winona LaDuke's idea of Indigenous North America can be extended to include Mexico and to portray the whole region as a set of islands in a continent, with each island representing an Indigenous people and territory. Thus, the Blackfoot, Crow, Cheyenne, Navaho, Yaqui, Mohawk, Cree, Aztecs, Zapotecs, and Mixtec islands, among others, existed and continue to exist as differentiated cultural entities.[2] Some of them have been larger than others, and all of them have had their distinctive political organizations. This continent of islands was extremely diverse and had its own social, cultural, political, and economic dynamics. Rather than east-west, this geographic space had a south-north logic of economic and cultural exchanges among the different Indigenous civilizations.

Such exchanges developed in "interaction spheres," which facilitated the exchange of gifts, ideas, trade, and the creation of alliances both political and military.[3] Interaction spheres can be understood as the spaces or centres where cultural innovation occurred and which influenced distant peripheries.[4] In fact, one of the issues that has received a great deal of attention from archaeologists and anthropologists has been the influence of Mesoamerican cultures such as those of the Mayans and Aztecs on the northern Indigenous cultures. Platform mounds with temples atop, standard community layouts with plazas, and certain artifacts and decorative motifs have, for several decades, induced scholars to speculate about the cultural connections and trade between the northern cultures and Mesoamerica or Middle America.[5]

Influence and exchange are not exclusive to archaeological remains, for oral history is also an important source for tracing back Indigenous interrelations between Mesoamerica and northern North America.

The Colonization of Diversity

Territories and borders are the result of human agency rather than changeless geographical spaces. The continent of islands or Indigenous North America and the interconnectedness of its peoples were gradually displaced by colonial processes and moral and racial discourses, and, later, by a new east-west logic that was imposed internally in each newly created national state in the region.

The colonization of the Americas by different European empires such as the British, Spanish, and French crowns initiated gigantic transformations in the dynamic of Indigenous interrelations by redefining North America's cultural, political, and economic interactions around the dichotomy "Old World" and "New World." As suggested by Gould,[6] far from being different, these competing empires were part of the same hemispherical system, which was extremely asymmetric, with

Spain being the most prominent member. This asymmetric relationship influenced the way in which British project was conceived, the arguments used to legitimize possessions, and the Indigenous peoples/colonizers relationships.

Scholars generally accept that the construction of the idea of the "New World" was based upon cultural representations as ideological legitimization for territorial expansion. Therefore, the "New World" became a place populated by pagan savages, who became the oppositional Other of the civilized West or the "Old World." Regardless of their background, European colonizers constructed these differences to legitimize their racial superiority. Colonizers' representations of the Other centred on similar strategies such as archives or travellers' information and tales, knowledge, religion, taboos, fear, and ethnography in order to describe and construct a world of Others.

Through these oppositions, colonial discourses perpetuated an ideology that justified European expansion and the aggression inflicted on Indigenous Peoples through genocide, slavery, and deterritorialization. The European colonial moral discourse was that of a civilizing mission oriented to save "savages." As Richard Harvey Brown argues, to justify their domination, colonizers created categories and moral hierarchies that distinguished between the pure and the impure, and the savages and the civilized, and turned cultural difference into natural, binary oppositions.[7]

The process of negotiating and imposing borders and constructing difference created a complex colonial hierarchy of peoples that continues to exist today in subtle forms. This hierarchy grouped/homogenized peoples into new racial categories that defined them in relation to the colonial history. First Nations, Métis, Inuit, Mixed Blood, Mestizos, Indians, and other labels are a reflection of the complex racial distinctions that today characterize North America and Indigenous peoples' relations to the national states. In fact, one of the most divisive issues afflicting Indigenous Peoples in this region involves who has a legitimate right to define his or her identity and by what criteria, and by whose definition this assertion may or may not be true. As the symbolic power of race continues to be strongly embedded in the construction of ambiguous Indigenous identities, further paradoxes are created. The Métis people of Canada, for example, are often irreducibly constructed as "mixed" regardless of how they perceived themselves and of how little metissage[8] may add to the understanding of their identity. Metissage, on the other hand, has also been used to undermine Indigenous place-based identities.

The racial reconstruction of difference in North America was not limited to only Europeans versus Amerindians. Rather, the discourses varied according to the contexts in which they were deployed and the competition among European empires that characterized the colonization of North America. For this reason, European rivalry and moral disqualification became the basis for constructing differences among Spanish, English, and, to some extent, French colonial adventures in North America. It was particularly clear between the British and the Spaniards.

According to Gedges Gonzalez, the British highlighted the violence that Spaniards had inflicted on Indigenous populations and insinuated that miscegenation had caused the decadence among the Indigenous Peoples.[9] English Protestants, in contrast, represented themselves and Indigenous Peoples as two separate worlds that never mixed. They represented British colonial enterprises as an orderly business carried out through treaty and trade relationships with Indigenous Peoples, punctuated by a few "accidental," regrettable episodes. The British adopted a doctrine of effective occupation, which was conceived to subvert Spanish claims to territory not directly under Spain's control. This doctrine also served to differentiate Britain's "libertarian" imperial project from the Spaniards.

Thus, the Black Legend, or the story about Spanish atrocities in the New World, became a way for English imperialists to distinguish their benign project from the Spaniards' destructive one.[10] According to Bernadette Bucher, this difference and the idea of two separate worlds would later be used for the normalization of interracial marriage taboos, racial segregation, and the creation of reservations, all characteristics of English colonial enterprises in North America.[11]

The opposing representations extended to people of mixed ancestry as well. Unlike the English, the Spanish colonial system needed Native people for its population base and as a major labour force. Thus,

Spanish authorities encouraged or tolerated miscegenation.[12] Unlike the interracial unions that occurred in British-controlled territories and that were undermined by whiteness, the ones developed in Spanish-controlled territories eventually resulted in a growing mixed population characterized by class distinctions and racial undertones.[13] This growing population eventually became the Mestizo mainstream society and not a different segment of the Indigenous population. Mestizos appropriated and transformed European notions of race and culture into similar mediations based on hybridity and metissage, that later became a mode of rationality and a new way of reifying culture and policing borders and identities, particularly after Mexico gained independence in 1810. Of course, while metissage celebrates an indigenous past, living Indigenous Peoples and identities were perceived as the internal Other.

From this perspective, both whiteness and metissage worked in these different contexts as regulatory mechanisms defining and circumscribing Indigenity and predicating racial and cultural difference internally. At the transnational level, whiteness emphasized an Anglo-North America and constructed metissage as a contaminated misfit that still haunt North American "post-colonial relations."

In the same way that colonial discourses characterized Indigenous Peoples' laws and politics as inferior, the Othering of other colonial enterprises by British colonizers also created social and geographical segregation that distinguish Indigenous Peoples in relation to who colonized their territories. The settler society encouraged Indigenous Peoples to perpetuate such differences and discourses.[14] As Homi Bhabha observes, colonial discourse tunes on the recognition and disavowal of races/cultural/historical differences and functions to create space for "subject peoples."[15] This function suggests that the geographical frontier also existed as a moral frontier.[16] While colonial racial/cultural/historical discourse separated Indigenous Peoples from Europeans, such rhetoric also created a difference between English/north/Indigenous Peoples and Spanish/south/Indigenous Peoples.

However, these historical differences, representations, and relationships between the colonizers and Indigenous Peoples and also between competing empires must be understood not as separate but as entangled histories influencing each other. Migration, dispossession, resettlement, the creation of markets, the construction of ethnic labour systems, and metropolitan growth have been common practices in the larger story of the colonization of Native North America by peoples from elsewhere. The European colonial competition for the control of the continent of islands altered not only the interconnectedness of the original peoples in the Americas, but also reshaped their identification along racial inclusions/exclusions. The historical reconfiguration of borders and difference created not only distinctive national histories, but also a complex racial hierarchy that places groups of people within borderlands where they are still subjected to racial discrimination and Othering at the present.

Ironically, this historical politics in the region has continued to transform the material and discursive legacies of contemporary Indigenous peoples and replaced them with an asymmetrical north-south/Anglo/Spanish relationship that subsumes Indigenous diversity and past interactions. Indigenous Peoples, who, prior to colonization, regarded themselves as distinct peoples and interacted based on their difference, now identify themselves along linguistic lines and pan-Indigenous legal categories amidst the many destructive effects of colonialism. This identification conceals the internal tension between frontiers and regions, the existing inequalities that characterize Indigenous Peoples both in Spanish and English North America. This also reflects the spatial genealogy of ideas and the contingency of the north and south relations in the construction of this region.[17] More importantly, such identification privileges separate colonial histories and undermine Indigenous past histories and normalized diversity.

From this point of view, race and the colonial in the Foucaultian sense continue to inform politics in present North America and continue to be a disciplinary tool that controls, regulates, and protects the settler/colonial population from itself and from its internal enemies, or those who do not conform to the ideal. Whiteness and metissage as regimes of truth continue to circumscribe the political possibilities of Indigenous Peoples both within national and across borders.[18]

The Possibilities of Indigenous Transnationalism

Contemporary global, national, and local developments signal markedly different contexts in normalizing (post?) colonial relations among Indigenous Peoples. Academic and political discourses have emphasized the increasingly complex forms of social interaction associated with global capital flow, technology, information, labour, and new forms of economic integration.

J.D. Sidaway has pointed out that the actors, including the state, in such dramas are neither innocent nor romantic resistance heroes struggling against Western culture and domination.[19] Rather, they are the result of systematic forms of exploitation and Othering, of ethnically or spatially distinct populations in colonial and post-colonial states reproducing racial and political hierarchies through negotiating meaning. Places or the local are not different because of who colonized those places. Rather, they are different because of their historical and contemporary linkages to broader political and economic processes. Thus, understanding the connection between colonialism and economic development involves realizing how the everyday enactments of development in the diverse landscapes of what is called global north and global south rest upon colonial relations and the social, political, and economic ties among regions.

Indigenous Peoples continue to be the most marginalized segments of the population in both the global north and global south. Nevertheless, these peoples' marginalization is often represented differently. What is neglected in these representations is how economic globalization affects Indigenous Peoples in particular ways because they are exposed to a complex system of oppression involving race, colonization, rules, and institutions in both north and south. Although this system of oppression is usually represented as inherent to the margins and as being hardest in the south, it is a creature of neo-liberal state formation and of colonialist discursive subject. In both north and south, Indigenous Peoples have struggled and continue to struggle to maintain control of their lives and lands, and to confront complex networks that traverse the boundaries between the state, the market, and civil society.

The growing importance of international corporations and global flows of capital puts pressure on Indigenous Peoples' lands and resources, regardless of where they are.

In North America, regional economic integration has involved transformations that are not only economic but dramatically political.[20] While neither Canada nor Mexico's close relationship with the US economy is new, the intensification of these relationships, and especially the neo-liberal reforms that have accompanied continental integration, have redefined how people relate to each other, to resources, and to the state. In this context, relationships between the state and Indigenous Peoples also have been transformed and new forms of governance negotiated. These understandings of governance are usually shaped in controversial ways because they both undermine collectivities and emphasizes market-oriented development.[21]

There are certainly important differences in terms of political strategies and actions that are place-specific. However, the question is, can North American Indigenous Peoples decolonize colonial representations and constructions in order to identify common issues, interests, allies, and enemies across borders and difference?

Decolonizing colonial constructions of Indigeneity requires us to recognize the diversity of Indigenous cultures and histories. It requires us to examine nation-specific, precolonial conceptualizations of citizenship, how our nations determined who were citizens, and how we related to other Indigenous peoples on Turtle Island. It is not colonial history that makes us different or similar; as Indigenous Peoples, we have always been different. What unites Hawai'ians with Zapotecs, what connects the Mohawks with Mayan activists or Inuit with Nahuatls and Mixtecs is neither colonial language nor their primordial attachments, but their long survival and resistance, and their will to continue to be who they are. As James Clifford argues, commonalities among diverse peoples are historically contingent, though no less real for all that. Indigenous Peoples and movements are positioned but not necessarily connected by similar experiences in relation to who colonized their territories.[22] Corporations and private investors pushing Indigenous Peoples to open their lands and resources to economic development neither work exclusively within national borders nor along cultural identification. They are, rather, transnational. This is not to suggest that Indigenous Peoples in the North American region do not have their own temporality or struggle strategies; rather, it is to argue that there are possibilities of networking, coalition building, and transformative actions in diversity across different Indigenous nations.

Conclusions

Turtle Island was a continent of islands with their own interactions, trade, and cultural exchanges. The colonial enterprises in North America radically changed those interactions. The representation and construction of Indigenous difference in North America have been informed by colonial discourses, which are still being deployed. Variations among representations depend upon the contexts in which discourses are deployed. Moreover, I have shown that the colonizers' representation and construction of difference was not limited to Indigenous Peoples but extended to European rivals in the struggle to control North America. Colonial competition in this region produced entangled histories, which shaped transitions from colonies to national states and blurred cross-cultural relations.

The historical reconfiguration of difference along colonial racial and linguistic lines subsumed the uneven and contradictory impacts of development among actors, institutions, and areas. This politics of representation and geographic construction continues to influence how Indigenous Peoples perceive themselves and how they relate to others. In addition, such representation continues to hide common origins and processes and to conceal some of the similar challenges faced by contemporary North America's Indigenous Peoples.

---

[1] Eliga H. Gould, 2007. "Entangled Histories. Entangled World: The English Speaking Atlantic as a Spanish Periphery," *Contemporary Review* 289 (1684): 764–786.

[2] W. LaDuke, "An Indigenous View of North America," Oral Presentation, North Carolina State University: Raleigh, NC, November 13, 1995.

[3] Joseph R. Caldwell, "Interaction Spheres in Prehistory," *Hopewellian Studies* 12, 6 (1964): 133–156.

[4] Ibid.

[5] Charles Hudson, *The Southeastern Indians* (Tennessee: Tennessee Press, 1982); Alfonso Ortiz, vol. ed, *Handbook of North American Indians* Vol. 10 (Washington: Smithsonian Institution, 1983); Michael S. Foster, "The Mesoamerican Connection: A View from the South" in *Ripples in the Chichimec Sea: New Considerations of Southwestern-Mesoamerican Interactions*, ed. Frances Mathien, and Randall McGuire (Carbondale: Southern Illinois University Press, 1986).

[6] Gould, "Entangled Histories," 764–786.

[7] Richard Harvey Brown, "Cultural Representations and Ideological Domination," *Social Forces* 71, 3 (1993): 660.

[8] Metissage roughly refers to "the mixing of races" or "cultural hybridization." In Mexico, metissage was used as an ideology to strategically construct a distinct and racialized national identity that synthesized both the Indigenous and colonial pasts. As such, it became the invisible norm through which Indigenous Peoples are judged and Indigenous political possibilities circumscribed.

[9] Henry Gedges González, "Icon, Conquest, Trasnationalism: The Visual Politics of Constructing Difference in the Americas," *Passages: A Journal of Trasnational and Transcultural Studies* 1, 1 (1999): 33–52.

[10] Brown, "Cultural Representations," 665.

[11] Bernadette Bucher, "Al Oeste del Eden: La Semiótica de la Conquista, Reconstrucción del Icono y Política Estructural" in Mercedes López-Baral, *Iconografía Política del Nuevo Mundo* (San Juan: Universidad de Puerto Rico, 1990), 18–20.

[12] James Axtell, *The European and the Indian: Essays in the Ethnohistory of Colonial North America* (New York: Oxford University Press, 1981), 206.

[13] Claudio Esteva-Fabregat, *Mestizaje in Ibero-America*, trans. John Wheat (Tucson: University of Arizona Press, 1995), 57.

[14] Jean Barman, "What a Difference a Border Makes: Aboriginal Racial Intermixture in the Pacific Northwest," *Journal of the West* 38 (1999):14–20; Jay Nelson, "'A Strange Revolution in the Manners of the Country': Aboriginal-Settler Intermarriage in Nineteenth-Century British Columbia," in *Regulating Lives: Historical Essays on the State, Society, the Individual, and the Law*, ed. John McLaren, Robert Menzies and Dorothy E. Chunn (Vancouver: UBC Press, 2003); Sylvia Van Kirk, "From 'Marrying-In' to 'Marrying-Out': Changing Patterns of Aboriginal/Non-Aboriginal Marriage in Colonial Canada," *Frontiers: A Journal of Women Studies* 23, 3 (2002): 2–11.

[15] Homi Bhabha, *The Location of Culture* (London: Routledge, 2004).

[16] Nelson, "'A Strange Revolution in the Manners of the Country,'" 24.

[17] M. Bell, "Inquiring Minds and Postcolonial Devices: Examining Poverty at a Distance," *Annals of the Association of American Geographers* 92, 77 (2002): 507–23.

[18] Aileen Moreton-Robinson, "A New Research Agenda? Foucault, Whiteness and Indigenous Sovereignty," *Journal of Sociology* 42,4 (2006): 383–395.

[19] J.D. Sidaway, "Postcolonial Geographies: Survey—Explore—Review," in *Postcolonial Geographies*, ed. A. Blunt and C. McEwan (New York: Continuum, 2002), 18–19.

[20] Laura Macdonald, "Governance and State Society Relations: The Challenges," in *Capacity for Choice: Canada in a North America*, ed. George Hoberg (Toronto: University of Toronto Press, 2002), 187–223.

[21] Makere Stewart-Harawira, *The Indigenous New Response to Imperial Globalization Order*, (London: Zed Books, 2005), 179.

[22] James Clifford, "Indigenous Articulations," in *Cultural Rupture and Indigeneity: The Challenge of (Re) Visioning "Place" in the Pacific*, ed. David Welchmean Gegeo (Honolulu: University of Hawai'i Press, 2001), 472.

Chapter 12

Beyond Recognition: Indigenous Self-Determination as Prefigurative Practice

GLEN COULTHARD

Over the past thirty years, the self-determination efforts and objectives of Indigenous Peoples in Canada have increasingly been cast in the language of "recognition." Consider, for example, the formative declaration issued by my community, the Dene Nation, in 1975:

> We the Dene of the NWT [Northwest Territories] insist on the right to be regarded by ourselves and the world as a nation. Our struggle is for the *recognition* of the Dene Nation by the Government and people of Canada and the peoples and governments of the world.[1]

Now, fast-forward to the 2005 policy position on self-determination issued by Canada's largest Aboriginal organization, the Assembly of First Nations (AFN). According to the AFN, "a consensus has emerged [...] around a vision of the relationship between First Nations and Canada which would lead to strengthening recognition and implementation of First Nations' governments."[2] This "vision," the AFN goes on to state, expands on the core principles outlined in the 1996 *Report of the Royal Commission on Aboriginal Peoples* (RCAP): that is, recognition of the nation-to-nation relationship between First Nations and the Crown; recognition of the equal right of First Nations to self-determination;

recognition of the Crown's fiduciary obligation to protect Aboriginal treaty rights; recognition of First Nations' inherent right to self-government; and recognition of the right of First Nations to economically benefit from the use of their lands and resources.[3] When considered from the vantage point of these perspectives, it would appear that recognition has emerged as the hegemonic expression of self-determination within the Indigenous rights movement in Canada.

The increase in recognition-demands made by Indigenous and other marginalized minorities over the last three decades has prompted a surge of intellectual activity that has sought to unpack the ethical, political, and legal significance of these types of claims. Influenced by Charles Taylor's catalytic 1992 essay "The Politics of Recognition,"[4] much of this literature focuses on the relationship between the affirmative recognition of societal cultural differences on the one hand, and the freedom and well-being of marginalized individuals and groups living in ethnically diverse states on the other. In Canada, it has been argued that this synthesis of theory and practice has forced the state to reconceptualize the tenets of its relationship with Aboriginal Peoples;[5] whereas prior to 1969, federal Indian policy was unapologetically assimilationist, now it is couched in the vernacular of "mutual recognition."[6]

In the following chapter I employ the work of anti-colonial theorist Frantz Fanon to challenge the idea that the colonial relationship between Indigenous Peoples and the Canadian state can be significantly transformed via a politics of recognition. Here I take "politics of recognition" to refer to the now expansive range of recognition-based models of liberal pluralism that seek to reconcile Indigenous claims to nationhood with Crown sovereignty via the accommodation of Indigenous identities in some form of renewed relationship with the Canadian state.[7] Although these models tend to vary in both theory and practice, most involve the delegation of land, capital, and political power from the state to Indigenous communities through a combination of land claim agreements, economic development initiatives, and self-government packages. Against this position, I argue that instead of ushering in an era of peaceful co-existence grounded on the ideal of *mutuality*, the politics of recognition in its contemporary form promises to reproduce the very configurations of colonial power that Indigenous Peoples' demands for recognition have historically sought to transcend.

Recognition and Freedom

Two interrelated Hegelian assumptions continue to ground the liberal recognition approach to Indigenous self-determination in Canada. The first assumption, which is now uncontroversial, involves recognition's perceived role in the constitution of human subjectivity: the notion that our identities are formed in complex ways through our relations with others. On this account, relations of recognition are deemed "constitutive of subjectivity: one becomes an individual subject only in virtue of recognizing, and being recognized by another subject."[8] The second, more contentious assumption is the one that I want to problematize below: namely, the notion that the specific institutional and interpersonal character of our relations of recognition can have a positive (when mutual) or detrimental (when hierarchical) effect on our status as *free agents*. Here it is not my intention to *reject* the correlation drawn between recognition and freedom as such, but rather to show how the *form of mutuality* envisioned by many advocates of the liberal recognition approach serves to foster unfree and non-mutual relations instead of free and mutual ones.

Let us take Charles Taylor's work as an example. In "The Politics of Recognition," Taylor draws on the insights of Hegel and others to critique what he claims to be the increasingly "impracticable"[9] nature of "difference-blind" (40) liberalism when applied to diverse settler polities such as the United States and Canada. As an alternative to this articulation of liberal thought and practice, Taylor defends a variant of liberalism that posits that, under certain circumstances, diverse states can indeed recognize and accommodate a range of group claims without abandoning their commitment to a core set of fundamental rights (61). According to Taylor, these types of claims can be justified on liberal grounds because it is within and against the "horizon" of one's cultural community that individuals come to develop their identities, and thus the capacity to make sense of their lives and life choices (23–33). In short, our identities provide the background "against which our tastes and desires and opinions and aspirations make sense" (33–34). Without this orienting framework, we would be unable to derive meaning from our lives—we would not know "who we are" or "where [we are] coming from." (33). We would be "at sea," as Taylor states elsewhere.[10]

At the core of Taylor's argument, then, is the idea that humans do not develop their identities in "isolation"—rather they are formed through "dialogue with others, in agreement or struggle with their recognition of us."[11] However, given that our identities are formed in this manner, it also follows that they can be significantly *de*formed when these processes run awry. This is what Taylor means when he asserts that our identities are not only shaped by recognition, but also its absence,

> often by the misrecognition of others. A person or a group of people can suffer real damage, real distortion, if the people or society around them mirror back to them a confining or demeaning or contemptible picture of themselves. Nonrecognition or misrecognition can inflict harm, can be a form of oppression, imprisoning one in a false, distorted, and reduced mode of being.[12]

It is this second assumption that unequal relations of recognition can impede human freedom and flourishing that continues to serve as one of the main theoretical justifications for state policies geared toward the recognition and protection of cultural differences, including those that Indigenous Peoples bring to the table.[13]

Frantz Fanon and the Problem of Recognition in Colonial Contexts

In the second half of "The Politics of Recognition," Taylor identifies Fanon's classic 1961 treatise on decolonization, *The Wretched of the Earth*,[14] as one of the first texts to elicit the role that misrecognition plays in propping up relations of domination. By extension, Fanon's analysis in *The Wretched* is also used to support one of the central political arguments undergirding Taylor's analysis: his call for the cultural recognition of sub-state groups that have suffered at the hands of a hegemonic political power. Although Taylor acknowledges that Fanon advocated "violent" struggle as the primary means of overcoming the "psycho-existential"[15] complexes instilled in colonial subjects by misrecognition, he nonetheless insists that Fanon's argument is applicable to contemporary debates surrounding the "politics of difference" more generally.[16] Below, I want to challenge Taylor's use of Fanon in this context: not by disputing Taylor's assertion that Fanon's work constitutes an important theorization of the ways in which the subjectivities of the oppressed can be deformed by mis- or non-recognition, but rather by contesting his assumption that a more accommodating, liberal regime of mutual recognition might be capable of addressing the types of relations typical of those between Indigenous Peoples and settler states. Presciently, Fanon posed a similar challenge in his earlier work, *Black Skin, White Masks (BSWM).*[17]

Fanon's concern with the relationship between human freedom and equality in relations of recognition represents a central and reoccurring theme in *BSWM*. It was there that Fanon first persuasively argued that the long-term stability of a colonial structure of dominance relies as much on the "internalization" of the racist forms of asymmetrical and non-mutual modes of recognition, either imposed or bestowed on the Indigenous population, as it does on brute force. Fanon argued that, in contexts of domination such as colonialism, not only are the terms of recognition usually determined by, and in the interests of, the colonizer, but also over time colonized populations tend to develop what he called "psycho-affective"[18] attachments to these master-sanctioned forms of recognition, and that this subjective attachment is essential in maintaining the economic and political structure of colonizer/colonized relations themselves. For Fanon, colonialism can thus be said to operate on two interrelated levels: it includes "not only the interrelations of *objective* historical conditions but also human *attitudes* to these conditions."[19] Fanon argued that it was the interplay between the structural/objective and the recognitive/subjective realms of colonialism that ensured its hegemony over time.

With respect to the subjective dimension, *BSWM* painstakingly outlines the myriad ways in which those "attitudes" conducive to colonial rule are cultivated amongst the colonized through the unequal exchange of institutionalized and interpersonal patterns of recognition between the colonial society and the Indigenous population. In effect, Fanon revealed how, over time, colonized populations tend to internalize the derogatory images imposed on them by their colonial "masters," and how, as a result of this process, these images, along with the structural relations with which they are entwined, come to be recognized (or endured) as more or less natural. This last point is made agonizingly clear in one of the most famous passages from *BSWM*, where Fanon shares an alienating encounter on the streets of Paris with a little white girl: "Look, a Negro!" Fanon recalled the girl saying, "Moma, see the Negro! I'm frightened! frightened!" (111–112) At that moment the imposition of the child's racist gaze "sealed" Fanon into a "crushing objecthood," fixing him "like a chemical solution is fixed by a dye" (109). He found himself temporarily *accepting* that he was indeed the subject of the girls call: "It was true, it amused me" (111), thought Fanon; but then "I subjected myself to an objective examination, I discovered my blackness, my ethnic characteristics; and I was battered down by tom-toms, cannibalism, intellectual deficiency, fetishism, racial defects" (112). Far from assuring Fanon's humanity, the other's recognition imprisoned him in an externally determined and devalued conception of himself. Instead of being acknowledged as a "man among men," he was reduced to "an object among other objects" (109).

Left as is, Fanon's insights into the ultimately objectifying nature of colonial recognition appear to square nicely with the politics of recognition as conceived of, and practised, in Canada today. For example, although Fanon never uses the word himself, he nonetheless appears to be describing the debilitating effects associated with misrecognition in the sense that Taylor and others use the term. In fact, *BSWM* is littered with passages that illustrate the innumerable ways in which the imposition of the settler's gaze can inflict damage on the Indigenous society at both the individual and collective levels. Even with this being the case, however, a close reading of *BSWM* renders problematic the liberal recognition approach in at least two crucial respects.

The first problem has to do with its failure to adequately confront the dual structure of colonialism noted above. Fanon insisted, for example, that to transform a colonial configuration of power, one had to attack it at both levels of operation: the objective and the subjective. This point is made at the outset of *BSWM* and reverberates throughout all of Fanon's work. As indicated in his introduction, although significant sections of *BSWM* would highlight and explore the "psychological" terrain of colonial rule, this would not be done in a manner decoupled from a radical structural/material analysis. Indeed, Fanon claimed that there will be an "authentic disalienation" of the colonized subject "only to the degree to which things, in the most materialistic meaning of the word, [are] restored to their proper places."[20] Here Fanon correctly situates colonial-capitalist exploitation and domination alongside misrecognition and alienation as foundational sources of colonial injustice. "The Negro problem," wrote Fanon, "does not resolve itself into the problem of Negroes living among white men [sic] but rather of Negroes being exploited, enslaved, despised by a colonialist, capitalist society that is only accidentally white."[21]

Although Fanon was enough of a Marxist to understand the role that capitalist economic relations played in exasperating asymmetrical relations of recognition, he was also much more perceptive than many of his Marxist contemporaries in recognizing the need to target and transform the subjective realm of colonialism along with the socio-economic structure. The colonized person "must wage war on both levels,"[22] insisted Fanon. "Since historically they influence each other, any unilateral liberation is incomplete, and the gravest mistake would be to believe in their automatic interdependence."[23] For Fanon, attacking colonial power on one front, in other words, would not guarantee the subversion of its effects on the other. "This is why a Marxist analysis should always be slightly stretched when it comes to addressing the colonial issue," Fanon would later write in *The Wretched*.[24]

Fanon's insights here clearly expose the limits of the politics of recognition for restructuring Indigenous-state relations in Canada. As mentioned at the outset of this chapter, this approach seeks to address colonial injustice in strictly reformist terms, like the promotion of state redistribution schemes that grant certain "cultural rights" and economic concessions to Indigenous communities through land claims, self-government agreements, and economic development initiatives. Although this approach may, at best, alter some of the worst effects of colonial-capitalist exploitation and domination, it does little to address their generative structures—in this case, a racist economy and a colonial state. When interrogated from this angle, it is clear that the contemporary politics of recognition leaves one of the two operative levels of colonial power identified by Fanon untouched.

The second key problem with the liberal recognition paradigm has to do with the subjective realm of power relations. Here it is important to note that most recognition-based proposals rest on the problematic assumption that the flourishing of Indigenous Peoples as distinct and self-determining agents is somehow dependent on their being granted recognition from the oppressive structures and institutions of the settler state and state society. For Fanon, there are at least two problems underlying the idea that freedom and independence can be achieved through such a delegated exchange of recognition. The first involves the relationship he draws between struggle and the disalienation of the colonized subject. Simply stated, for Fanon, it is through struggle and conflict (and for the later Fanon, *violent* struggle and conflict) that the colonized come to purge the "arsenal of complexes"[25] driven into the core of their being through the colonial process. In this sense, struggle—or, as I will argue later, *transformative practice*—serves as a mediating force through which the colonized shed their colonial mentalities and imperial modes of conduct. In contexts where recognition is conferred without struggle and conflict, this fundamental self-transformation—or as Lou Turner has put it, this "inner-differentiation"[26] at the level at one's being—cannot occur, thus foreclosing the possibility of achieving real freedom. Although the formal political structure of domination may change in these situations—for example, the colonized may be afforded constitutionally protected "rights" to land and self-government—the subjective life of the colonized will tend to remain the same—they become "emancipated slaves."[27]

It should be noted that when Fanon speaks of a lack of struggle in the decolonization movements of his day, he does not mean to suggest that the Indigenous population in these contexts simply remained passive recipients of colonial practices. He readily admits, for example, that the colonized may indeed fight "for Liberty and Justice."[28] However, the point to highlight here is that when this fight is carried out in a manner that fails to challenge the background discursive and non-discursive structures of colonial power as such—which, for Fanon, will *always* involve struggle and conflict—then the best the colonized can hope for is "white liberty and white justice; that is, values secreted by [their] masters."[29] This brings us to the second problem Fanon identifies with the recognition paradigm when conceptualized as a conferral of freedom without conflict: when struggle does not constitute a central feature of the decolonization movement, not only will the terms of recognition tend to remain the property of those in power to grant to their inferiors in ways that they deem appropriate,[30] but also under these conditions, the Indigenous population will often come to see the limited and structurally constrained terms of recognition granted to them *as their own.* In effect, they will begin to *identify* with "white liberty and white justice." Either way, for Fanon, in situations such as this, the colonized will have failed to re-establish themselves as truly self-determining, that is, as the creators of the terms and values *of their own recognition.*

Anyone familiar with the power dynamics that currently structure the Aboriginal rights movement in Canada should immediately see the applicability of Fanon's insights here. Indeed, one need not expend much effort at all to elicit the countless ways in which the liberal discourse of recognition has been limited and constrained by the state, politicians, corporations and the courts in ways that pose no fundamental challenge to the colonial relationship. With respect to the law, for example, over the last thirty years, the Supreme Court of Canada has consistently refused to recognize Indigenous Peoples' equal and self-determining status, based on the Court's adherence to legal precedent founded on the white supremacist myth that Indigenous societies were too primitive to bear fundamental political rights when they first encountered European powers.[31] Thus, even though the Court has secured an unprecedented degree of recognition for certain "cultural" practices within the colonial state, it has nonetheless failed to challenge the racist origin of Canada's assumed authority over Indigenous Peoples and their territories.

The political and economic ramifications of the Court's actions have been clear-cut. In *Delgamuukw v. British Columbia*, for example, it was declared that any residual Aboriginal rights that may have survived the unilateral assertion of Crown sovereignty could be infringed upon by the federal and provincial governments so long as this action could be shown to further a "compelling and substantial legislative objective" consistent with the "fiduciary relationship" between the state and Indigenous Peoples.[32] What "substantial objectives" might justify infringement? According to the Court, virtually any exploitative economic venture, including the "development of agriculture, forestry, mining, and hydroelectric power, the general economic development of the interior of British Columbia, protection of the environment or endangered species and the building of infrastructure and the settlement of foreign populations to support those aims."[33] So today it appears, much as it did in Fanon's day, that colonial powers will recognize the collective rights and identities of Indigenous Peoples only insofar as this recognition does not obstruct the imperatives of state and capital.[34]

But the above examples confirm only one aspect of Fanon's insights into the problem of recognition when applied to the colonial setting: the limitations that it runs up against when pitted against these overtly structural expressions of colonial power. Can the same be said for the subjective dimension of colonial power relations?

With respect to the forms of racist recognition pounded into the psyches of Indigenous Peoples through the institutions of the state, church, schools, and media, and by racists within the dominant society, the answer is surely yes. Countless studies, novels, and autobiographical narratives have outlined, in painful detail, the ways in which these expressions of recognition have saddled Indigenous people with low self-esteem, depression, alcohol and drug abuse, and violent behaviour directed both inward and outward.

However, similarly convincing arguments have been made concerning the limited forms of recognition and accommodation offered to Indigenous communities through the law, self-government and land claims, and economic development. The recent work of Isabel Altamirano-Jiménez,[35] Taiaiake Alfred,[36] and Paul Nadasdy,[37] for example, have all demonstrated the ways in which the state institutional and discursive fields within and against which Indigenous demands for recognition are made and adjudicated can subtly shape the subjectivities and world views of the Indigenous claimants involved. The problem here, of course, is that these fields are by no means neutral: they are profoundly hierarchical and power-laden, and, as such, have the ability to asymmetrically mould and govern how Indigenous subjects think and act, not only in relation to the topic at hand (the recognition claim), but also to themselves and to others. This is what I take Alfred to mean when he suggests, echoing Fanon, that the dominance of the legal approach to self-determination has, over time, helped produce a class of Aboriginal "citizens" whose rights and identities have become defined solely in relation to the colonial state and its legal apparatus. Similarly, strategies that have sought self-determination via mainstream economic development have facilitated the creation of a new elite of Aboriginal capitalists whose unquenchable thirst for profit has come to outweigh their ancestral obligations to the land and to others. And land-claims processes, which are couched almost exclusively in the language of property,[38] are now threatening to produce a new breed of Aboriginal property owner, whose territories, and thus whose very indentity, risk becoming subject to expropriation and alienation. Whatever the method, for Alfred, all these approaches, even when carried out by sincere and well-intentioned individuals, threaten to erode the most traditionally egalitarian aspects of Indigenous ethical systems, ways of life, and forms of social organization.

Indigenous Peoples and Transformative Self-Empowerment

As argued throughout the preceding pages, Fanon did not attribute much emancipatory potential to a politics of recognition when applied to the colonial arena. Yet this is not to say that he rejected the recognition paradigm entirely. As we have seen, like Taylor after him, Fanon ascribed to the idea that relations of recognition are constitutive of subjectivity and that, when unequal, can foreclose the realization of human freedom. On the latter point, however, he was deeply skeptical as to whether reaching a level of mutuality in relations of recognition was possible in the conditions indicative of contemporary settler colonialism. But if Fanon did not see freedom as naturally emanating from the colonial subject being granted recognition from his or her master, where, if at all, did it originate?

In effect, Fanon claimed that the road to *self*-determination instead lay in a quasi-Nietzschean form of personal and collective self-affirmation.[39] Rather than remaining dependent on their oppressors for their freedom and self-worth, Fanon argued, the colonized must struggle to critically reclaim and revaluate the worth of *their own* histories and traditions against the subjectifying gaze and assimilative lure of colonial recognition. According to Fanon, it is this *self-initiated* process that "triggers a change of fundamental importance in the colonized's psycho-affective equilibrium."[40] For Fanon, the colonized must instigate decolonization by recognizing *themselves* as free, dignified, and distinct contributors to humanity.[41]

Although Fanon's argument remains an innovative and important contribution to anti-colonial thought and practice, in the end his endorsement of self-empowerment over colonial dependency does not push far enough. By the time Fanon was immersed in writing *The Wretched of the Earth*, he had come to see the empowering process of self-recognition in strictly instrumental terms; that is, although he saw the critical revaluation of culture and tradition as an important, even necessary, means of temporarily breaking the colonized free from the subjectifying effects of being exposed to structured patterns of colonial misrecognition, he was decidedly less willing to explore the role that Indigenous ways of life might play in providing a substantive *alternative* to the oppressive social relations that produced colonized subjects to begin with. In this sense, Fanon appears to have remained *too much* of a Marxist in that his work tends to treat "culture" in a manner similar to "class"; that is, as a category of identification that subaltern groups must struggle to transcend as soon as they become conscious of its existence.

If one examines the grassroots strategies and tactics adopted by a growing number of today's Indigenous activists—whether in reserve settings like Grassy Narrows and Six Nations, or in urban centres such as Vancouver and Victoria—the revaluation of Indigenous traditions and cultures in a manner akin to Fanon's notion of self-empowerment becomes apparent. However, unlike the later Fanon, who saw the "moment" of cultural self-recognition as only that—a moment in a dialectical progression beyond itself—the best of today's Indigenous movements articulate a far more substantive relationship between identity and freedom insofar as they are attempting to critically reconstruct and deploy previously disparaged traditions and practices in a manner that consciously seeks to prefigure a lasting alternative to the colonial present.

This form of prefigurative/transformative praxis is evident in a recent and ongoing initiative carried out by a number of Nuu-chah-nulth activists in their attempt to curb the proliferation of colonial-patriarchal practices within their communities. Initiated by Chiinuuks Ogilvie and several other members of the now disbanded West Coast Warrior Society,[42] this project seeks not only to raise awareness of the mutually reinforcing relationship between sexual violence, patriarchy and the operation of colonial relations of power, but also to *break* this relationship by critically revisiting Nuu-chah-nulth teachings and traditions regarding the proper ordering of community gender relations.[43] However, unlike most liberal approaches to the problem of violence against Native women, which tend to call for *more* state and police intervention into the lives of their communities, these activists are explicitly attempting to undercut their nation's dependence on the colonial state to redress problems that the state itself has played a fundamental role in creating. As Na'cha'uaht explains:

> For me, the colonial state system was never meant to liberate us or allow us to be ourselves and craft our futures as we see fit. [When we rely on the state,] well-intentioned people and efforts get swallowed up by the band councils and government programs where they, at best, prop-up a corrupt social-safety net, or worse, *fundamentally change who we are as [I]ndigenous [P]eoples.*
>
> The benefit of organizing outside this system has been the opportunity to show people that we can achieve tangible results without relying on government funding or direction. It has been an awesome experience to see people realize that our ways, Nuu-chah-nulth ways and teachings, are still

valid and can guide us in a way that could never be achieved within the state system.[44]

I mention the Nuu-chah-nulth example because of two illustrative similarities it shares with Fanon's critique of the recognition paradigm. First, it identifies well the always potentially risky and subjectifying nature of strategies that aim to harness the discursive and institutional tools of colonial law and politics as a means of addressing problems that those tools have themselves helped produce. This is what I take Na'cha'uaht to mean when he suggests that state-sanctioned forms of recognition, such as self-government and band council social programming, have served to "at best, prop-up a corrupt social-safety net, or worse, *fundamentally change who we are as [I]ndigenous [P]eoples.*" In Fanon's terms, these forms of recognition have caused certain segments of the community to identify more with "white liberty and white justice" than with Nuu-chah-nulth perspectives on these matters. And second, I think that their efforts attempt to address the dual-structured character of colonial power identified by Fanon as well. On the one hand, they have begun to creatively work over the more subjective/psycho-affective terrain of colonialism by critically revaluating what their history and teachings have to say about gender parity, which has, on the other hand, cashed out in the transformative practice of confronting the structural/material realm of colonial patriarchy in their communities. Again, the important difference is that unlike the instrumental (and one could argue, class and race-centric) view espoused by Fanon, the transformative praxis indicative of Nuu-chah-nulth self-recognition and revaluation seeks to prefigure practices that aspire to subvert and replace the colonial social relations that presently undercut the freedom and health of Nuu-chah-nulth communities.

Conclusion

Throughout this chapter, I have argued that Fanon's insights into the subjectifying nature of colonial recognition are as applicable today to the liberal politics of recognition as they were when he first formulated his thoughts on the matter. I have also shown that Fanon's dual-structured conception of colonial power still captures the subtle (and not so subtle) ways in which a system of imperial domination that does not sustain itself exclusively by force is reproduced over time. As Taiaiake Alfred has recently argued, under these "post-modern" imperial conditions, "[o]pression has become increasingly invisible; [it is] no longer constituted in conventional terms of military occupation, onerous taxation burdens, blatant land thefts, etc.,"[45] but rather through a "fluid confluence of politics, economics, psychology, and culture."[46] But if the dispersal and effects of colonial and state power are now so diffuse, how is one to transform or resist them? Here I believe that the central insight underlying Fanon's earlier work remains key: that Indigenous societies must begin to "turn away"[47] from the assimilative lure of settler-state recognition and instead find in their own transformative praxis the source of their liberation. I think that today this process will and must continue to involve some form of critical individual and collective self-recognition on the part of Indigenous societies, not only in an instrumental sense like Fanon seemed to have envisioned it, but with the understanding that our cultures have much to teach the Western world about the establishment of relationships within and between peoples and the natural world that are profoundly non-imperialist.

AUTHOR'S NOTE: Significant parts of this chapter are drawn from a much longer essay first published under the title "Subjects of Empire: Indigenous Peoples and the 'Politics of Recognition' in Canada." *Contemporary Political Theory* 6,4 (2007), reproduced with permission of Palgrave Macmillan.

[1] Dene Nation, "Dene Declaration" in *Dene Nation: The Colony Within*, ed. Mel Watkins (Toronto: University of Toronto Press, 1977), 3–4.

[2] Assembly of First Nations (AFN), *Our Nations, Our Governments: Choosing our own Paths* (Ottawa: Assembly of First Nations, 2005), 18.

[3] Ibid., 18–19.

[4] Charles Taylor, "The Politics of Recognition" in *Re-examining the Politics of Recognition*, ed. Amy Guttman (Princeton: Princeton University Press, 1994).

[5] Alan Cairns, *Citizens Plus: Aboriginal Peoples and the Canadian State* (Vancouver: University of British Columbia Press, 2000) and *First Nations and the Canadian State: In Search of Co-existence* (Kingston: Institute of Intergovernmental Relations, 2005).

[6] Department of Indian Affairs and Northern Development, *Gathering Strength: Canada's Aboriginal Action Plan* (Ottawa: Published under the authority of the Minister of Indian Affairs and Northern Development, 1997) and *A First Nations-Crown Political Accord on the Recognition and Implementation of First Nation's Governments* (Ottawa: Published under the authority of the Minister of Indian Affairs and Northern Development, 2005).

[7] For a similar articulation, see Richard J.F. Day, *Multiculturalism and the History of Canadian Diversity* (Toronto: University of Toronto Press, 2000).

[8] Nancy Fraser and Axel Honneth, *Redistribution or Recognition? A Political-Philosophical Exchange* (London: Verso, 2003), 11.

[9] Taylor, "The Politics of Recognition," 61.

[10] Charles Taylor, *Sources of the Self* (Cambridge UK: Cambridge University Press, 1989), 27.

[11] Charles Taylor, *The Malaise of Modernity* (Toronto: Anansi Press, 1991), 45–46.

[12] Taylor, "Politics of Recognition," 25.

[13] For example, the *Report of the Royal Commission for Aboriginal Peoples* situates "mutual recognition" as one of the central normative principles around which to reconstruct Indigenous/state relations based on freedom rather than domination. See Royal Commission on Aboriginal Peoples, *Report of the Royal Commission on Aboriginal Peoples*, 5 Volumes (Ottawa: Minister of supply and Services, 1996).

[14] Frantz Fanon, *The Wretched of the Earth* (Boston: Grove Press, 2005).

[15] Frantz Fanon, *Black Skin, White Masks* (Boston: Grove Press, 1967), 12.

[16] Taylor, *The Politics of Recognition*, 65–66.

[17] Fanon, *Black Skin, White Masks*.

[18] Fanon, *Black Skin, White Masks*, 148.

[19] Ibid., 84, emphasis added.

[20] Fanon, *Black Skin, White Masks*, 11–12.

[21] Ibid., 202.

[22] Ibid.,11.

[23] Ibid.

[24] Fanon, *The Wretched of the Earth*, 5. Fanon's "stretching" of the Marxist paradigm constitutes one of the most innovative contributions to classical Marxist debates on ideology. In Fanon's work, not only is the relationship between base and superstructure posited as both interdependent and semi-autonomous, but, more significantly, those axes of domination historically relegated in Marxism to the superstructural realm—such as racism and the effects it has on those subject to it—are attributed a substantive capacity to structure the character of social relations.

[25] Fanon, *Black Skin, White Masks*, 18.

[26] Lou Turner, "On the Differnce between the Hegelian and Fanonian Dialectic of Lordship and Bondage" in *Fanon: A Critical Reader*, ed. Lewis Gordon, T. Denean Sharpley-Whiting, and Rene T. White (New York: Routledge, 1996), 146.

[27] Ibid.

[28] Fanon, *Black Skin, White Masks*, 221.

[29] Ibid., 221.

[30] Kelly Oliver, *Witnessing: Beyond Recognition* (Minneapolis: University of Minnesota Press, 2001).

[31] Michael Asch, "From 'Calder' to 'Van der Peet': Aboriginal Rights and Canadian Law" in *Indigenous Peoples' Rights in Australia, Canada, and New Zealand*, ed. Paul Havemann (Auckland: University of Cambridge Press, 1999). Also see Patrick Macklem, *Indigenous Difference and the Constitution of Canada* (Toronto: University of Toronto Press, 2001); and James Tully, "Aboriginal Peoples: Negotiating Reconciliation" in *Canadian Politics*, 3rd ed., ed. James Bickerton and Alain-G Gagnon (Peterborough: Broadview Press, 2000).

[32] Quoted in Tully, "Aboriginal Peoples," 413.

[33] Ibid., 413.

[34] Elizabeth Povinelli, *The Cunning of Recognition: Indigenous Alterities and the Making of Australian Multiculturalism* (Durham: Duke University Press, 2002).

[35] Isabel Altamirano-Jiménez, "North American First Peoples: Slipping into Market Citizenship" *Citizenship Studies* 8,4 (2004), 349–365.

[36] Taiaiake Alfred, *Wasáse: Indigenous Pathways of Action and Freedom* (Peterborough: Broadview Press, 2005).

[37] Paul Nadasdy, *Hunters and Bureaucrats: Power, Knowledge, and Aboriginal/State Relations in the Southwest Yukon* (Vancouver: University of British Columbia Press, 2005).

[38] Ibid.

[39] Fanon, *Black Skin, White Masks*, 222.

[40] Fanon, *The Wretched of the Earth*, 148.

[41] Fanon, *Black Skin, White Masks*, 222.

[42] For a succinct genealogy of Indigenous warrior societies in North America, see Taiaiake Alfred and Lana Lowe, "What are Warrior Societies?" in *New Socialist: Special Issue on Indigenous Resurgence*, 58, ed. Taiaiake Alfred, Glen Coulthard, and Deborah Simmons (September–October, 2006).

[43] Chiinuuks (Ruth Ogilvie) and Nu'cha'uaht (Cliff Atleo Jr.), "Nuu-chah-nulth Struggles Against Sexual Violence," in *New Socialist: Special Issue on Indigenous Resurgence*, 58, ed. Taiaiake Alfred, Glen Coulthard, and Deborah Simmons (September–October, 2006).

[44] Ibid.,31, emphasis added.

[45] Alfred, *Wasáse*, 58.

[46] Ibid., 30.

[47] Fanon, *Black Skin, White Masks*, 221.

Chapter 13

Nogojiwanong: The Place at the Foot of the Rapids

LEANNE SIMPSON

Spring comes early to the eastern doorway of the Nishnaabeg[1] Nation, where the Mississaugas sit. The bear returns from her spiritual journey in the dreamworld to nurse her cubs. The medicines return to us. The people engage in purification rituals and prepare to fast. The rivers are full. The rains are coming and the land is gently cleansed with the flooding. We tap Ninaatig, the maple, and hear that drumbeat as the first sap drips into the bucket, so we can cleanse ourselves with the sweet water. It is a time of birth, and a time to celebrate mno-bimadziwin,[2] continuous rebirth.

It is also a time for remembering and recommitting to our responsibilities as individuals, communities, and nations. Nishnaabe-kwewag, as grandmothers, mothers, aunties, sisters, and daughters, have some very important responsibilities when it comes to the land and the matters concerning the nation. Our relationship with the land is based on those responsibilities and our relationship to water is central. The water, Nibi, teaches us about relationships, interconnection, interdependence, and renewal.

Nishnaabe-kwewag learn about water through pregnancy and by giving birth.[3] As we carry the children of our nation through our pregnancy ceremony, we carry them in water, and we become the water carriers.

Water is our first home, the lifeblood, protecting unborn babies and nurturing them until they are ready to pass through the doorway to this world. When a pregnant woman's water breaks, it cleans the path for the baby to follow. Women know that the water inside their wombs is the same water that is in our rivers and our lakes. We drink lots of water during pregnancy. We drink lots of water nursing our babies. We are the water.

In our bodies, water acts as a purifier, cleansing us and protecting us from disease. Similarly, water is the lifeblood of ecosystems, purifying the land through melting, through rain and natural flooding. The waters bring forth new life each spring, cleansing the land and running off into the streams, the rivers, the lakes, and the Big Lakes, Gizhe Gaming. In our traditions, the Great Lakes are the liver and the kidneys of the land, filtering out contaminants and sending the water through the rest of the system. It is a system women have been honouring and protecting for countless generations.

A few years ago, Peterborough, the city where I live, celebrated the 100-year anniversary of the Peterborough Lift Lock, part of the Trent Severn Waterway. The waterway is a system of locks from Lake Ontario through the Trent River, Pamitaskwotayong—Lake of Burning Plains (now known as Rice Lake), the Otonaabe River, the Kawartha Lakes, Lake Simcoe, the Severn River, and into Georgian Bay, Wasigaming. It is an ancient waterway, travelled by different Indigenous Nations for generations.[4]

It seemed like everyone in Peterborough was in on the celebrations—there were concerts and art shows, kids' activities, and fireworks. Everyone was enthusiastic, except for the Mississaugas. To us, the Trent Severn Waterway meant the loss of territory, as the natural flow of the water was artificially altered. It meant the flooding of cemeteries and sacred sites, and it meant the destruction of our rice beds. Today, the lift locks act like a system of dams constricting and constraining and controlling what the river can do. The lift locks block and disrupt the power of that flowing water with handcuffs and shackles, interfering with the cleansing, with bringing forth new life, and with the river's responsibility of sustaining the territory. When the construction of the lift locks colonized an ancient travel route, it also colonized the life-blood of our first mother.

The towering, concrete hydraulic lift lock in downtown Peterborough is a vivid, tragic representation of the colonization of women and the colonization of Mississauga territorial lands. The image of the locks holding back the power of the river system reminds me of the medicalization of birth so many of our women have experienced and continue to experience. We used to believe that our bodies were powerful and knew how to give birth on their own. We used to believe that the pregnancy ceremony was beautiful and a celebration of our ability to bring forth new life.[5] Giving birth was transformative, a ceremony with particular songs and traditions to support women and new babies. Colonialism stripped women of our power through the life-changing and life-giving ceremony of birth. For so many of our women, it meant being alone in the hospital far away from those support systems, with doctors replacing midwives and aunties, our men not allowed to participate. The medicalization of the birthing ceremony makes it more difficult for our women to bring forth the new life of our nation—just like those lift locks make it more difficult for the river to bring forth new life, the new life that upon which we are utterly dependent.

The construction of the Trent Severn waterway also had other impacts on the land and the Mississaugas. It meant the end of nishnaabeg-mnoomin (wild rice) on Pamitaskwotayong. That rice sustained our community; it was the grain that provided balanced nutrition through our traditional foodways. It was the sacred rice that held our fall ceremonies, dances, and songs, and our traditional ways of governance. The rice cannot grow on Rice Lake to this day because of the fluctuating water levels of the lake caused by the lock system.

Mnoomin sustained our people. Just like nursing sustained our little ones. Our grandmothers knew that breastmilk was the perfect food for babies, but they were made to feel ashamed because they did not bottle feed, and told they were not doing the best thing for our babies. So we were given bottles, our children forgoing their first teachings about treaty relationships, the symbiotic agreement of sharing between mothers and babies at the breast.

There were more impacts of the Trent Severn waterway on the land. Our Clans relate us to the land, and our system of governance comes from the land through our relationship with our Clans. The people of the Fish Clans, who are the intellectuals of the nation, have important responsibilities, and they have an important relationship with the Fish Nations. Twice a year for thousands of years, those Fish Nations have met at Mnjikaning, in small narrows between Lake Simcoe and Lake Couchiching. The Fish Nations gathered to talk, to tend to their treaty relationships, as the Gizhe-mnido had instructed them. The people came as well, to fish, to talk, to meet with the Fish Nations. Indigenous Peoples tended those complex fish weirs at Mnjikaning for thousands of years, but we were forced to stop about 100 years ago.

Governance Begins with Mothers

In the past few years I have done a lot of listening about our traditional political systems and governments. Taiaiake Alfred, talks about how we need to pull back dealing with "territorial losses and political disempowerment,"[6] and how we must look inward, into our own communities and nations. We have to rebuild and figure out how to live our traditions in contemporary times.[7] We must build strong leaders according to our own traditions. This begins with women, the centre of the family, the mothers. Our traditional models of governance flow out from the centre of the family, to clans, communities, and nation, and lastly to our relationship with other nations. Our political systems were non-hierarchical, non-coercive, and non-authoritarian.[8] Our political systems begin with how we mother.

In pre-contact times, children were powerful spiritual teachers because they had only recently come to the physical world from the spiritual world. Children were respected as persons. They are Gifts from the Creator, and as gifts they were honoured. They were treated with gentleness, patience, compassion, and kindness, and we had the support of extended family and communities. They were not endlessly controlled, but allowed freedom within our extended families and Clans to experience life in a responsible manner and to discover their own gifts.

In pre-contact time, those first "explorers" wrote about how the land was wild and untamed, about how our women were wild and unruly, and they said the same thing about our children. Our cultures were designed to produce individuals who had a lot of individual freedom and a strong sense of belonging, as well as a sense of collective responsibility in the absence of coercive or authoritarian restrictions on freedoms. That is such a radical notion to me, because it flies in the face of colonialism and it flies in the face of how we practise some of our traditions today. It is a challenge to do better, to listen closely to those old ones who are so soft-spoken, so careful with their words, so gentle, and full of compassion and patience, and so full of humility.

Colonialism created residential schools and the child welfare system, poverty, despair, and discrimination, and these forces changed how we mother. It created boys capable of patriarchy and abuse; it created communities where we collectively reproduce colonialism rather than rally against it. All the while, that colonial machine was destroying our forests, erasing habitats for our Clans, building dams, and releasing toxic chemicals and pollutants. All the while that colonial attack on women continued—removing us from having any political power, narrowing gender roles, attacking mothering, birth, breastfeeding, and attachment-style parenting. This led to the breakdown of extended family and social support systems, the normalization of the exploitation and abuse of women and land, and the rise of authoritarian relationships.

And that is why it is our individual and collective responsibility to decolonize—ourselves, our families, our communities, our nations, and Canada. We need to get that lifeblood of our cultures flowing back through ourselves and our families, flowing back through the land.

Lighting the Eighth Fire

Our Nishnaabeg Seven Fires prophecy talks about a time when it was not safe to practise our cultures, when certain families had the responsibility of hanging on, of hiding and protecting it. That time passed, and then led to a time where the next generation could pick up those beautiful things left along the path and bring life to them once again. If we are going to make it to that Eighth fire, then we all have the responsibility for picking up those Gifts—for honouring them and making them relevant in our lives and in our nations, without rigidity and without exclusion.

In order to perpetuate the patriarchy that is entrenched in colonialism, both the internal colonialism within Indigenous Nations and colonialism perpetuated by the state, boys are raised to uphold the values of state colonialism. Holding a newborn baby boy, or watching a little toddler boy play, you know that boys are not born abusers or patriarchs or colonizers. The societies they are born into make them that, and that conditioning starts at birth. We dress baby boys in manly blue instead of "sissy" pink. We don't attend to their cries in order to "toughen them up." If they are sensitive, they are labelled "cry babies," and it becomes very important that boys become tough, independent, and strong. Even when they are just babies, even when they are just kids, patriarchy becomes entrenched in them and it continues as they grow. Boy culture does not permit boys to express a full and normal range of human emotions. Boys are "allowed" to express happiness when they win at sports, and to express anger and frustration. For other emotions, like empathy, caring, nurturing, sadness, worry, boys are teased and ridiculed. Yet these emotions are normal, healthy and absolutely necessary.[9]

When boys are not encouraged to express all their emotions in an appropriate way, over time, they stop feeling those particular unexpressed emotions. This is a danger, because it sets the conditions up for our men to behave in a disconnected way, a way that is not responsible to the whole family or the whole community. They will displace these feelings, and they often come out in inappropriate ways. If we do not allow boys to be nurturing, caring, responsible individuals, then they cannot learn to empathize with those who have different experiences and with those who come from different cultures or genders. If we create boys who cannot empathize, we create men who cannot empathize, men who are detached, unable to appreciate the experiences or perspectives of others; we create men who are able to engage in patriarchy and able to perpetuate the injustices of colonialism.

I believe it is our responsibility as mothers and aunties, and as fathers and uncles, to nurture boys who are incapable of upholding that system of patriarchy and colonialism. We must work with our men to redefine masculinity so that the gentleness with the land, with the women, and with our children is honoured as it once was. We must create communities in which we value the contributions of individuals, in which we have once again a fluidity around gender roles and responsibilities, and in which we respect all the forms of diversity that our societies used to foster so beautifully.

The essays in this book talk about planting the seeds of Indigenous resurgence. The contributors recognize that we are collectively at a place of rebirth, and that the seeds we plant now will determine what the coming summer will bring. It is our collective hope that Indigenous Peoples will immerse themselves in the swirling waters of the rapids, finding within their knowledge systems cleansing, renewal, and freedom, and that within that renewal, we will collectively awaken to our responsibilities to realize an Indigenous resurgence. Our book is a challenge for Indigenous and non-Indigenous Peoples to go and sit with the rapids, to allow that water to carry us on a journey of cleansing, renewal, justice, and freedom so that we may once again be able "to hear the life of the river above all other sounds."[10]

AUTHOR'S NOTE: This is the Mississauga name for Peterborough ON. This chapter is based upon my keynote address given at the 8th Annual Indigenous Women's Symposium at Trent University, March 17, 2007.

[1] Nishnaabeg is translated as "the people" and refers to Ojibwe, Odawa (Ottawa), Potawatomi, Mississauga, Saulteaux, and Omàmìwinini (Algonquin) Peoples. Nishnaabeg peoples are also known as Nishinaabeg, Anishinaabeg, and Anishinaabek in adjacent dialects. All words in Nishnaabemwin (Ojibwe language) in this chapter are in the eastern Manitoulin dialect of the language.

[2] Translated as the "good life" or continuous rebirth.

[3] Edna Manitowabi taught me about Nibi, and guided me through both of my pregnancy and birth ceremonies.

[4] See <www.mnjikaningfishweirs.org> for more information.

[5] For a more detailed discussion see Leanne Simpson, "Birthing an Indigenous Resurgence: Decolonizing our Pregnancy and Birth Ceremonies," *Until Our Hearts Are On the Ground: Aboriginal Mothering, Oppression, Resistance and Rebirth*, ed. D.M. Lavell-Harvard and J. Corbiere Lavell (Toronto: Demeter Press, 2006), 25–34.

[6] See Taiaiake Alfred's, *Wasáse: Indigenous Pathways of Action and Freedom*, (Peterborough, ON: Broadview Press, 2006), particularly page 38.

[7] By this I mean we need to reclaim the "radical" and "revolutionary" parts of Nishnaabeg Knowledge, the parts that encouraged what Alfred calls "free philosophical thinking" (197), and encourage self-reflection, a fluidity regarding individuality while maintaining responsibility to the collective. I believe that the fundamentalism that is sometimes seen in Nishnaabeg and other Indigenous communities is a facet of colonialism, and comes from a misunderstanding of Nishnaabemwin and Nishnaabeg philosophy.

[8] For a discussion of this topic within a Blackfoot context, see Kiera Ladner, "Women in Blackfoot Nationalism," *Journal of Canadian Studies* 35, 2 (2000): 35–60; and "Governing Within an Ecological Context: Creating an AlterNative Understanding of Blackfoot Governance," *Studies in Political Economy* 70 (2003): 125–152.

[9] For a similar discussion in a Eurocentric context, see Mary Polce-Lynch, *Boy Talk: How You Can Help Your Son Express His Emotions* (Oakland CA: New Harbinger Publications, 2002).

[10] A few years ago I had the honour of working with Renée Bédard on her MA thesis, "An Anishinaabekwe Writes History: An Alternative Understanding of Indigenous Intellectual and Historical Traditions," (Frost Centre for Native and Canadian Studies, Trent University, 2004) on Nishnaabeg intellectual traditions as they relate to history. One of the most powerful sections of her thesis is when she talks about rapids. Renée's territory is along the French River and so the river plays a very important role. It grounded her knowledge and her cultural traditions. She talks about how rapids are a place of cleansing, renewal, and of freedom, "where the life of the river is heard above all other sounds." The swirling waters of the rapids remind Renée of an individual's responsibilities to the past, the present, and future, and to oneself, one's family, community, and nation.

Closing Words

Go Fish

EDEN ROBINSON

Dad pauses, leaning on his wooden dip net like it's a staff. He patiently scans the shore for signs of jak'wun. With his grizzled hair and weather-beaten face, with the snow-capped mountains jutting up behind him and the ocean waves swelling beside him, Dad is strikingly Tolkienesque. I have a white plastic grocery bag over my head and I'm wearing rain clogs and a novelty Christmas sweater I don't mind getting fish guts on. Windblown sleet has numbed my face and makes my flared jeans flap sullenly against my calves. Early this morning when we started off, it was all sunshine and southerly breezes. I pooh-poohed the rain slickers and gumboots Dad tried to foist on me as overly cautious and sweat inducing.

My father and I are on a sandbar off the Prince Rupert highway in British Columbia, dip-net fishing for jak'wun, a small, smelt-like fish more commonly referred to as eulachon or "candle-fish." We aren't alone. A mass of screeching seagulls dives and rises continuously over the choppy ocean. The gnarled roots of a two-storey-high cedar stump washed onto the bar acts as a perch to both seagulls and a dozen pot-bellied eagles too fat to fish anymore. A pack of seals herds a school of jak'wun to a more convenient snacking location.

I wish we could sit in our car parked on the shoulder of the highway with the slicker-suited Kitsumkalum and Kitselas locals, who are waiting for a break in the weather comfortably in their SUVs and Ford F-150s. When we stopped at the Kitsumkalum Tempo Gas station, the attendants recognized the dip net immediately and knew where we were headed. The young Native cashier wrinkled her nose and said her granny still ate eulachons but she didn't really care for them. Dad chatted up the gas attendants, trying to find out how the run was going and if anyone was selling fresh eulachons. Dad wants to try to drive up to Canyon City tomorrow if we get skunked today.

None of this driving around would be necessary if the eulachons were still running in Haisla Territory, but eulachon are sensitive fish and won't run if they're too stressed, or if the water is too fast or too warm. The runs near Kitimat are compromised by effluent from Eurocan Pulp and Paper and Alcan Aluminum smelters. The runs further down the Douglas channel in the Kitlope and Kemano areas have always been spotty, but lately have been non-existent. We haven't had a decent eulachon run in three years, which is worrying many people, especially the Elders. A couple of families in the village still know how to render the eulachons into a traditional oil affectionately known as "grease." But the commitment of time and money coupled with the bad runs has meant that no grease has been made and the price of the stockpiled grease has shot up to $300 a gallon. Dad's house was broken into last year and the big-screen TV and stereo systems and DVD collection were untouched. The only thing taken was a jar of grease.

I keep glancing at the road in case someone comes stomping down and asks us what the hell we're doing here. I'm only reassured that we aren't breaching protocol when Dad wanders back to the road to question the locals about how long they've been waiting. He played basketball with one of the Elders and they shoot the breeze. I go back to sit in the car and thaw out while listening to Wild William Wesley on CFNR, the local Aboriginal station, mentally taking notes about the irony of food fishing in the imperial era of McDonald's. For instance, you have to be fairly well-off to eat traditional Haisla cuisine. Sure, the fish and game are free, but after factoring in fuel, time, equipment, and maintenance of various vehicles, it's cheaper to buy frozen fish from the grocery store than it is to physically go out and get it.

Morning turns into afternoon and we're still waiting. Dad lopes back to the car with news that someone is trading eulachons from the Nass for cigarettes. We drive to a small house near the Terrace Wal-Mart and Dad strikes a deal. We end up with a bucket of less than fresh eulachons, but, as Dad says, resigned, beggars can't be choosers.

When we return home, the afternoon is already darkening, but Dad can't wait to put the eulachons up in the smokehouse. He scrubs off a single dom, a thin cedar stick about four feet long, and teaches me how to thread the dom in through the eulachon's gills and out its mouth. One dom easily holds thirty small fish. "Your ma-ma-oo used to put up 500 doms a day all by herself," he says.

As he tells me about the eulachon runs of old, it's easy to imagine Ma-ma-oo bustling cheerfully though the smokehouse, making it look effortless. I hate to think of thousands of years of tradition dying with my generation. Because if the eulachon don't return to our rivers, we lose more than a species. We lose a connection with our history, a thread of tradition that ties us to this particular piece of the earth, that ties our ancestors to our children.

For tonight, we'll invite family over for a feed. Even if the kids wrinkle their noses at "granny food," we'll get together and celebrate the beginning of spring with fish I haven't completely mangled in a hopeful attempt to reclaim my heritage.

AUTHOR'S NOTE: This article was previously published by *SPIRIT Magazine* and is reprinted here with permission.

Contributors

Charlie Greg Sark

Charlie Greg Sark is a cross-blood who maintains and exercises his inherent rights, roles, and responsibilities as a member of the Mi'kmaq Nation. His writing has appeared in a few places, and sometimes under assumed identities. Currently, he is passively assembling his writing into a collection of prose, poetry, and rants. He sometimes lives on Prince Edward Island, and he sometimes lives in Ottawa. Someday, he would like to go to the moon (but, the Whitehouse would do).

Taiaiake Alfred

Taiaiake Alfred is a Kahnawake Mohawk educator and writer. He has long been involved in the public life of his own and other Indigenous Nations. He holds a PhD in political science from Cornell University and is the founding director of the University of Victoria's Indigenous Governance Programs. His awards include the Native American Journalists Association award for column writing and a National Aboriginal Achievement Award in the field of education. Taiaiake's publications include three books: *Heeding the Voices of Our Ancestors* and *Peace, Power, Righteousness* from Oxford University Press, and *Wasáse: Indigenous Pathways of Action and Freedom*, from Broadview Press.

Susan M. Hill

Susan M. Hill is a Haudenosaunee citizen and resident of Ohswe:ken (Grand River Territory). She holds a PhD in Indigenous Studies from Trent University and is an Assistant Professor of Indigenous Studies and Contemporary Studies at Wilfrid Laurier University, Brantford. Her work focuses on Haudenosaunee relationships to land stretching from the cultural history through contemporary history and into the present day.

Nicholas Xumthoult Claxton

Nicholas Claxton's WSÁNEĆ (Saanich) name is Xumthoult, and he was born and raised in WSÁNEĆ Territory. He is from the Tsawout Band of the WSÁNEĆ Nation, on southern Vancouver Island. Nick is an instructor on First Nations Studies at Malaspina University-College and is currently working on his PhD in environmental studies at the University of Victoria.

Fred (Gopit) Metallic

Fred Metallic is from a Mi'gmaq family of fishers. His family lives in the traditional territory of Gespe'gewa'gi, the seventh district of Mi'gma'gi. In addition to being a PhD candidate in environmental studies at York University, Fred Metallic is currently working as the Director of Research at the Migmawei Mawiomi Secretariat in Listuguj. Recently, Fred Metallic taught literature and history courses, in the Mi'gmaq language, for St. Thomas University (New Brunswick). Fred has written several research reports, and has presented numerously to Mi'gmaq and non-Mi'gmaq communities, on topics related to Mi'gmaq history, Mi'gmaq political traditions, governance, and research ethics and protocols. Through his academic, professional, and personal pursuits, Fred advocates for the necessity to reconcile pre- and post-colonial visions of the land and waters. To reconcile competing visions, we need to respect, listen, and follow those who still understand the voices of the land and waters.

Renée Elizabeth Mzinegiizhigo-kwe Bédard

Renée Elizabeth Mzinegiizhigo-kwe Bédard is a Nishnaabekwe (Ojibwe) from Dokis First Nation, Marten Clan. She holds a BA in History from Nipissing University and an MA in Canadian/Native Studies from Trent University. Currently, she is completing her doctoral degree in the Indigenous Studies PhD program at Trent University. As a scholar, painter, and craftswoman, she focuses both her writing and art on issues that have an impact on the lives of Nishnaabe-women, specifically their cultural traditions, their knowledge, and their roles and responsibilities as Nishnaabe-kwewag.

Paula Sherman

Dr. Paula Sherman is Omàmìwinini (Algonquin) and Family Head on Ka-Pishkawandemin, the traditional Council from Ardoch. She is also an assistant professor in Indigenous Studies at Trent University in Peterborough, ON.

Jackie Price

Jackie Price is Inuk from Nunavut, and grew up in Rankin Inlet and Iqaluit. Jackie received her BA in political science from the University of New Brunswick, and her MA from the Indigenous Governance Program at the University of Victoria. Jackie held various policy posts within the Government of Nunavut and was an instructor at Nunavut Sivuniksavut, a college-level program specifically for Inuit students from Nunavut in Ottawa. Jackie is currently a PhD student with the Scott Polar Research Institute at the University of Cambridge.

Jocelyn Cheechoo

Jocelyn Cheechoo is from Moose Cree First Nation and is the former Old Growth Organizer for the Rain Forest Action Network in San Francisco. She is currently completing her MA in Native Studies at the University of Manitoba.

Laura Hall

Of Kanienkehaka, Irish, French, Métis, and English heritage, Laura Hall was born and raised in Sudbury, Ontario, and currently lives and breathes in downtown Toronto. She is completing her PhD in the Faculty of Environmental Studies at York University. Her theoretical focus is on Indigenous, and in particular Haudenosaunee, economic philosophies and practices, land reclamation and self-determination. Her practical focus is on sustainable economic initiatives. She hopes that this work will soon include a bio-diesel vehicle-sharing project, which will allow Indigenous researchers to travel off the concrete "grid" in cheaper and less polluting ways.

Brock Pitawanakwat

Brock Pitawanakwat (Nishnaabe-Whitefish River First Nation) was born and raised off-reserve and, since 2003, has taught Indigenous Studies at First Nations University (Regina Campus). He was also a doctoral student in the University of Victoria's Indigenous Governance Programs with a dissertation that explores how Nishnaabeg maintain and revitalize Nishnaabemwin in urban centres. Other Indigenous research interests include anti-oppressive social movements, fundamentalism, language revitalization, and ethno-political/social mobilization in Abya Yala and Tahuantinsuyu. Brock is now Assistant Professor in the Aboriginal Governance Program at the University of Winnipeg.

Isabel Altamirano-Jiménez

Isabel Altamirano-Jiménez is a Zapotec woman from southern Mexico and holds a joint appointment as assistant professor in the Department of Political Science and the Faculty of Native Studies at the University of Alberta. She has done extensive research comparing Indigenous politics in Canada and Mexico. Among her recent publications are "The Construction of Difference and Indigenous Transnationalism in North America"; "Indigenous Peoples and the Topography of Gender in Mexico and Canada"; and "North American First Peoples Slipping up into Market Citizenship?" Her research interests are: Indigenous comparative politics, nationalism, gender issues, Indigenous development, self-government, and land rights.

Glen Coulthard

Glen Coulthard was a Yellowknives Dene PhD candidate in political theory at the University of Victoria and taught in the Indigenous Governance Programs and the Department of Political Science. Glen is now an Assistant Professor in First Nations Studies and Political Science at the University of British Columbia.

Eden Robinson

Eden Robinson is a Haisla/Heiltsuk author who grew up in Haisla, British Columbia. Her first book, *Traplines*, a collection of short stories, won the Winifred Holtby Memorial Prize and was a *New York Times* Notable Book of the Year in 1998. *Monkey Beach*, her first novel, was shortlisted for both The Giller Prize and the Governor General's Literary Award for fiction in 2000 and named a notable book by *The Globe and Mail*. Her most recent novel is *Blood Sports*.

Rebecca Belmore (cover artist)

Born in Ontario, Rebecca Belmore (Anishinabekwe) works in a variety of media, including sculpture, installation, video, and performance. Currently living and working in Vancouver, Belmore has long been creating work about the plight of the disenfranchised and marginalized in society. In her poignant and dramatic performances, the artist's own body becomes the site of historical, cultural, and political investigations as she explores self and community, boundaries between public and private, chaos, and linear narrative. The official representative for Canada at the 2005 Venice Biennale, Belmore's work has been exhibited internationally since 1987 and can be found in the collections of the National Gallery of Canada, Art Gallery of Ontario, and the Canada Council Art Bank. In 2004, Belmore received the prestigious VIVA award from the Jack and Doris Shadbolt foundation.

From the editor

In the context of the installation, as Belmore states on her website, "the image references historic and current cycles of oppression, greed, and theft—theft of land, theft of language, theft of identity, and theft of human rights." In the context of this book, it also invokes imagery around the eighth fire and decolonization and reflects the content and the politics of the essays. I like that this image challenges a romantic vision of decolonization—decolonizing isn't easy or pretty. The image of a scared fire burning in a tire is about starting with what we have. The important thing is that the fire gets started.

Leanne Simpson

Leanne Betasamosake Simpson is a leading Indigenous researcher, writer, educator, and activist. She is a citizen of the Nishnaabeg nation, with roots in the Mississaugas of Alderville First Nation, and obtained her PhD from the University of Manitoba in 1999.

Leanne's work has appeared in the *Wicazo Sa Review, American Indian Quarterly, American Indian Cultural Journal, Canadian Journal of Native Studies, Journal of Aboriginal Health, Tribal College Journal, Spirit Magazine,* and *Now Magazine.* She has also written chapters for *Native Historians Write Back: Decolonizing American Indian History,* forthcoming from the University of Texas Press; *The Politics of Participation in Sustainable Development Governance,* United Nations University Press; *Until our Hearts are on the Ground: Aboriginal Mothering: Oppression, Resistance, and Transformation,* Demeter Press; and *Every Grain of Sand: Canadian Perspectives on Ecology and Environment,* Wilfred Laurier Press.

Leanne has taught courses at the University of Manitoba, Trent University, and the University of Victoria, and is currently teaching at the Centre for World Indigenous Knowledge, Athabasca University. She also works with Indigenous communities and organizations across Canada and internationally on issues regarding land, politics, governance, and Indigenous Knowledge. She lives in Nogojiwanong (Peterborough, Ontario) with her partner and her two young children, Nishna and Minowewebeneshiinh.

Index